Divine Love
and
Wisdom

Angelic Wisdom concerning

Divine Love
and
Wisdom

EMANUEL SWEDENBORG

Translated from the Original Latin by
John C. Ager

STANDARD EDITION

SWEDENBORG FOUNDATION
West Chester, Pennsylvania

First published in Latin, London, 1763
First English translation, by Nathaniel Tucker, Manchester, England, 1788
First translation by J. C. Ager, Swedenborg Foundation, 1885
Second Ager edition, 1995
Printed in the United States of America

Library of Congress Cataloging-in-Publication Data

Swedenborg, Emanuel, 1688–1772.
  [Sapientia angelica de divino amore et de divina sapientia, English.]
  Angelic wisdom concerning the divine love and the divine wisdom /
  by Emanuel Swedenborg ; translated from the original Latin by
  John C. Ager. — 2nd Ager ed.
    p.   cm.
  Includes indexes.

  ISBN 0-87785-274-X (casebound)
  ISBN 0-87785-277-4 (paperback)
  ISBN 0-87785-282-0 (boxed set with *Heaven and Hell*
    and *Divine Providence*)

    1. God—Love. 2. God—Wisdom.   I. Ager, John C. (John Curtis),
  1835–1913.   II. Title.

BX8712.D4 1995
231'.6—dc20
                                      95—36404
                                             CIP

Typeset in Garamond by William Ross Woofenden
Designed by Joanna V. Hill
Printed and bound by BookCrafters, Inc.

For information contact:
  Swedenborg Foundation
  320 North Church Street
  West Chester, PA 19380

Contents

2. [The Means of Creation]

Editor's Preface

Divine Love and Wisdom is a philosophical work that was first published in Latin in 1763. It states in a concise and orderly way the philosophy of creation that underlies all of Emanuel Swedenborg's theological writings. This philosophy of creation can first be unquestionably identified in two works he published in 1734, the *Principia* and the *Infinite and Final Cause of Creation*, both of which are based on the premise that this is a created universe. Swedenborg held consistently to this belief from at least this time through the rest of his life.

In chapter 3, paragraph 188, Swedenborg states that "it is the object of this little work to uncover causes, that effects may be seen from them, and thus the darkness may be dispelled in which the man of the church is in respect to God and the Lord, and in respect to Divine things in general which are called spiritual things."

Divine Love and Wisdom was first translated into English in 1788 by Nathaniel Tucker and printed in Manchester, England. There is a copy of this edition in the library of the British Museum with manuscript notes by William Blake. The present version was translated by John C. Ager and first published by the Swedenborg Foundation in 1885. This work has also been printed in several other languages, including Danish, French, German, Icelandic, Italian, Russian, and Swedish.

Although this work is Swedenborg's most orderly presentation of a philosophic concept, its five chapters are untitled. Descriptive titles have been supplied by the present editor and added in brackets on the first page of each chapter; they also have been placed in the running heads.

As was the custom in his day, Swedenborg referred to the Psalms as the book of David, and to the Pentateuch (Genesis, Exodus, Leviticus, Numbers, and Deuteronomy) as the books of Moses. As with previous printings, the bold numerals in brackets, [2], [3], etc., indicate divisions of Swedenborg's long numbered sections, made for the convenience of the reader by John Faulkner Potts in his six-volume *Swedenborg Concordance* (London: Swedenborg Society, 1888–1902).

William Ross Woofenden
Sharon, Massachusetts

Divine Love
and
Wisdom

Chapter 1
[The Creator]

Love is the life of man

1. Man knows that there is such a thing as love, but he does not know what love is. He knows that there is such a thing as love from common speech, as when it is said, he loves me, a king loves his subjects, and subjects love their king, a husband loves his wife, a mother her children, and conversely; also, this or that one loves his country, his fellow citizens, his neighbor; and likewise of things abstracted from person, as when it is said, one loves this or that thing. But although the word love is so universally used, hardly anybody knows what love is. And because one is unable, when he reflects upon it, to form to himself any idea of thought about it, he says either that it is not anything, or that it is merely something flowing in from sight, hearing, touch, or conversation with others, and thus affecting him. He is wholly unaware that love is his very life; not only the general life of his whole body, and the general life of all his thoughts, but also the life of all their particulars. This a man of discernment can perceive when it is said: If you remove the affection which is from love, can you think anything, or do anything? Do not thought, speech, and action grow cold in the measure in which the affection which is from love grows cold? And do they not grow warm in the measure in which this affection grows warm? But this a man of discernment perceives simply by observing that such is the case, and not from any knowledge that love is the life of man.

2. What the life of man is, no one knows unless he knows that it is love. If this is not known, one person may believe

that man's life is nothing but perceiving with the senses and acting, and another that it is merely thinking; and yet thought is the first effect of life, and sensation and action are the second effect of life. Thought is here said to be the first effect of life, yet there is thought which is interior and more interior, also exterior and more exterior. What is actually the first effect of life is inmost thought, which is the perception of ends. But of all this hereafter, when the degrees of life are considered.

3. Some idea of love, as being the life of man, may be had from the sun's heat in the world. This heat is well known to be the common life, as it were, of all the vegetations of the earth. For by virtue of heat, coming forth in springtime, plants of every kind rise from the ground, deck themselves with leaves, then with blossoms, and finally with fruits, and thus, in a sense, live. But when, in the time of autumn and winter, heat withdraws, the plants are stripped of these signs of their life, and they wither. So it is with love in man; for heat and love mutually correspond. Therefore love also is warm.

God alone, consequently the Lord, is love itself, because he is life itself, and angels and men are recipients of life

4. This will be fully shown in treatises on *Divine Providence* and on *Life;* it is sufficient here to say that the Lord, who is the God of the universe, is uncreate and infinite, whereas man and angel are created and finite. And because the Lord is uncreate and infinite, he is being *[esse]* itself, which is called "Jehovah," and life itself, or life in itself. From the uncreate, the infinite, being itself and life itself, no one can be created immediately, because the Divine is one and indivisible; but their creation must be out of things created and finited, and so formed that the Divine can be in them. Because men and angels are such, they are recipients of life. Consequently, if any man suffers himself to be so far misled as to think that he is not a recipient of life but is life, he cannot be withheld from the thought that he is God. A man's feeling as if he were life, and therefore believing himself to be so, arises from fallacy; for the principal cause is not perceived in the instrumental cause otherwise than as one with it. That the Lord is life in himself, he himself teaches in John:

> As the Father hath life in himself, so also hath he given to the Son to have life in himself (5:26).

> He declares also that he is life itself (John 11:25; 14:6).

Now since life and love are one (as is apparent from what has been said above, n. 1, 2), it follows that the Lord, because he is life itself, is love itself.

5. But that this may reach the understanding, it must needs be known positively that the Lord, because he is love in its very essence, that is, Divine love, appears before the angels in heaven as a sun, and that from that sun heat and light go forth; the heat which goes forth therefrom being in its essence love, and the light which goes forth therefrom being in its essence wisdom; and that so far as the angels are recipients of that spiritual heat and of that spiritual light, they are loves and wisdoms; not loves and wisdoms from themselves, but from the Lord. That spiritual heat and that spiritual light not only flow into angels and affect them, but they also flow into men and affect them just to the extent that they become recipients; and they become recipients in the measure of their love to the Lord and love towards the neighbor. That sun itself, that is, the Divine love, by its heat and its light, cannot create anyone immediately from itself; for one so created would be love in its essence, which love is the Lord himself; but it can create from substances and matters so formed as to be capable of receiving the very heat and the very light; comparatively as the sun of the world cannot by its heat and light produce germinations on the earth immediately, but only out of earthy matters in which

ıt can be present by its heat and light, and cause vegetation. In the spiritual world the Divine love of the Lord appears as a sun, and from it proceed the spiritual heat and the spiritual light from which the angels derive love and wisdom, as may be seen in the work on *Heaven and Hell* (n. 116–140).

6. Since, then, man is not life, but is a recipient of life, it follows that the conception of a man from his father is not a conception of life, but only a conception of the first and purest form capable of receiving life; and to this, as to a nucleus or starting point in the womb, are successively added substances and matters in forms adapted to the reception of life, in their order and degree.

The Divine is not in space

7. That the Divine, that is, God, is not in space, although omnipresent and with every man in the world, and with every angel in heaven, and with every spirit under heaven, cannot be comprehended by a merely natural idea, but it can by a spiritual idea. It cannot be comprehended by a natural idea, because in the natural idea there is space; since it is formed out of such things as are in the world, and in each and all of these, as seen by the eye, there is space. In the world, everything great and small is of space; everything long, broad, and high is of space; in short, every measure, figure, and form is of space. This is why it has been said that it cannot be comprehended by a merely natural idea that the Divine is not in space, when it is said that the Divine is everywhere. Still, by natural thought, a man may comprehend this, if only he admit into it something of spiritual light. For this reason something shall first be said about spiritual idea, and thought therefrom. Spiritual idea derives nothing from space, but it derives its all from state. State is predicated of love, of life, of wisdom, of affections, of joys therefrom; in general, of good and of truth. An idea of

these things which is truly spiritual has nothing in common with space; it is higher and looks down upon the ideas of space which are under it as heaven looks down upon the earth. But since angels and spirits see with eyes, just as men in the world do, and since objects cannot be seen except in space, therefore in the spiritual world where angels and spirits are, there appear to be spaces like the spaces on earth; yet they are not spaces, but appearances, since they are not fixed and constant, as spaces are on earth; for they can be lengthened or shortened; they can be changed or varied.

Thus because they cannot be determined in that world by measure, they cannot be comprehended there by any natural idea, but only by a spiritual idea. The spiritual idea of distances of space is the same as of distances of good or distances of truth, which are affinities and likenesses according to states of goodness and truth.

8. From this it may be seen that man is unable, by a merely natural idea, to comprehend that the Divine is everywhere, and yet not in space; but that angels and spirits comprehend this clearly; consequently that a man also may, provided he admits into his thought something of spiritual light; and this for the reason that it is not his body that thinks, but his spirit, thus not his natural, but his spiritual.

9. But many fail to comprehend this because of their love of the natural, which makes them unwilling to raise the thoughts of their understanding above the natural into spiritual light; and those who are unwilling to do this can think only from space, even concerning God; and to think according to space concerning God is to think concerning the expanse of nature. This has to be premised, because without a knowledge and some perception that the Divine is not in space, nothing can be understood about the Divine life, which is love and wisdom, of which subjects this volume treats; and hence little, if anything, about divine providence, omnipresence, omniscience, omnipotence, infinity and eternity, which will be treated of in succession.

10. It has been said that in the spiritual world, just as in the natural world, there appear to be spaces, consequently also distances, but that these are appearances according to spiritual affinities which are of love and wisdom, or of good and truth. From this it is that the Lord, although everywhere in the heavens with angels, nevertheless appears high above them as a sun. Furthermore, since reception of love and wisdom causes affinity with the Lord, those heavens in which the angels are, from reception, in closer affinity with him, appear nearer to him than those in which the affinity is more remote. From this it is also that the heavens, of which there are three, are distinct from each other, likewise the societies of each heaven; and further, that the hells under them are remote according to their rejection of love and wisdom. The same is true of men, in whom and with whom the Lord is present throughout the whole earth; and this solely for the reason that the Lord is not in space.

God is very man

11. In all the heavens there is no other idea of God than that he is a man. This is because heaven as a whole and in part is in form like a man, and because it is the Divine which is with the angels that constitutes heaven and inasmuch as thought proceeds according to the form of heaven, it is impossible for the angels to think of God in any other way. From this it is that all those in the world who are conjoined with heaven think of God in the same way when they think interiorly in themselves, that is, in their spirit. From this fact that God is a man, all angels and all spirits, in their complete form, are men. This results from the form of heaven, which is like itself in its greatest and in its least parts. That heaven as a whole and in

part is in form like a man may be seen in the work *Heaven and Hell* (n. 59–87); and that thoughts proceed according to the form of heaven (n. 203, 204). It is known from Genesis (1:26, 27), that men were created after the image and likeness of God. God also appeared as a man to Abraham and to others. The ancients, from the wise even to the simple, thought of God no otherwise than as being a man; and when at length they began to worship a plurality of gods, as at Athens and Rome, they worshiped them all as men. What is here said may be illustrated by the following extract from a small treatise already published:

> The Gentiles, especially the Africans, who acknowledge and worship one God, the Creator of the universe, have concerning God the idea that he is a man, and declare that no one can have any other idea of God. When they learn that there are many who cherish an idea of God as something cloud-like in the midst of things, they ask where such persons are; and on being told that they are among Christians, they declare it to be impossible. They are informed, however, that this idea arises from the fact that God in the Word is called "a spirit," and of a spirit they have no other idea than of a bit of cloud, not knowing that every spirit and every angel is a man. An examination, nevertheless, was made, whether the spiritual idea of such persons was like their natural idea, and it was found not to be so with those who acknowledge the Lord interiorly as God of heaven and earth. I heard a certain elder from the Christians say that no one can have an idea of a human Divine; and I saw him taken about to various gentile nations, and successively to such as were more and more interior, and from them to their heavens, and finally to the Christian heaven; and everywhere their interior perception concerning God was communicated to him, and he observed that they had no other idea of God than that he is a man, which is the same as the idea of a human Divine (*Continuation Concerning the Last Judgment*, n. 74).

12. The common people in Christendom have an idea that God is a man, because God in the Athanasian doctrine of the trinity is called a "person." But those who are more learned than the common people pronounce God to be invisible; and this for the reason that they cannot comprehend how God, as a man, could have created heaven and earth, and then fill the universe with his presence, and many things besides, which cannot enter the understanding so long as the truth that the Divine is not in space is ignored. Those, however, who go to the Lord alone think of a human Divine, thus of God as a man.

13. How important it is to have a correct idea of God can be known from the truth that the idea of God constitutes the inmost of thought with all who have religion, for all things of religion and all things of worship look to God. And since God, universally and in particular, is in all things of religion and of worship, without a proper idea of God no communication with the heavens is possible. From this it is that in the spiritual world every nation has its place allotted in accordance with its idea of God as a man; for in this idea, and in no other, is the idea of the Lord. That man's state of life after death is according to the idea of God in which he has become confirmed, is manifest from the opposite of this, namely, that the denial of God, and, in the Christian world, the denial of the divinity of the Lord, constitutes hell.

In God-man esse and existere[1] are one distinguishably[2]

14. Where there is *esse* [being] there is *existere* [taking form]; one is not possible apart from the other. For *esse* is by means of *existere*, and not apart from it. This the rational mind comprehends when it thinks whether there can possibly be any *esse* [being] which does not exist [take form], and whether there

---

1. "To be and to exist." Swedenborg seems to use this word "exist" nearly in the classical sense of springing or standing forth, becoming manifest, taking form. The distinction between *esse* and *existere* is essentially the same as between substance and form.

2. For the meaning of this phrase, *"distincte unum,"* see below in this paragraph; also n. 17, 22, 34, 223, and *Divine Providence,* n. 4.

can possibly be *existere* except from *esse*. And since one is possible with the other, and not apart from the other, it follows that they are one, but one distinguishably. They are one distinguishably, like love and wisdom; in fact, love is *esse*, and wisdom is *existere*, for there can be no love except in wisdom, nor can there be any wisdom except from love; consequently when love is in wisdom, then it exists. These two are one in such a way that they may be distinguished in thought but not in operation, and because they may be distinguished in thought though not in operation, it is said that they are one distinguishably. *Esse* and *existere* in God-man are also one distinguishably like soul and body. There can be no soul apart from its body, nor body apart from its soul. The Divine soul of God-man is what is meant by Divine *esse*, and the Divine body is what is meant by Divine *existere*. That a soul can exist apart from a body, and can think and be wise, is an error springing from fallacies; for every man's soul is in a spiritual body after it has cast off the material coverings which it carried about in the world.

15. *Esse* is not *esse* unless it exists, because until then it is not in a form, and if not in a form it has no quality; and what has no quality is not anything. That which exists from *esse*, for the reason that it is from *esse*, makes one with it. From this there is a uniting of the two into one; and from this each is the other's mutually and interchangeably, and each is all in all things of the other as in itself.

16. From this it can be seen that God is man, and consequently he is God-existing; not existing from himself but in himself. He who has existence in himself is God from whom all things are.

In God-man infinite things are one distinguishably

17. That God is infinite is well known, for he is called the Infinite; and he is called the Infinite because he is infinite. He is infinite not from this alone, that he is very *esse* and *existere* in itself, but because in him there are infinite things. An infinite without infinite things in it, is infinite in name only. The infinite things in him cannot be called infinitely many, nor infinitely all, because of the natural idea of many and of all; for the natural idea of infinitely many is limited, and the natural idea of infinitely all, though not limited, is derived from limited things in the universe. Therefore man, because his ideas are natural, is unable by any refinement or approximation, to come into a perception of the infinite things in God; and an angel, while he is able, because he is in spiritual ideas, to rise by refinement and approximation above the degree of man, is still unable to attain to that perception.

18. That in God there are infinite things, anyone may convince himself who believes that God is a man; for, being a man, he has a body and everything pertaining to it, that is, a face, breast, abdomen, loins and feet; for without these he would not be a man. And having these, he also has eyes, ears, nose, mouth, and tongue; also the parts within man, as the heart and lungs, and their dependencies, all of which, taken together, make man to be a man. In a created man these parts are many, and regarded in their details of structure are numberless; but in God-man they are infinite, nothing whatever is lacking, and from this he has infinite perfection. This comparison holds between the uncreated man who is God and created man, because God is a man; and he himself says that the man of this world was created after his image and into his likeness (Gen. 1:26, 27).

19. That in God there are infinite things, is still more evident to the angels from the heavens in which they dwell. The whole heaven, consisting of myriads of myriads of angels, in its universal form is like a man. So is each society of heaven, be it larger or smaller. From this, too, an angel is a man, for an angel

is a heaven in least form. (This is shown in the work *Heaven and Hell*, n. 51–86.) Heaven as a whole, in part, and in the individual, is in that form by virtue of the Divine which angels receive; for in the measure in which an angel receives from the Divine is he in complete form a man. From this it is that angels are said to be in God, and God in them; also, that God is their all. How many things there are in heaven cannot be told; and because the Divine is what makes heaven, and consequently these unspeakably many things are from the Divine, it is clearly evident that there are infinite things in very man, who is God.

20. From the created universe a like conclusion may be drawn when it is regarded from uses and their correspondences. But before this can be understood some preliminary illustrations must be given.

21. Because in God-man there are infinite things which appear in heaven, in angel, and in man, as in a mirror; and because God-man is not in space (as was shown above, n. 7–10), it can, to some extent, be seen and comprehended how God can be omnipresent, omniscient, and all-providing; and how, as man, he could create all things, and as man can hold the things created by himself in their order to eternity.

22. That in God-man infinite things are one distinguishably, can also be seen, as in a mirror, from man. In man there are many and numberless things, as said above; but still man feels them all as one. From sensation he knows nothing of his brains, of his heart and lungs, of his liver, spleen, and pancreas; or of the numberless things in his eyes, ears, tongue, stomach, generative organs, and the remaining parts; and because from sensation he has no knowledge of these things, he is to himself as a one. The reason is that all these are in such a form that not one can be lacking; for it is a form recipient of life from God-man (as was shown above, n. 4–6). From the order and connection of all things in such a form there comes the feeling, and

from that the idea, as if they were not many and numberless, but were one. From this it may be concluded that the many and numberless things which make in man a seeming one, a very man who is God, are one distinguishably, yea, most distinguishably.

There is one God-man, from whom all things come

23. All things of human wisdom unite, and as it were center in this, that there is one God, the creator of the universe; consequently a man who has reason, from the general nature of his understanding, does not and cannot think otherwise. Say to any man of sound reason that there are two creators of the universe, and you will be sensible of his repugnance, and this, perhaps, from the mere sound of the phrase in his ear; from which it appears that all things of human reason unite and center in this, that God is one. There are two reasons for this. First, the very capacity to think rationally, viewed in itself, is not man's, but is God's in man; upon this capacity human reason in its general nature depends, and this general nature of reason causes man to see as from himself that God is one. Secondly, by means of that capacity man either is in the light of heaven, or he derives the generals of his thought therefrom; and it is a universal of the light of heaven that God is one. It is otherwise when man by that capacity has perverted the lower parts of his understanding; such a man indeed is endowed with that capacity, but by the twist given to these lower parts, he turns it contrariwise, and thereby his reason becomes unsound.

24. Every man, even if unconsciously, thinks of a body of men as of one man; therefore he instantly perceives what is meant when it is said that a king is the head, and the subjects are the body, also that this or that person has such a place in the general body, that is, in the kingdom. As it is with the body politic, so is it with the body spiritual. The body spiritual is the church; its head is God-man; and from this it is plain how the church thus viewed as a man would appear if instead of one God, the creator and sustainer of the universe, several were thought of. The church thus viewed would appear as one body with several heads; thus not as a man, but as a monster. If it be said that these heads have one essence, and that thus together they make one head, the only conception possible is either that of one head with several faces or of several heads with one face; thus making the church, viewed as a whole, appear deformed. But in truth, the one God is the head, and the church is the body, which acts under the command of the head, and not from itself; as is also the case in man; and from this it is that there can be only one king in a kingdom, for several kings would rend it asunder, but one is able to preserve its unity.

25. So would it be with the church scattered throughout the whole globe, which is called a communion, because it is as one body under one head. It is known that the head rules the body under it at will; for understanding and will have their seat in the head; and in conformity to the understanding and will the body is directed, even to the extent that the body is nothing but obedience. As the body can do nothing except from the understanding and will in the head, so the man of the church can do nothing except from God.

The body seems to act of itself, as if the hands and feet in acting are moved of themselves; or the mouth and tongue in speaking vibrate of themselves, when, in fact, they do not in the slightest degree act of themselves, but only from an affection of the will and the consequent thought of the understanding in the head. Suppose, now, one body to have several heads and each head to be free to act from its own understanding and its own will, could such a body continue to exist? For among several heads singleness of purpose, such as results from one head, would be impossible. As in the church, so in the heavens; heaven consists of myriads of myriads of angels, and unless these all and each looked to one God, they would fall away from one another and heaven would be broken up. Consequently, if an angel of heaven but thinks of a plurality of gods he is at once separated; for he is cast out into the outmost boundary of the heavens, and sinks downward.

26. Because the whole heaven and all things of heaven have relation to one God, angelic speech is such that by a certain unison flowing from the unison of heaven it closes in a single cadence—a proof that it is impossible for the angels to think otherwise than of one God; for speech is from thought.

27. Who that has sound reason can help seeing that the Divine is not divisible? Also that a plurality of infinites, of uncreates, of omnipotents, and of gods, is impossible? Suppose one destitute of reason were to declare that a plurality of infinites, of uncreates, of omnipotents, and of gods is possible, if only they have one identical essence, and this would make of them one infinite, uncreate, omnipotent, and God, would not the one identical essence be one identity? And one identity is not possible to several. If it should be said that one is from the other, the one who is from the other is not God in himself; nevertheless, God in himself is the God from whom all things are (see above, n. 16).

The Divine essence itself is love and wisdom

28. Sum up all things you know and submit them to careful inspection, and in some elevation of spirit search for the universal of all things, and you cannot conclude otherwise than that it is love and wisdom. For these are the two essentials of all things of man's life; everything of that life, civil, moral, and spiritual, hinges upon these two, and apart from these two is

nothing. It is the same with all things of the life of the composite man, which is, as was said above, a society, larger or smaller, a kingdom, an empire, a church, and also the angelic heaven. Take away love and wisdom from these, and consider whether they be anything, and you will find that apart from love and wisdom as their origin they are nothing.

29. Love together with wisdom in its very essence is in God. This no one can deny; for God loves everyone from love in himself, and leads everyone from wisdom in himself. The created universe, too, viewed in relation to its order, is so full of wisdom coming forth from love that all things in the aggregate may be said to be wisdom itself. For things limitless are in such order, successively and simultaneously, that taken together they make a one. It is from this, and this alone, that they can be held together and continually preserved.

30. It is because the Divine essence itself is love and wisdom that man has two capacities for life; from one of these he has understanding, from the other will. The capacity from which he has understanding derives everything it has from the influx of wisdom from God, and the capacity from which he has will derives everything it has from the influx of love from God. Man's not being truly wise and not loving rightly does not take away these capacities, but merely closes them up; and so long as they are closed up, although the understanding is still called understanding and the will is called will, they are not such in essence. If these two capacities, therefore, were to be taken away, all that is human would perish; for the human is to think and to speak from thought, and to will and to act from will. From this it is clear that the Divine has its seat in man in these two capacities, the capacity to be wise and the capacity to love (that is, that one may be wise and may love). That in man there is a possibility of loving [and of being wise], even when he is not wise as he might be and does not love as he might,

has been made known to me from much experience, and will be abundantly shown elsewhere.

31. It is because the Divine essence itself is love and wisdom, that all things in the universe have relation to good and truth; for everything that proceeds from love is called good, and everything that proceeds from wisdom is called truth. But of this more hereafter.

32. It is because the Divine essence itself is love and wisdom, that the universe and all things in it, alive and not alive, have unceasing existence from heat and light; for heat corresponds to love, and light corresponds to wisdom; and therefore spiritual heat is love and spiritual light is wisdom. But of this, also, more hereafter.

33. From Divine love and from Divine wisdom, which make the very essence that is God, all affections and thoughts with man have their rise—affections from Divine love, and thoughts from Divine wisdom; and each and all things of man are nothing but affection and thought; these two are like fountains of all things of man's life. All the enjoyments and pleasant- nesses of his life are from these—enjoyments from the affection of his love, and pleasantnesses from the thought therefrom. Now since man was created to be a recipient, and is a recipient in the degree in which he loves God and from love to God is wise, in other words, in the degree in which he is affected by those things which are from God and thinks from that affec- tion, it follows that the Divine essence, which is the creator *[creatrix]*, is Divine love and Divine wisdom.

Divine love is of Divine wisdom and Divine wisdom of Divine love

34. In God-man Divine *esse* [being] and Divine *existere* [taking form] are one distinguishably (as may be seen above, n. 14–16). And because Divine *esse* is Divine love, and Divine *existere* is

Divine wisdom, these are likewise one distinguishably. They are said to be one distinguishably, because love and wisdom are two distinct things, yet so united that love is of wisdom, and wisdom is of love, for in wisdom love is, and in love wisdom exists; and since wisdom derives its *existere* from love (as was said above, n. 15), therefore Divine wisdom also is *esse*. From this it follows that love and wisdom taken together are the Divine *esse*, but taken distinguishably love is called Divine *esse*, and wisdom Divine *existere*. Such is the angelic idea of Divine love and of Divine wisdom.

35. Since there is such a union of love and wisdom and of wisdom and love in God-man, there is one Divine essence. For the Divine essence is Divine love because it is of Divine wisdom, and is Divine wisdom because it is of Divine love. And since there is such a union of these, the Divine life also is one. Life is the Divine essence. Divine love and Divine wisdom are a one because the union is reciprocal, and reciprocal union causes oneness. Of reciprocal union, however, more will be said elsewhere.

36. There is also a union of love and wisdom in every Divine work; from which it has perpetuity, yea, its everlasting duration. If there were more of Divine love than of Divine wisdom, or more of Divine wisdom than of Divine love, in any created work, it could have continued existence only in the measure in which the two were equally in it, anything in excess passing off.

37. The Divine providence in the reforming, regenerating, and saving of men, partakes equally of Divine love and of Divine wisdom. From more of Divine love than of Divine wisdom, or from more of Divine wisdom than of Divine love, man cannot be reformed, regenerated, and saved. Divine love wills to save all, but it can save only by means of Divine wisdom; to Divine wisdom belong all the laws through which salvation is effected; and these laws love cannot transcend, because Divine love and Divine wisdom are one and act in unison.

38. In the Word, Divine love and Divine wisdom are meant by "righteousness" and "judgment," Divine love by "righteousness," and Divine wisdom by "judgment"; for this reason "righteousness" and "judgment" are predicated in the Word of God; as in David:

> Righteousness and judgment are the support of Thy Throne (Ps. 89:14).

> Jehovah shall bring forth righteousness as the light, and judgment as the noonday (Ps. 37:6).

In Hosea:

> I will betroth thee unto Me forever, in righteousness, and in judgment (2:19).

In Jeremiah:

> I will raise unto David a righteous Branch, who shall reign as King and shall execute judgment and righteousness in the earth (23:5).

In Isaiah:

> He shall sit upon the throne of David, and upon his kingdom, to establish it in judgment and in righteousness (9:7).

> Jehovah shall be exalted, because he hath filled the earth with judgment and righteousness (33:5).

In David:

> When I shall have learned the judgments of Thy righteousness. . . .
> Seven times a day do I praise Thee, because of the judgments of Thy righteousness (Ps. 119:7, 164).

The same is meant by "life" and "light" in John:

> In him was life, and the life was the light of men (1:4).

By "life" in this passage is meant the Lord's Divine love, and by "light" his Divine wisdom. The same also is meant by "life" and "spirit" in John:

Jesus said, The words which I speak unto you, they are spirit, and they are life (6:63).

39. In man love and wisdom appear as two separate things, yet in themselves they are one distinguishably, because with man wisdom is such as the love is, and love is such as the wisdom is. The wisdom that does not make one with its love appears to be wisdom, but it is not; and the love that does not make one with its wisdom appears to be the love of wisdom, but it is not; for the one must derive its essence and its life reciprocally from the other. With man love and wisdom appear as two separate things, because with him the capacity for understanding may be elevated into the light of heaven, but not the capacity for loving, except so far as he acts according to his understanding. Any apparent wisdom, therefore, which does not make one with the love of wisdom, sinks back into the love which does make one with it; and this may be a love of unwisdom, yea, of insanity. Thus a man may know from wisdom that he ought to do this or that, and yet he does not do it, because he does not love it. But so far as a man does from love what wisdom teaches, he is an image of God.

Divine love and Divine wisdom are substance and are form

40. The idea of men in general about love and about wisdom is that they are like something hovering and floating in thin air or ether or like what exhales from something of this kind. Scarcely anyone believes that they are really and actually substance and form. Even those who recognize that they are substance and form still think of the love and the wisdom as outside the subject and as issuing from it. For they call substance and form that which they think of as outside the subject and as issuing from it, even though it be something hovering and floating; not knowing that love and wisdom are the subject itself, and that what is perceived outside of it and as hovering

and floating is nothing but an appearance of the state of the subject in itself. There are several reasons why this has not hitherto been seen, one of which is, that appearances are the first things out of which the human mind forms its understanding, and these appearances the mind can shake off only by the exploration of the cause; and if the cause lies deeply hidden, the mind can explore it only by keeping the understanding for a long time in spiritual light; and this it cannot do by reason of the natural light which continually withdraws it. The truth is, however, that love and wisdom are the real and actual substance and form that constitute the subject itself.

41. But as this is contrary to appearance, it may seem not to merit belief unless it be proved; and since it can be proved only by such things as man can apprehend by his bodily senses, by these it shall be proved. Man has five external senses, called touch, taste, smell, hearing, and sight. The subject of touch is the skin by which man is enveloped, the very substance and form of the skin causing it to feel whatever is applied to it. The sense of touch is not in the things applied, but in the substance and form of the skin, which are the subject; the sense itself is nothing but an affecting of the subject by the things applied. It is the same with taste; this sense is only an affecting of the substance and form of the tongue; the tongue is the subject.

It is the same with smell; it is well known that odor affects the nostrils, and that it is in the nostrils, and that the nostrils are affected by the odoriferous particles touching them. It is the same with hearing, which seems to be in the place where the sound originates; but the hearing is in the ear, and is an affecting of its substance and form; that the hearing is at a distance from the ear is an appearance.

It is the same with sight. When a man sees objects at a distance, the seeing appears to be there; yet the seeing is in the eye, which is the subject, and is likewise an affecting of the subject. Distance is solely from the judgment concluding about space from things intermediate, or from the diminution and consequent indistinctness of the object, an image of which is produced interiorly in the eye according to the angle of incidence. From this it is evident that sight does not go out from the eye to the object, but that the image of the object enters the eye and affects its substance and form. Thus it is just the same with sight as with hearing; hearing does not go out from the ear to catch the sound, but the sound enters the ear and affects it. From all this it can be seen that the affecting of the substance and form which causes sense is not a something separate from the subject, but only causes a change in it, the subject remaining the subject then as before and afterwards.

From this it follows that seeing, hearing, smell, taste, and touch, are not a something volatile flowing from their organs, but are the organs themselves, considered in their substance and form, and that when the organs are affected sense is produced.

42. It is the same with love and wisdom, with this difference only, that the substances and forms which are love and wisdom are not obvious to the eyes as the organs of the external senses are. Nevertheless, no one can deny that those things of wisdom and love, which are called thoughts, perceptions, and affections, are substances and forms, and not entities flying and flowing out of nothing, or abstracted from real and actual substance and form, which are subjects. For in the brain are substances and forms innumerable, in which every interior sense which pertains to the understanding and will has its seat. The affections, perceptions, and thoughts there are not exhalations from these substances, but are all actually and really subjects emitting nothing from themselves, but merely undergoing changes according to whatever flows against and affects them. This may be seen from what has been said above about the external senses. Of what thus flows against and affects more will be said below.

43. From all this it may now first be seen that Divine love and Divine wisdom in themselves are substance and form; for they are very *esse* and *existere;* and unless they were such *esse* and *existere* as they are substance and form, they would be a mere thing of reasoning, which in itself is nothing.

Divine love and Divine wisdom are substance and form in itself, thus the very and the only

44. That Divine love and Divine wisdom are substance and form has been proved just above; and that Divine *esse* [being] and *existere* [taking form] are *esse* and *existere* in itself, has also been said above. It cannot be said to be *esse* and *existere* from itself, because this involves a beginning, and a beginning from something within in which would be *esse* and *existere* in itself. But very *esse* and *existere* in itself is from eternity. Very *esse* and *existere* in itself is also uncreated, and everything created must needs be from an uncreate. What is created is also finite, and the finite can exist only from the Infinite.

45. He who by exercise of thought is able to grasp the idea of and to comprehend *esse* and *existere* in itself, can certainly perceive and comprehend that it is the very and the only. That is called the very which alone is; and that is called the only from which everything else proceeds. Now because the very and the only is substance and form, it follows that it is the very and only substance and form. Because this very substance and form is Divine love and Divine wisdom, it follows that it is the very and only love, and the very and only wisdom; consequently, that it is the very and only essence, as well as the very and only life; for life is love and wisdom.

46. From all this it can be seen how sensually (that is, how much from the bodily senses and their blindness in spiritual matters) do those think who maintain that nature is from herself. They think from the eye, and are not able to think from the understanding. Thought from the eye closes the understanding, but thought from the understanding opens the eye. Such persons cannot think at all of *esse* and *existere* in itself, and that it is eternal, uncreate, and infinite; neither can they think at all of life, except as a something fleeting and vanishing into nothingness; nor can they think otherwise of love and wisdom, nor at all that from these are all things of nature. Neither can it be seen that from these are all things of nature, unless nature is regarded, not from some of its forms, which are merely objects of sight, but from uses in their succession and order. For uses are from life alone, and their succession and order are from wisdom and love alone; while forms are only containers of uses. Consequently, if forms alone are regarded, nothing of life, still less anything of love and wisdom, thus nothing of God, can be seen in nature.

Divine love and Divine wisdom must necessarily have being [esse] *and have form* [existere] *in others created by itself*

47. It is the essential of love not to love self, but to love others, and to be conjoined with others by love. It is the essential of love, moreover, to be loved by others, for thus conjunction is effected. The essence of all love consists in conjunction; this, in fact, is its life, which is called enjoyment, pleasantness, delight, sweetness, bliss, happiness, and felicity. love consists in this, that its own should be another's; to feel the joy of another as joy in oneself, that is loving. But to feel one's own joy in another and not the other's joy in oneself is not loving; for this is loving self, while the former is loving the neighbor. These two kinds of love are diametrically opposed to each other. Either, it is true, conjoins; and to love one's own, that is, oneself, in another does not seem to divide; but it does so effectually divide that so far as anyone has loved another in

this manner, so far he afterwards hates him. For such conjunction is by its own action gradually loosened, and then, in like
measure, love is turned to hate.

48. Who that is capable of discerning the essential character
of love cannot see this? For what is it to love self alone, instead
of loving someone outside of self by whom one may be loved
in return? Is not this separation rather than conjunction?
Conjunction of love is by reciprocation; and there can be no
reciprocation in self alone. If there is thought to be, it is from
an imagined reciprocation in others. From this it is clear that
Divine love must necessarily have being and have form in
others whom it may love, and by whom it may be loved. For
as there is such a need in all love, it must be to the fullest
extent, that is, infinitely in love itself.

49. With respect to God, it is impossible for him to love
others and to be loved reciprocally by others in whom there
is anything of infinity, that is, anything of the essence and
life of love in itself, or anything of the Divine. For if there
were beings having in them anything of infinity, that is, of
the essence and life of love in itself, that is, of the Divine, it
would not be God loved by others, but God loving himself;
since the Infinite, that is, the Divine, is one only, and if this
were in others, itself would be in them, and would be the
love of self itself; and of that love not the least trace can
possibly be in God, since it is wholly opposed to the Divine
essence. Consequently, for this relation to be possible there
must be others in whom there is nothing of the Divine in
itself.

That it is possible in beings created from the Divine will be
seen below. But that it may be possible, there must be
infinite wisdom making one with infinite love; that is, there
must be the Divine love of Divine wisdom, and the Divine
wisdom of Divine love (concerning which see above, n. 34-39).

50. Upon a perception and knowledge of this mystery depend a perception and knowledge of all things of existence, that is, creation; also of all things of continued existence, that is, preservation by God; in other words, of all the works of God in the created universe, of which the following pages treat.

51. But do not, I entreat you, confuse your ideas with time and with space, for so far as time and space enter into your ideas when you read what follows, you will not understand it; for the Divine is not in time and space. This will be seen clearly in the progress of this work, and in particular from what is said of eternity, infinity, and omnipresence.

All things in the universe were created from the Divine love and the Divine wisdom of God-man

52. So full of Divine love and Divine wisdom is the universe in greatest and least, and in first and last things, that it may be said to be Divine love and Divine wisdom in an image. That this is so is clearly evident from the correspondence of all things of the universe with all things of man. There is such correspondence of each and every thing that takes form in the created universe with each and every thing of man, that man may be said to be a sort of universe. There is a correspondence of his affections, and thence of his thoughts, with all things of the animal kingdom; of his will, and thence of his understanding, with all things of the vegetable kingdom; and of his outmost life with all things of the mineral kingdom. That there is such a correspondence is not apparent to anyone in the natural world, but it is apparent to everyone who gives heed to it in the spiritual world. In that world there are all things that take form in the natural world in its three kingdoms, and they are correspondences of affections and thoughts, that is, of affections from the will and of thoughts from the understanding, also of the outmost things of the life, of those who are in that world, around whom all these things are visible, presenting an appearance like that of the created universe, with the difference that it is in lesser form.

From this it is very evident to angels, that the created universe is an image representative of God-man, and that it is his love and wisdom which are presented, in an image, in the universe. Not that the created universe is God-man, but that it is from him; for nothing whatever in the created universe is substance and form in itself, or life in itself, or love and wisdom in itself, yea, neither is man a man in himself, but all is from God, who is man, wisdom, and love, also form and substance, in itself. That which has being-in-itself is uncreate and infinite; but whatever is from very being, since it contains in it nothing of Being-in-itself, is created and finite, and this exhibits an image of him from whom it has being and has form.

53. Of things created and finite *esse* [being] and *existere* [taking form] can be predicated, likewise substance and form, also life, and even love and wisdom; but these are all created and finite. This can be said of things created and finite, not because they possess anything Divine, but because they are in the Divine, and the Divine is in them. For everything that has been created is, in itself, inanimate and dead, but all things are animated and made alive by this, that the Divine is in them, and that they are in the Divine.

54. The Divine is not in one subject differently from what it is in another, but one created subject differs from another; for no two things can be precisely alike, consequently each thing is a different container. On this account, the Divine as imaged forth presents a variety of appearances. Its presence in opposites will be discussed hereafter.

*All things in the created universe are recipients of the Divine love
and the Divine wisdom of God-man*

55. It is well known that each and all things of the universe
were created by God; hence the universe, with each and every
thing pertaining to it, is called in the Word the work of the
hands of Jehovah. There are those who maintain that the
world, with everything it includes, was created out of nothing,
and of that nothing an idea of absolute nothingness is entertained. From absolute nothingness, however, nothing is or can
be made. This is an established truth. The universe, therefore,
which is God's image, and consequently full of God, could be
created only in God from God; for God is *esse* itself, and from
esse must be whatever is. To create what is, from nothing which
is not, is an utter contradiction. But still, that which is created
in God from God is not continuous from him; for God is *esse*
in itself, and in created things there is not any *esse* in itself. If
there were in created things any *esse* in itself, this would be
continuous from God, and that which is continuous from God
is God.

The angelic idea of this is, that what is created in God from
God, is like that in man which has been derived from his life,
but from which the life has been withdrawn, which is of such a
nature as to be in accord with his life, and yet it is not his life.
The angels confirm this by many things which have existence in
their heaven, where they say they are in God, and God is in
them, and still that they have, in their *esse*, nothing of God
which is God. Many things whereby they prove this will be
presented hereafter; let this serve for present information.

56. Every created thing, by virtue of this origin, is such in its
nature as to be a recipient of God, not by continuity, but by
contiguity. By the latter and not the former comes its capacity
for conjunction. For having been created in God from God, it
is adapted to conjunction; and because it has been so created, it

is an analogue, and through such conjunction it is like an image of God in a mirror.

57. From this it is that angels are angels, not from themselves, but by virtue of this conjunction with God-man; and this conjunction is according to the reception of Divine good and Divine truth, which are God, and which seem to proceed from him, though really they are in him. This reception is according to their application to themselves of the laws of order, which are Divine truths, in the exercise of that freedom of thinking and willing according to reason, which they possess from the Lord as if it were their own. By this they have a reception, as if from themselves, of Divine good and of Divine truth, and by this there is a reciprocation of love; for, as was said above, love is impossible unless it is reciprocal. The same is true of men on the earth. From what has been said it can now first be seen that all things of the created universe are recipients of the Divine love and the Divine wisdom of God-man.

58. It cannot yet be intelligibly explained how all other things of the universe which are unlike angels and men, that is, the things below man in the animal kingdom, and the things below these in the vegetable kingdom, and the things still below these in the mineral kingdom, are also recipients of the Divine love and of the Divine wisdom of God-man; for many things need to be said first about degrees of life, and degrees of the recipients of life. Conjunction with these things is according to their uses; for no good use has any other origin than through a like conjunction with God, but yet different according to degrees.

This conjunction in its descent becomes successively such that nothing of freedom is left therein, because nothing of reason, and therefore nothing of the appearance of life; but still they are recipients. Because they are recipients, they are also reagents; and forasmuch as they are reagents, they are containers.

Conjunction with uses which are not good will be discussed when the origin of evil has been made known.

59. From the above it can be seen that the Divine is in each and every thing of the created universe, and consequently that the created universe is the work of the hands of Jehovah, as is said in the Word; that is, the work of Divine love and Divine wisdom, for these are meant by the hands of Jehovah. But though the Divine is in each and all things of the created universe there is in their *esse* nothing of the Divine in itself; for the created universe is not God, but is from God; and since it is from God, there is in it an image of him like the image of a man in a mirror, wherein indeed the man appears, but still there is nothing of the man in it.

60. I heard several about me in the spiritual world talking together, who said that they were quite willing to acknowledge that the Divine is in each and every thing of the universe, because they behold therein the wonderful works of God, and these are the more wonderful the more interiorly they are examined. And yet, when they were told that the Divine is actually in each and every thing of the universe, they were displeased; which is a proof that although they assert this they do not believe it. They were therefore asked whether this cannot be seen simply from the marvelous power which is in every seed, of producing its own vegetable form in like order, even to new seeds; also because in every seed an idea of the infinite and eternal is presented; since there is in seeds an endeavor to multiply themselves and to fructify infinitely and eternally? Is not this evident also in every living creature, even the smallest?

In that there are in it organs of sense, also brains, a heart, lungs, and other parts; with arteries, veins, fibers, muscles, and the activities proceeding therefrom; besides the surpassing marvels of animal nature, about which whole volumes have been written. All these wonderful things are from God; but the forms with which they are clothed are from earthy matters, out of which come plants, and in their order, men. Therefore it is said of man,

That he was created out of the ground, and that he is dust of the earth, and that the breath of lives was breathed into him (Genesis 2:7).

From which it is plain that the Divine is not man's own, but is adjoined to him.

All created things have relation in a kind of image to man

61. This can be seen from each and all things of the animal kingdom, from each and all things of the vegetable kingdom, and from each and all things of the mineral kingdom.

A relation to man in each and all things of the animal kingdom is evident from the following. Animals of every kind have limbs by which they move, organs by which they feel, and viscera by which these are exercised; these they have in common with man. They have also appetites and affections similar to man's natural appetites and affections; and they have inborn knowledges corresponding to their affections, in some of which there appears a resemblance to what is spiritual, which is more or less evident in beasts of the earth, and birds of the air, and in bees, silkworms, ants, etc. From this it is that merely natural men consider the living creatures of this kingdom to be like themselves, except in the matter of speech.

A relation to man arising out of each and all things of the vegetable kingdom is evident from this: they spring forth from seed, and thereafter proceed step by step through their periods of growth; they have something akin to marriage, followed by prolification; their vegetative soul is use, and they are forms thereof; besides many other particulars which have relation to man. These also have been described by various authors.

A relation to man deducible from each and every thing of the mineral kingdom is seen only in an endeavor to produce forms which exhibit such a relation (which forms, as said above, are each and all things of the vegetable kingdom), and in an endeavor to perform uses thereby. For when first a seed falls into the bosom of the earth, she cherishes it, and out of herself provides it with nourishment from every source, that it may shoot up and present itself in a form representative of man. That such an endeavor exists also in its solid parts is evident from corals at the bottom of the seas and from flowers in mines, where they originate from minerals, also from metals. This endeavor towards vegetating, and performing uses thereby, is the outmost derivation from the Divine in created things.

62. As there is an endeavor of the minerals of the earth towards vegetation, so there is an endeavor of the plants towards vivification: this accounts for insects of various kinds corresponding to the odors emanating from plants. This does not arise from the heat of this world's sun, but from life operating through that heat according to the state of its recipients (as will be seen in what follows).

63. That there is a relation of all things of the created universe to man may be known from the foregoing statements, yet it can be seen only obscurely; whereas in the spiritual world this is seen clearly. In that world, also, there are all things of the three kingdoms, and in the midst of them the angel; he sees them about him, and also knows that they are representations of himself; yea, when the inmost of his understanding is opened he recognizes himself in them, and sees his image in them, hardly otherwise than as in a mirror.

64. From these and from many other concurring facts which there is not time to adduce now, it may be known with certainty that God is a man; and that the created universe is an image of him; for there is a general relation of all things to him, as well as a particular relation of all things to man.

The uses of all created things ascend by degrees from last things to
man, and through man to God the creator, from whom they are

65. Last things, as was said above, are each and all things of
the mineral kingdom, which are materials of various kinds, of
a stony, saline, oily, mineral, or metallic nature, covered over
with soil formed of vegetable and animal matters reduced to the
finest dust. In these lie concealed both the end and the beginning of all uses which are from life. The end of all uses is the
endeavor to produce uses, and the beginning is the acting force
from that endeavor. These pertain to the mineral kingdom.
Middle things are each and all things of the vegetable kingdom,
such as grasses and herbs of every kind, plants and shrubs of
every kind, and trees of every kind. The uses of these are for
the service of each and all things of the animal kingdom, both
imperfect and perfect. These they nourish, delight, and vivify;
nourishing the bellies of animals with their vegetable substances, delighting the animal senses with taste, fragrance, and
beauty, and vivifying their affections.

The endeavor towards this is in these also from life. First
things are each and all things of the animal kingdom. Those are
lowest therein which are called worms and insects, the middle
are birds and beasts, and the highest, men; for in each kingdom
there are lowest, middle and highest things, the lowest for the
use of the middle, and the middle for the use of the highest.
Thus the uses of all created things ascend in order from
outmost things to man, who is first in order.

66. In the natural world there are three degrees of ascent, and
in the spiritual world there are three degrees of ascent. All
animals are recipients of life. The more perfect are recipients of
the life and the three degrees of the natural world, the less
perfect of the life of two degrees of that world, and the
imperfect of one of its degrees. But man alone is a recipient of
the life both of the three degrees of the natural world and of

the three degrees of the spiritual world. From this it is that man can be elevated above nature, while the animal cannot. Man can think analytically and rationally of the civil and moral things that are within nature, also of the spiritual and celestial things that are above nature, yea, he can be so elevated into wisdom as even to see God. But the six degrees by which the uses of all created things ascend in their order even to God the creator, will be treated of in their proper place. From this summary, however, it can be seen that there is an ascent of all created things to the first, who alone is life, and that the uses of all things are the very recipients of life; and from this are the forms of uses.

67. It shall also be stated briefly how man ascends, that is, is elevated, from the lowest degree to the first. He is born into the lowest degree of the natural world; then, by means of knowledges, he is elevated into the second degree; and as he perfects his understanding by knowledges he is elevated into the third degree, and then becomes rational. The three degrees of ascent in the spiritual world are in man above the three natural degrees, and do not appear until he has put off the earthly body. When this takes place the first spiritual degree is open to him, afterwards the second, and finally the third; but this only with those who become angels of the third heaven; these are they that see God. Those become angels of the second heaven and of the last heaven in whom the second degree and the last degree can be opened.

Each spiritual degree in man is opened according to his reception of Divine love and Divine wisdom from the Lord. Those who receive something thereof come into the first or lowest spiritual degree, those who receive more into the second or middle spiritual degree, those who receive much into the third or highest degree. But those who receive nothing thereof remain in the natural degrees, and derive from the spiritual degrees nothing more than an ability to think and thence to speak, and to will and thence to act, but not with intelligence.

68. Of the elevation of the interiors of man, which belong to his mind, this also should be known. In everything created by God there is reaction. In life alone there is action; reaction is caused by the action of life. Because reaction takes place when any created thing is acted upon, it appears as if it belonged to what is created. Thus in man it appears as if the reaction were his, because he has no other feeling than that life is his, when yet man is only a recipient of life. From this cause it is that man, by reason of his hereditary evil, reacts against God. But so far as man believes that all his life is from God, and that all good of life is from the action of God, and all evil of life from the reaction of man, so far his reaction comes to be from [God's] action, and man acts with God as if from himself. The equilibrium of all things is from action and simultaneous reaction, and in equilibrium everything must be. These things have been said lest man should believe that he himself ascends toward God from himself, and not from the Lord.

The Divine, apart from space, fills all spaces of the universe

69. There are two things proper to nature—space and time. From these man in the natural world forms the ideas of his thought, and thereby his understanding. If he remains in these ideas, and does not raise his mind above them, he is in no wise able to perceive things spiritual and Divine, for these he involves in ideas drawn from space and time; and so far as that is done the light of his understanding becomes merely natural. To think from this *lumen* in reasoning about spiritual and Divine things, is like thinking from the thick darkness of night about those things that appear only in the light of day. From this comes worship of nature. But he who knows how to raise his mind above ideas of thought drawn from space and time passes from thick darkness into light, and has discernment in things spiritual and Divine, and finally sees the things which are in and from what is spiritual and Divine; and then from that light he dispels the thick darkness of the natural *lumen,* and banishes its fallacies from the middle to the sides. Every man who has understanding is able to transcend in thought these properties of nature, and actually does so; and he then affirms and sees that the Divine, because omnipresent, is not in space. He is also able to affirm and to see the things that have been adduced above. But if he denies the Divine omnipresence, and ascribes all things to nature, then he has no wish to be elevated, though he can be.

70. All who die and become angels put off the two above-mentioned properties of nature, namely, space and time; for they then enter into spiritual light, in which objects of thought are truths, and objects of sight are like those in the natural world, but are correspondent to their thoughts. The objects of their thought which, as just said, are truths, derive nothing at all from space and time; and though the objects of their sight appear as if in space and in time, still the angels do not think from space and time.

The reason is, that spaces and times there are not fixed, as in the natural world, but are changeable according to the states of their life. In the ideas of their thought, therefore, instead of space and time there are states of life, instead of spaces such things as have reference to states of love, and instead of times such things as have reference to states of wisdom. From this it is that spiritual thought, and spiritual speech therefrom, differ so much from natural thought and natural speech therefrom, as to have nothing in common except as regards the interiors of things, which are all spiritual. Of this difference more will be said elsewhere. Now, because the thoughts of angels derive nothing from space and time, but everything from states of life,

when it is said that the Divine fills spaces angels evidently
cannot comprehend it, for they do not know what spaces are;
but when, apart from any idea of space, it is said that the
Divine fills all things, they clearly comprehend it.

71. To make it clear that the merely natural man thinks of
spiritual and Divine things from space, and the spiritual man
apart from space, let the following serve for illustration. The
merely natural man thinks by means of ideas which he has
acquired from objects of sight, in all of which there is figure
partaking of length, breadth, and height, and of shape determined by these, either angular or circular. These [conceptions]
are manifestly present in the ideas of his thought concerning
things visible on earth; they are also in the ideas of his thought
concerning those not visible, such as civil and moral affairs.

This he is unconscious of; but they are nevertheless there, as
continuations. With a spiritual man it is different, especially
with an angel of heaven, whose thought has nothing in common with figure and form that derives anything from spiritual
length, breadth, and height, but only with figure and form
derived from the state of a thing resulting from the state of its
life. Consequently, instead of length of space he thinks of the
good of a thing from good of life; instead of breadth of space,
of the truth of a thing from truth of life; and instead of height,
of the degrees of these. Thus he thinks from the correspondence there is between things spiritual and things natural. From
this correspondence it is that in the Word "length" signifies the
good of a thing, "breadth" the truth of a thing, and "height"
the degrees of these.

From this it is evident that an angel of heaven, when he
thinks of the Divine Omnipresence, can by no means think
otherwise than that the Divine, apart from space, fills all things.
And that which an angel thinks is truth, because the light
which enlightens his understanding is Divine wisdom.

72. This is the basis of thought concerning God; for without it, what is to be said of the creation of the universe by God-man, of his providence, omnipotence, omnipresence and omniscience, even if understood, cannot be kept in mind; since the merely natural man, even while he has these things in his understanding, sinks back into his life's love, which is that of his will; and that love dissipates these truths, and immerses his thought in space, where his *lumen*, which he calls rational, abides, not knowing that so far as he denies these things, he is irrational. That this is so, may be confirmed by the idea entertained of this truth, that God is a man. Read with attention, I pray you, what has been said above (n. 11–13) and what follows after, and your understanding will accept it. But when you let your thought down into the natural *lumen* which derives from space, will not these things be seen as paradoxes? And if you let it down far, will you not reject them? This is why it is said that the Divine fills all spaces of the universe, and why it is not said that God-man fills them. For if this were said, the merely natural *lumen* would not assent. But to the proposition that the Divine fills all space, it does assent, because this agrees with the mode of speech of the theologians, that God is omnipresent, and hears and knows all things. (On this subject, more may be seen above, n. 7–10.)

The Divine is in all time, apart from time

73. As the Divine, apart from space, is in all space, so also, apart from time, is it in all time. For nothing which is proper to nature can be predicated of the Divine, and space and time are proper to nature. Space in nature is measurable, and so is time. This is measured by days, weeks, months, years, and centuries; days are measured by hours; weeks and months by days; years by the four seasons; and centuries by years. Nature derives this measurement from the apparent revolution and annual motion of the sun of the world. But in the spiritual world it is different. The progressions of life in that world appear in like manner to be in time, for those there live with one another as men in the world live with one another; and this is not possible without the appearance of time. But time there is not divided into periods as in the world, for their sun is constantly in the east and is never moved away; for it is the Lord's Divine love that appears to them as a sun. Wherefore they have no days, weeks, months, years, centuries, but in place of these there are states of life, by which a distinction is made which cannot be called, however, a distinction into periods, but into states. Consequently, the angels do not know what time is, and when it is mentioned they perceive in place of it state; and when state determines time, time is only an appearance. For joyfulness of state makes time seem short, and joylessness of state makes time seem long; from which it is evident that time in the spiritual world is nothing but quality of state. It is from this that in the Word, "hours," "days," "weeks," "months," and "years," signify states and progressions of state in series and in the aggregate; and when times are predicated of the church, by its "morning" is meant its first state, by "midday" its fullness, by "evening" its decline, and by "night" its end. The four seasons of the year, "spring," "summer," "autumn," and "winter," have a like meaning.

74. From the above it can be seen that time makes one with thought from affection; for from that is the quality of man's state. And with progressions of time, in the spiritual world, distances in progress through space coincide; as may be shown from many things. For instance, in the spiritual world ways are actually shortened or are lengthened in accordance with the longings that are of thought from affection. From this, also, comes the expression, "spaces of time." Moreover, in cases where thought does not join itself to its proper affection in man, as in sleep, the lapse of time is not noticed.

75. Now as times which are proper to nature in its world are in the spiritual world pure states, which appear progressive because angels and spirits are finite, it may be seen that in God they are not progressive because he is infinite, and infinite things in him are one (as has been shown above, n. 17–22). From this it follows that the Divine in all time is apart from time.

76. He who has no knowledge of God apart from time and is unable from any perception to think of him, is thus utterly unable to conceive of eternity in any other way than as an eternity of time; in which case, in thinking of God from eternity he must needs become bewildered; for he thinks with regard to a beginning, and beginning has exclusive reference to time. His bewilderment arises from the idea that God had existence from himself, from which he rushes headlong into an origin of nature from herself; and from this idea he can be extricated only by a spiritual or angelic idea of eternity, which is an idea apart from time; and when time is separated, the Eternal and the Divine are the same, and the Divine is the Divine in itself, not from itself.

The angels declare that while they can conceive of God from eternity, they can in no way conceive of nature from eternity, still less of nature from herself and not at all of nature as nature in herself. For that which is in itself is the very *esse*, from which all things are; *esse* in itself is very life, which is the Divine love of Divine wisdom and the Divine wisdom of Divine love. For the angels this is the eternal, an eternal as removed from time as the uncreated is from the created, or the infinite from the finite, between which, in fact, there is no ratio.

The Divine in things greatest and least is the same

77. This follows from the two preceding articles, that the Divine apart from space is in all space, and apart from time is

in all time. Moreover, there are spaces greater and greatest, and lesser and least; and since spaces and times, as said above, make one, it is the same with times. In these the Divine is the same, because the Divine is not varying and changeable, as everything is which belongs to nature, but is unvarying and unchangeable, consequently the same everywhere and always.

78. It seems as if the Divine were not the same in one person as in another; as if, for instance, it were different in the wise and in the simple, or in an old man and in a child. But this is a fallacy arising from appearance; the man is different, but the Divine in him is not different. Man is a recipient, and the recipient or receptacle is what varies. A wise man is a recipient of Divine love and Divine wisdom more adequately, and therefore more fully, than a simple man; and an old man who is also wise, more than a little child or boy; yet the Divine is the same in the one as in the other. It is in like manner a fallacy arising from appearance, that the Divine is different with angels of heaven from what it is with men on the earth, because the angels of heaven are in wisdom ineffable, while men are not; but the seeming difference is not in the Lord but in the subjects, according to the quality of their reception of the Divine.

79. That the Divine is the same in things greatest and least, may be shown by means of heaven and by means of an angel there. The Divine in the whole heaven and the Divine in an angel is the same; therefore even the whole heaven may appear as one angel. So is it with the church, and with a man of the church. The greatest form receptive of the Divine is the whole heaven together with the whole church; the least is an angel of heaven and a man of the church. Sometimes an entire society of heaven has appeared to me as one angel-man; and it was told that it may appear like a man as large as a giant, or like a man as small as an infant; and this, because the Divine in things greatest and least is the same.

80. The Divine is also the same in the greatest and in the least of all created things that are not alive; for it is in all the good of their use. These, moreover, are not alive for the reason that they are not forms of life but forms of uses; and the form varies according to the excellence of the use. But how the Divine is in these things will be stated in what follows, where creation is treated of.

81. Put away space, and deny the possibility of a vacuum, and then think of Divine love and of Divine wisdom as being essence itself, space having been put away and a vacuum denied. Then think according to space; and you will perceive that the Divine, in the greatest and in the least things of space, is the same; for in essence abstracted from space there is neither great nor small, but only the same.

82. Something shall now be said about vacuum. I once heard angels talking with Newton about vacuum, and saying that they could not tolerate the idea of a vacuum as being nothing, for the reason that in their world which is spiritual, and which is within or above the spaces and times of the natural world, they equally feel, think, are affected, love, will, breathe, yea, speak and act, which would be utterly impossible in a vacuum which is nothing, since nothing is nothing, and of nothing not anything can be affirmed. Newton said that he now knew that the Divine, which is being itself, fills all things, and that to him the idea of nothing as applied to vacuum is horrible, because that idea is destructive of all things; and he exhorts those who talk with him about vacuum to guard against the idea of nothing, comparing it to a swoon, because in nothing no real activity of mind is possible.

Chapter 2
[The Means of Creation]

Divine love and Divine wisdom appear in the spiritual world as a sun

83. There are two worlds, the spiritual and the natural. The spiritual world does not draw anything from the natural, nor the natural world from the spiritual. The two are totally distinct, and communicate only by correspondences, the nature of which has been abundantly shown elsewhere. To illustrate this by an example: heat in the natural world corresponds to the good of charity in the spiritual world, and light in the natural world corresponds to the truth of faith in the spiritual world; and who does not see that heat and the good of charity, and that light and the truth of faith, are wholly distinct? At first sight they appear as distinct as two entirely different things.

They so appear when one inquires what the good of charity has in common with heat, or the truth of faith with light; when in fact, spiritual heat is that good, and spiritual light is that truth. Although these things are in themselves so distinct, they make one by correspondence. They make one in this way: when man reads, in the Word, of heat and light, the spirits and angels who are with the man perceive charity instead of heat, and faith instead of light. This example is adduced, in order that it may be known that the two worlds, the spiritual and the natural, are so distinct as to have nothing in common with each other; yet are so created as to have communication, yea, conjunction by means of correspondences.

84. Since these two worlds are so distinct, it can be seen very clearly that the spiritual world is under another sun than the natural world. For in the spiritual world, just as in the natural, there is heat and light; but the heat there, as well as the light, is spiritual; and spiritual heat is the good of charity, and spiritual light is the truth of faith. Now since heat and light can originate only in a sun, it is evident that the spiritual world has a different sun from the natural world; and further, that the sun of the spiritual world in its essence is such that spiritual heat and light can come forth from it; whereas the sun of the natural world in its essence is such that natural heat can come forth from it. Everything spiritual has relation to good and truth, and can spring from no other source than Divine love and Divine wisdom; for all good is of love and all truth is of wisdom; that they have no other origin any discerning man can see.

85. That there is any other sun than that of the natural world has hitherto been unknown. The reason is, that the spiritual of man has so far passed over into his natural, that he does not know what the spiritual is, and thus does not know that there is a spiritual world, the abode of spirits and angels, other than and different from the natural world. Since the spiritual world has lain so deeply hidden from the knowledge of those who are in the natural world, it has pleased the Lord to open the sight of my spirit, that I might see the things which are in that world, just as I see those in the natural world, and might afterwards describe that world; which has been done in the work *Heaven and Hell,* in one chapter of which the sun of the spiritual world is treated of. For that sun has been seen by me; and it appeared of the same size as the sun of the natural world; also fiery like it, but more glowing. It has also been made known to me that the whole angelic heaven is under that sun; and that angels of the third heaven see it constantly, angels of the second heaven very often, and angels of the first or outmost heaven sometimes. That all their heat and all their light, as well as all things that are manifest in that world, are from that sun will be seen in what follows.

86. That sun is not the Lord himself, but is from the Lord. It is the Divine love and the divine wisdom proceeding from him that appear as a sun in that world. And because love and wisdom in the Lord are one (as shown in chapter 1), that sun is said to be Divine love; for Divine wisdom is of Divine love, consequently is love.

87. Since love and fire mutually correspond, that sun appears before the eyes of the angels as fiery; for angels cannot see love with their eyes, but they see in the place of love what corresponds to it. For angels, equally with men, have an internal and an external; it is their internal that thinks and is wise, and that wills and loves; it is their external that feels, sees, speaks and acts. All their externals are correspondences of internals; but the correspondences are spiritual, not natural. Moreover, Divine love is felt as fire by spiritual beings. For this reason "fire," when mentioned in the Word, signifies love. In the Israelitish church, "holy fire" signified love; and this is why, in prayers to God, it is customary to ask that "heavenly fire," that is, Divine love, "may kindle the heart."

88. With such a difference between the spiritual and the natural (as shown above, n. 83), nothing from the sun of the natural world, that is, nothing of its heat and light, nor anything pertaining to any earthly object, can pass over into the spiritual world. To the spiritual world the light of the natural world is thick darkness, and its heat is death. Nevertheless, the heat of the world can be vivified by the influx of heavenly heat, and the light of the world can be illumined by the influx of heavenly light. Influx is effected by correspondences; and it cannot be effected by continuity.

Out of the sun that takes form [existit] *from Divine love and Divine wisdom, heat and light go forth*

89. In the spiritual world where angels and spirits are there are heat and light, just as in the natural world where men are; moreover in like manner as heat, the heat is felt and the light is seen as light. Still the heat and light of the spiritual world and of the natural world are (as said above) so entirely different as to have nothing in common. They differ one from the other as what is alive differs from what is dead. The heat of the spiritual world in itself is alive; so is the light; but the heat of the natural world in itself is dead; so is its light. For the heat and light of the spiritual world go forth from a sun that is pure love, while the heat and light of the natural world go forth from a sun that is pure fire; and love is alive, and the Divine love is life itself; while fire is dead, and solar fire is death itself, and may be so called because it has nothing whatever of life in it.

90. Since angels are spiritual they can live in no other than spiritual heat and light, while men can live in no other than natural heat and light; for what is spiritual accords with what is spiritual, and what is natural with what is natural. If an angel were to derive the least particle from natural heat and light he would perish; for it is totally discordant with his life. As to the interiors of the mind every man is a spirit. When he dies he withdraws entirely from the world of nature, leaving behind him all its belongings, and enters a world where there is nothing of nature.

In that world he lives so separated from nature that there is no communication whatever by continuity, that is, as between what is purer and grosser, but only like that between what is prior and posterior; and between such no communication is possible except by correspondences. From this it can be seen that spiritual heat is not a purer natural heat, or spiritual light a purer natural light, but that they are altogether of a different essence; for spiritual heat and light derive their essence from a sun which is pure Love, and this is life itself; while natural heat and light derive their essence from a sun which is pure fire, in which (as said above) there is absolutely nothing of life.

91. Such being the difference between the heat and light of the two worlds, it is very evident why those who are in the one world cannot see those who are in the other world. For the eyes of man, who sees from natural light, are of the substance of his world, and the eyes of an angel are of the substance of his world; thus in both cases they are formed for the proper reception of their own light. From all this it can be seen from how much ignorance those think who, because they cannot see angels and spirits with their eyes, are unwilling to believe them to be men.

92. Hitherto it has not been known that angels and spirits are in a totally different light and different heat from men. It has not been known even that another light and another heat are possible. For man in his thought has not penetrated beyond the interior or purer things of nature. And for this reason many have placed the abodes of angels and spirits in the ether, and some in the stars—thus within nature, and not above or outside of it. But, in truth, angels and spirits are entirely above or outside of nature, and are in their own world, which is under another sun.

And since in that world spaces are appearances (as was shown above), angels and spirits cannot be said to be in the ether or in the stars; in fact, they are present with man, conjoined to the affection and thought of his spirit; since man is a spirit, and because of that thinks and wills; consequently the spiritual world is wherever man is, and in no wise away from him. In a word, every man as regards the interiors of his mind is in that world, in the midst of spirits and angels there; and he thinks from its light, and loves from its heat.

The sun of the spiritual world is not God, but is a proceeding from the Divine love and Divine wisdom of God-man; so also are the heat and light from that sun

93. By that sun which is before the eyes of the angels, and from which they have heat and light, is not meant the Lord himself, but the first proceeding from him, which is the highest [degree] of spiritual heat. The highest [degree] of spiritual heat is spiritual fire, which is Divine love and Divine wisdom in their first correspondence. On this account that sun appears fiery, and to the angels is fiery, but not to men. Fire which is fire to men is not spiritual, but natural; and between the two fires there is a difference like the difference between what is alive and what is dead. Therefore the spiritual sun by its heat vivifies spiritual beings and renews spiritual objects. The natural sun does the same for natural beings and natural objects; yet not from itself, but by means of an influx of spiritual heat, to which it renders aid as a kind of substitute.

94. This spiritual fire, in which also there is light in its origin, becomes spiritual heat and light, which decrease in their going forth. This decrease is effected by degrees, which will be treated of in what follows. The ancients represented this by circles glowing with fire and resplendent with light around the head of God, as is common also at the present day in paintings representing God as a man.

95. That love begets heat, and wisdom light, is manifest from actual experience. When man loves he grows warm, and when he thinks from wisdom he sees things as it were in light. And from this it is evident that the first proceeding of love is heat, and that the first proceeding of wisdom is light. That they are also correspondences is obvious; for heat takes place *[existit]* not in love itself, but from love in the will, and thence in the body; and light takes place not in wisdom, but in the thought of the understanding, and thence in the speech. Consequently

love and wisdom are the essence and life of heat and light. Heat and light are what proceed, and because they are what proceed, they are also correspondences.

96. That spiritual light is altogether distinct from natural light, anyone may know if he observes the thoughts of his mind. For when the mind thinks, it sees its objects in light, and they who think spiritually see truths, and this at midnight just as well as in the daytime. For this reason light is predicated of the understanding, and the understanding is said to see; thus one sometimes declares of something which another says that he sees (that is, understands) that it is so. The understanding, because it is spiritual, cannot thus see by natural light, for natural light does not inhere in man, but withdraws with the sun. From this it is obvious that the understanding enjoys a light different from that of the eye, and that this light is from a different origin.

97. Let everyone beware of thinking that the sun of the spiritual world is God himself. God himself is a man. The first proceeding from his love and wisdom is that fiery spiritual [substance] which appears before the angels as a sun. When, therefore, the Lord manifests himself to the angels in person, he manifests himself as a man; and this sometimes in the sun, sometimes outside of it.

98. It is from this correspondence that in the Word the Lord is called not only a "sun" but also "fire" and "light." And by the "sun" is meant himself as to Divine love and Divine wisdom together; by "fire" himself in respect to Divine love, and by "light" himself in respect to Divine wisdom.

Spiritual heat and light in proceeding from the Lord as a sun, make one, just as his Divine love and Divine wisdom make one

99. How Divine love and Divine wisdom in the Lord make one has been explained in chapter 1; in like manner heat and

light make one, because they proceed from these, and the things which proceed make one by virtue of their correspondence, heat corresponding to love, and light to wisdom.

From this it follows that as Divine love is Divine *esse* [being] and Divine wisdom is Divine *existere* [taking form] (as shown above, n. 14-16), so spiritual heat is the Divine proceeding from Divine *esse*, and spiritual light is the Divine proceeding from Divine *existere*. And as by that union Divine love is of Divine wisdom, and Divine wisdom is of Divine love (as shown above, n. 34-39), so spiritual heat is of spiritual light, and spiritual light is of spiritual heat. And because there is such a union it follows that heat and light, in proceeding from the Lord as a sun, are one. It will be seen, however, in what follows, that they are not received as one by angels and men.

100. The heat and light that proceed from the Lord as a sun are what in an eminent sense are called the spiritual, and they are called the spiritual in the singular number, because they are one; when, therefore, the spiritual is mentioned in the following pages, it is meant both these together. From that spiritual it is that the whole of that world is called spiritual. Through that spiritual, all things of that world derive their origin, and also their name. That heat and that light are called the spiritual, because God is called spirit, and God as spirit is the spiritual going forth. God, by virtue of his own very essence, is called Jehovah; but by means of that going forth He vivifies and enlightens angels of heaven and men of the church. Consequently, vivification and enlightenment are said to be effected by the spirit of Jehovah.

101. That heat and light, that is, the spiritual going forth from the Lord as a sun, make one, may be illustrated by the heat and light that go forth from the sun of the natural world. These two also make one in their going out from that sun. That they do not make one on earth is owing not to the

sun, but to the earth. For the earth revolves daily round its axis, and has a yearly motion following the ecliptic, which gives the appearance that heat and light do not make one. For in the middle of summer there is more of heat than of light, and in the middle of winter more of light than of heat. In the spiritual world it is the same, except that there is in that world no daily or yearly motion of the earth; but the angels turn themselves, some more, some less, to the Lord; those who turn themselves more, receive more from heat and less from light, and those who turn themselves less to the Lord receive more from light and less from heat.

From this it is that the heavens, which consist of angels, are divided into two kingdoms, one called celestial, the other spiritual. The celestial angels receive more from heat, and the spiritual angels more from light. Moreover, the lands they inhabit vary in appearance according to their reception of heat and light. If this change of state of the angels is substituted for the motion of the earth, the correspondence is complete.

102. In what follows it will be seen, also, that all spiritual things that originate through the heat and light of their sun, make one in like manner when regarded in themselves, but when regarded as proceeding from the affections of the angels do not make one. When heat and light make one in the heavens, it is with the angels as if it were spring; but when they do not make one, it is either like summer or like winter—not like the winter in the frigid zones, but like the winter in the warmer zone. Thus reception of love and wisdom in equal measure is the very angelic state, and therefore an angel is an angel of heaven according to the union in him of love and wisdom. It is the same with the man of the church, when love and wisdom, that is, charity and faith, make one in him.

The sun of the spiritual world appears at a middle altitude, far off from the angels, like the sun of the natural world from men

103. Most people take with them out of the world an idea of God, as being above the head, on high, and an idea of the Lord, as living in heaven among the angels. They take with them this idea of God because, in the Word, God is called the "most high," and is said to "dwell on high"; therefore in prayer and worship men raise their eyes and hands upwards, not knowing that by the "most high" is signified the inmost.

They take with them the idea of the Lord as being in heaven among the angels, because men think of him as they think of another man, some thinking of him as they think of an angel, not knowing that the Lord is the very and only God who rules the universe, who if he were among the angels in heaven, could not have the universe under his gaze and under his care and government. And unless he shone as a sun before those who are in the spiritual world, angels could have no light; for angels are spiritual, and therefore no other than spiritual light is in accord with their essence. That there is light in the heavens, immensely exceeding the light on earth, will be seen below where degrees are discussed.

104. As regards the sun, therefore, from which angels have light and heat, it appears above the lands on which the angels dwell, at an elevation of about forty-five degrees, which is the middle altitude; it also appears far off from the angels like the sun of the world from men. The sun appears constantly at that altitude and at that distance, and does not move from its place. Hence it is that angels have no times divided into days and years, nor any progression of the day from morning, through midday to evening and into night; nor any progression of the year from spring, through summer to autumn, into winter; but there is perpetual light and perpetual spring; consequently, with the angels, as was said above, in place of times there are states.

105. The sun of the spiritual world appears at a middle altitude chiefly for the following reasons: First, the heat and light which proceed from that sun are thus at their medium intensity, consequently are equally proportioned and thus properly attempered. For if the sun were to appear above the middle altitude more heat than light would be perceived, if below it more light than heat; as is the case on earth when the sun is above or below the middle of the sky; when above, the heat increases beyond the light, when below, the light increases beyond the heat; for light remains the same in summer and in winter, but heat increases and diminishes according to the degree of the sun's altitude. Second, the sun of the spiritual world appears in a middle altitude above the angelic heaven, because there is thus a perpetual spring in all the angelic heavens, whereby the angels are in a state of peace; for this state corresponds to springtime on earth. Third, angels are thus enabled to turn their faces constantly to the Lord, and behold him with their eyes. For at every turn of their bodies, the angels have the east, thus the Lord, before their faces. This is peculiar to that world, and would not be the case if the sun of that world were to appear above or below the middle altitude, and least of all if it were to appear overhead in the zenith.

106. If the sun of the spiritual world did not appear far off from the angels, like the sun of the natural world from men, the whole angelic heaven, and hell under it, and our terraqueous globe under these, would not be under the view, the care, the omnipresence, omniscience, omnipotence, and providence of the Lord; comparatively as the sun of our world, if it were not at such a distance from the earth as it appears, could not be present and powerful in all lands by its heat and light, and therefore could not render its aid, as a kind of substitute, to the sun of the spiritual world.

107. It is very necessary to be known that there are two suns, one spiritual, the other natural: a spiritual sun for those who are in the spiritual world, and a natural sun for those who are in the natural world. Unless this is known, nothing can be properly understood about creation and about man, which are the subjects here to be treated of. Effects may, it is true, be observed, but unless at the same time the causes of effects are seen, effects can only appear as it were in the darkness of night.

The distance between the sun and the angels in the spiritual world is an appearance according to reception by them of Divine love and Divine wisdom

108. All fallacies which prevail with the evil and the simple arise from appearances which have been confirmed. So long as appearances remain appearances, they are apparent truths, according to which everyone may think and speak; but when they are accepted as real truths, which is done when they are confirmed, then apparent truths become falsities and fallacies. For example: it is an appearance that the sun is borne around the earth daily, and follows yearly the path of the ecliptic. So long as this appearance is not confirmed it is an apparent truth, according to which anyone may think and speak; for he may say that the sun rises and sets and thereby causes morning, midday, evening, and night; also that the sun is now in such or such a degree of the ecliptic or of its altitude, and thereby causes spring, summer, autumn, and winter. But when this appearance is confirmed as the real truth, then the confirmer thinks and utters a falsity springing from a fallacy. It is the same with innumerable other appearances, not only in natural, civil, and moral, but also in spiritual affairs.

109. It is the same with the distance of the sun of the spiritual world, which sun is the first proceeding of the Lord's Divine love and Divine wisdom. The truth is that there is no distance, but that the distance is an appearance according to the reception of Divine love and Wisdom by the angels in their degree.

That distances, in the spiritual world, are appearances may be seen from what has been shown above (as in n. 7–9, that the Divine is not in space; and in n. 69–72, that the Divine, apart from space, fills all spaces). If there are no spaces, there are no distances, or, what is the same, if spaces are appearances, distances also are appearances, for distances are of space.

110. The sun of the spiritual world appears at a distance from the angels, because they receive Divine love and Divine wisdom in the measure of heat and light that is adequate to their states. For an angel, because created and finite, cannot receive the Lord in the first degree of heat and light, such as is in the sun; if he did he would be entirely consumed. The Lord, therefore, is received by angels in a degree of heat and light corresponding to their love and wisdom. The following may serve for illustration. An angel of the lowest heaven cannot ascend to the angels of the third heaven; for if he ascends and enters their heaven, he falls into a kind of swoon, and his life, as it were, strives with death; the reason is that he has a less degree of love and wisdom, and the heat of his love and the light of his wisdom are in the same degree as his love and wisdom. What, then, would be the result if an angel were even to ascend toward the sun, and come into its fire? On account of the differences of reception of the Lord by the angels, the heavens also appear separate from one another. The highest heaven, which is called the third, appears above the second, and the second above the first; not that the heavens are apart, but they appear to be apart, for the Lord is present equally with those who are in the lowest heaven and with those who are in the third heaven. That which causes the appearance of distance is not in the Lord but in the subjects, that is, the angels.

111. That this is so can hardly be comprehended by a natural idea, because in such there is space, but by a spiritual idea, such as angels have, it can be comprehended, because in such there

is no space. Yet even by a natural idea this much can be comprehended, that love and wisdom (or what is the same, the Lord, who is Divine love and Divine wisdom) cannot advance through spaces, but is present with each one according to reception. That the Lord is present with all, he teaches in Matthew (28:20), and that he makes his abode with those who love him, in John (14:23).

112. As this has been proved by means of the heavens and the angels, it may seem a matter of too exalted wisdom; but the same is true of men. Men, as to the interiors of their minds, are warmed and illuminated by that same sun. They are warmed by its heat and illuminated by its light in the measure in which they receive love and wisdom from the Lord. The difference between angels and men is that angels are under the spiritual sun only, but men are not only under that sun, but also under the sun of this world; for men's bodies can begin and continue to exist only under both suns; but not so the bodies of angels, which are spiritual.

Angels are in the Lord, and the Lord in them; and because angels are recipients, the Lord alone is heaven

113. Heaven is called "the dwelling place of God," also "the throne of God," and from this it is believed that God is there as is a king in his kingdom. But God (that is, the Lord) is in the sun above the heavens, and by his presence in heat and light, is in the heavens (as is shown in the last two paragraphs). But although the Lord is present in heaven in that manner, still he is there as he is in himself.

For (as shown just above, n. 108–112) the distance between the sun and heaven is not distance, but appearance of distance; and since that distance is only an appearance it follows that the Lord himself is in heaven, for he is in the love and wisdom of the angels of heaven; and since he is in the love and wisdom of all angels, and the angels constitute heaven, he is in the whole heaven.

114. The Lord not only is in heaven, but also is heaven itself; for love and wisdom are what make the angel, and these two are the Lord's in the angels; from which it follows that the Lord is heaven. For angels are not angels from what is their own; what is their own is altogether like what is man's own, which is evil. An angel's own is such because all angels were once men, and this own clings to the angels from their birth. It is only put aside, and so far as it is put aside the angels receive love and wisdom, that is, the Lord, in themselves. Anyone, if he will only elevate his understanding a little, can see that the Lord can dwell in angels, only in what is his, that is, in what is his very own, which is love and wisdom, and not at all in the selfhood of angels, which is evil. From this it is, that so far as evil is put away so far the Lord is in them, and so far they are angels. The very angelic of heaven is Love Divine and Wisdom Divine. This Divine is called the angelic when it is in angels. From this, again, it is evident that angels are angels from the Lord, and not from themselves; consequently, the same is true of heaven.

115. But how the Lord is in an angel and an angel in the Lord cannot be comprehended, unless the nature of their conjunction is known. Conjunction is of the Lord with the angel and of the angel with the Lord; conjunction, therefore, is reciprocal. On the part of the angel it is as follows. The angel, in like manner as man, has no other perception than that he is in love and wisdom from himself, consequently that love and wisdom are, as it were, his or his own. Unless he so perceived there would be no conjunction, thus the Lord would not be in him, nor he in the Lord. Nor can it be possible for the Lord to be in any angel or man, unless the

one in whom the Lord is, with love and wisdom, has a perception and sense as if they were his. By this means the Lord is not only received, but also, when received, is retained, and likewise loved in return. And by this, also, the angel is made wise and continues wise. Who can wish to love the Lord and his neighbor, and who can wish to be wise, without a sense and perception that what he loves, learns, and imbibes is, as it were, his own? Who otherwise can retain it in himself? If this were not so, the inflowing love and wisdom would have no abiding place, for it would flow through and not affect; thus an angel would not be an angel, nor would man be a man; he would be merely like something inanimate. From all this it can be seen that there must be an ability to reciprocate that there may be conjunction.

116. It shall now be explained how it comes that an angel perceives and feels as his, and thus receives and retains that which yet is not his; for, as was said above, an angel is not an angel from what is his, but from those things which he has from the Lord. The essence of the matter is this: Every angel has freedom and rationality; these two he has to the end that he may be capable of receiving love and wisdom from the Lord. Yet neither of these, freedom nor rationality, is his; they are the Lord's in him. But since the two are intimately conjoined to his life, so intimately that they may be said to be joined into it, they appear to be his own. It is from them that he is able to think and will, and to speak and act; and what he thinks, wills, speaks, and does from them, appears as if it were from himself.

This gives him the ability to reciprocate, and by means of this conjunction is possible. Yet so far as an angel believes that love and wisdom are really in him, and thus lays claim to them for himself as if they were his, so far the angelic is not in him, and therefore he has no conjunction with the Lord; for he is not in truth, and as truth makes one with the light of heaven, so far he cannot be in heaven; for he thereby denies that he lives from the Lord, and believes that he lives from himself, and that he therefore possesses Divine essence. In these two, freedom and rationality, the life which is called angelic and human consists. From all this it can be seen that for the sake of conjunction with the Lord, the angel has the ability to reciprocate, but that this ability, in itself considered, is not his but the Lord's.

From this it is, that if he abuses his ability to reciprocate, by which he perceives and feels as his what is the Lord's, which is done by appropriating it to himself, he falls from the angelic state. That conjunction is reciprocal, the Lord himself teaches (John 14:20-24; 15:4-6); also that the conjunction of the Lord with man and of man with the Lord, is in those things of the Lord that are called his words (John 15:7).

117. Some are of the opinion that Adam was in such liberty or freedom of choice as to be able to love God and be wise from himself, and that this freedom of choice was lost in his posterity. But this is an error; for man is not life, but is a recipient of life (see above, n. 4-6, 54-60); and he who is a recipient of life cannot love and be wise from anything of his own; consequently, when Adam willed to be wise and to love from what was his own he fell from wisdom and love, and was cast out of paradise.

118. What has just been said of an angel is likewise true of heaven, which consists of angels, since the Divine in greatest and least things is the same (as was shown above n. 77-82). What is said of an angel and of heaven is likewise true of man and the church, for the angel of heaven and the man of the church act as one through conjunction; in fact, a man of the church is an angel, in respect to the interiors which are of his mind. By a man of the church is meant a man in whom the church is.

In the spiritual world the east is where the Lord appears as a sun, and from that the other quarters are determined

119. The sun of the spiritual world and its essence, also its heat and light, and the presence of the Lord thereby, have been treated of; a description is now to be given of the quarters in the spiritual world. That sun and that world are treated of, because God and love and wisdom are treated of; and to treat of those subjects except from their very origin would be to proceed from effects, not from causes. Yet from effects nothing but effects can be learned; when effects alone are considered no cause is brought to light; but causes reveal effects. To know effects from causes is to be wise; but to search for causes from effects is not to be wise, because fallacies then present themselves, which the investigator calls causes, and this is to turn wisdom into foolishness. Causes are things prior, and effects are things posterior; and things prior cannot be seen from things posterior, but things posterior can be seen from things prior. This is order. For this reason the spiritual world is here first treated of, for all causes are there; and afterwards the natural world, where all things that appear are effects.

120. The quarters in the spiritual world shall now be spoken of. There are quarters there in like manner as in the natural world, but like that world itself, they are spiritual; while the quarters in the natural world, like that world itself, are natural; the difference between them therefore is so great that they have nothing in common. In each world there are four quarters, which are called east, west, south, and north. In the natural world, these four quarters are constant, determined by the sun on the meridian; opposite this is north, on one side is east, on the other, west. These quarters are determined by the meridian of each place; for the sun's station on the meridian at each point is always the same, and is therefore fixed. In the spiritual world it is different. The quarters there are determined by the sun of that world, which appears constantly in its own place, and where it appears is the east; consequently the determination of the quarters in that world is not from the south, as in the natural world, but from the east, opposite to this is west, on one side is south, and on the other, north. But that these quarters are not determined by the sun, but by the inhabitants of that world, who are angels and spirits, will be seen in what follows.

121. As these quarters, by virtue of their origin, which is the Lord as a sun, are spiritual, so the dwelling places of angels and spirits, all of which are according to these quarters, are also spiritual. They are spiritual, because angels and spirits have their places of abode according to their reception of love and wisdom from the Lord. Those in a higher degree of love dwell in the east; those in a lower degree of love in the west; those in a higher degree of wisdom, in the south; and those in a lower degree of wisdom, in the north. From this it is that, in the Word, by "the east," in the highest sense, is meant the Lord, and in a relative sense love to him; by the "west," a diminishing love to him; by the "south" wisdom in light; and by the "north" wisdom in shade; or similar things relatively to the state of those who are treated of.

122. Since the east is the point from which all quarters in the spiritual world are determined, and by the east, in the highest sense, is meant the Lord, and also Divine love, it is evident that the source from which all things are is the Lord and love to him, and that one is remote from the Lord in the measure in which he is not in that love, and dwells either in the west, or in the south, or in the north, at distances corresponding to the reception of love.

123. Since the Lord as a sun is constantly in the east, the ancients, with whom all things of worship were representative of spiritual things, turned their faces to the east in their devotions; and that they might do the like in all worship, they

turned their temples also in that direction. From this it is that, at the present day, churches are built in like manner.

The quarters in the spiritual world are not from the Lord as a sun, but from the angels according to reception

124. It has been stated that the angels dwell separate from each other; some in the eastern quarter, some in the western, some in the southern, and some in the northern; and that those who dwell in the eastern quarter are in a higher degree of love; those in the western, in a lower degree of love; those in the southern, in the light of wisdom; and those in the northern, in the shade of wisdom. This diversity of dwelling places appears as though it were from the Lord as a sun, when, in fact it is from the angels. The Lord is not in a greater and lesser degree of love and wisdom, that is, as a sun he is not in a greater or lesser degree of heat and light with one than with another, for he is everywhere the same. But he is not received by one in the same degree as by another; and this makes them appear to themselves to be more or less distant from one another, and also variously as regards the quarters. From this it follows that quarters in the spiritual world are nothing else than various receptions of love and wisdom, and thence of heat and light from the Lord as a sun. That this is so is plain from what was shown above (n. 108–112), that in the spiritual world distances are appearances.

125. As the quarters are various receptions of love and wisdom by angels, the variety from which that appearance springs shall now be explained. The Lord is in the angel, and the angel in the Lord (as was shown in a preceding article). But on account of the appearance that the Lord as a sun is outside of the angel, there is also the appearance that the Lord sees him from the sun, and that he sees the Lord in the sun. This is almost like the appearance of an image in a mirror. Speaking,

therefore, according to that appearance, it may be said that the Lord sees and looks at each one face to face, but that angels, on their part, do not thus behold the Lord. Those who are in love to the Lord from the Lord see him directly in front; these, therefore, are in the east and the west; but those who are more in wisdom see the Lord obliquely to the right, and those who are less in wisdom obliquely to the left; therefore the former are in the south, and the latter in the north. The view of these is oblique because love and wisdom (as has been said before), although they proceed from the Lord as one, are not received as one by angels; and the wisdom which is in excess of the love, while it appears as wisdom, is not wisdom, because in the overplus of wisdom there is no life from love. From all this it is evident whence comes the diversity of reception according to which angels appear to dwell according to quarters in the spiritual world.

126. That this variety of reception of love and wisdom is what gives rise to the quarters in the spiritual world can be seen from the fact that an angel changes his quarter according to the increase or decrease of love with him; from which it is evident that the quarter is not from the Lord as a sun, but from the angel according to reception. It is the same with man as regards his spirit. In respect to his spirit, he is in some quarter of the spiritual world, whatever quarter of the natural world he may be in, for quarters in the spiritual world, as has been said above, have nothing in common with quarters in the natural world. Man is in the latter as regards his body, but in the former as regards his spirit.

127. In order that love and wisdom may make one in an angel or in a man, there are pairs in all the things of his body. The eyes, ears, and nostrils are pairs; the hands, loins, and feet are pairs; the brain is divided into two hemispheres, the heart into two chambers, the lungs into two lobes, and in like

manner the other parts. Thus in angel and man there is right and left; and all their right parts have relation to the love from which wisdom comes; and all the left parts, to the wisdom which is from love; or, what is the same, all the right parts have relation to the good from which truth comes; and all the left parts, to the truth that is from good. Angel and man have these pairs in order that love and wisdom, or good and truth, may act as one, and as one, may have regard to the Lord. But of this more in what follows.

128. From all this it can be seen in what fallacy and consequent falsity those are, who suppose that the Lord bestows heaven arbitrarily, or arbitrarily grants one to become wise and loving more than another, when, in truth, the Lord is just as desirous that one may become wise and be saved as another. For he provides means for all; and everyone becomes wise and is saved in the measure in which he accepts these means, and lives in accordance with them. For the Lord is the same with one as with another; but the recipients, who are angels and men, are unlike by reason of unlike reception and life. That this is so can be seen from what has just been said of spiritual quarters, and of the dwelling places of the angels in accordance with them; namely, that this diversity is not from the Lord but from the recipients.

Angels turn their faces constantly to the Lord as a sun, and thus have the south to the right, the north to the left, and the west behind them

129. All that is here said of angels, and of their turning to the Lord as a sun, is to be understood also of man, as regards his spirit. For man in respect to his mind is a spirit, and if he be in love and wisdom, is an angel; consequently, after death, when he has put off his externals, which he had derived from the natural world, he becomes a spirit or an angel. And because

angels turn their faces constantly toward the sun in the east, thus toward the Lord, it is said also of any man who is in love and wisdom from the Lord, that "he sees God," that "he looks to God," that "he has God before his eyes," by which is meant that he lives as an angel does. Such things are spoken of in the world, because they actually take place [existunt] both in heaven and in the spirit of man. Who does not look before himself to God when he prays, to whatever quarter his face may be turned?

130. Angels turn their faces constantly to the Lord as a sun, because they are in the Lord, and the Lord in them; and the Lord interiorly leads their affections and thoughts, and turns them constantly to himself; consequently they cannot do otherwise than look towards the east where the Lord appears as a sun; from which it is evident that angels do not turn themselves to the Lord, but the Lord turns them to himself. For when angels think interiorly of the Lord, they do not think of him otherwise than as being in themselves. Real interior thought does not cause distance, but exterior thought, which acts as one with the sight of the eyes; and for the reason that exterior thought, but not interior, is in space; and when not in space, as in the spiritual world, it is still in an appearance of space. But these things can be little understood by the man who thinks about God from space. For God is everywhere, yet not in space.

Thus he is both within and without an angel; consequently an angel can see God, that is, the Lord, both within himself and without himself; within himself when he thinks from love and wisdom, without himself when he thinks about love and wisdom. But these things will be treated of in detail in treatises on the Lord's omnipresence, omniscience, and omnipotence. Let every man guard himself against falling into the detestable false doctrine that God has infused himself into men, and that he is in them, and no longer in himself; for God is everywhere, as well within man as without, for apart from space he is in all space (as was shown above, n. 7–10, 69–72); whereas if he were in man, he would be not only divisible, but also shut up in space; yea, man then might even think himself to be God. This heresy is so abominable, that in the spiritual world it stinks like carrion.

131. The turning of angels to the Lord is such that at every turn of their bodies they look toward the Lord as a sun in front of them. An angel may turn himself round and round, and thereby see the various things that are about him, still the Lord as a sun appears constantly before his face. This may seem wonderful, yet it is the truth. It has also been granted me to see the Lord thus as a sun. I see him now before my face; and for several years I have so seen him, to whatever quarter of the world I have turned.

132. Since the Lord as a sun, consequently the east, is before the faces of all angels of heaven, it follows that to their right is the south; to their left the north; and behind them the west; and this, too, at every turn of the body. For, as was said before, all quarters in the spiritual world are determined from the east; therefore those who have the east before their eyes are in these very quarters, yea, are themselves what determine the quarters; for (as was shown above, n. 124–128) the quarters are not from the Lord as a sun, but from the angels according to reception.

133. Now since heaven is made up of angels, and angels are of such a nature, it follows that all heaven turns itself to the Lord, and that, by means of this turning, heaven is ruled by the Lord as one man, as in his sight it is one man. That heaven is as one man in the sight of the Lord may be seen in the work *Heaven and Hell* (n. 59–87). Also from this are the quarters of heaven.

134. Since the quarters are thus inscribed as it were on the angel, as well as on the whole heaven, an angel, unlike man in the world, knows his own home and his own dwelling place wherever he goes. Man does not know his home and dwelling place from the spiritual quarter in himself, because he thinks from space, thus from the quarters of the natural world, which have nothing in common with the quarters of the spiritual world. But birds and beasts have such knowledge, for it is implanted in them to know of themselves their homes and dwelling places, as is evident from abundant observation; a proof that such is the case in the spiritual world; for all things that have form [existunt] in the natural world are effects, and all things that have form in the spiritual world are the causes of these effects. There does not take place [existit] a natural that does not derive its cause from a spiritual.

All interior things of the angels, both of mind and body, are turned to the Lord as a sun

135. Angels have understanding and will, and they have a face and body. They have also the interior things of the understanding and will, and of the face and body. The interiors of the understanding and will are such as pertain to their interior affection and thought; the interiors of the face are the brains; and the interiors of the body are the viscera, chief among which are the heart and lungs. In a word, angels have each and all things that men on earth have; it is from these things that angels are men. External form, apart from these internal things, does not make them men, but external form together with, yea, from, internals; for otherwise they would be only images of man, in which there would be no life, because inwardly there would be no form of life.

136. It is well known that the will and understanding rule the body at pleasure, for what the understanding thinks, the mouth speaks, and what the will wills, the body does. From this it is plain that the body is a form corresponding to the understanding and will. And because form also is predicated of understanding and will, it is plain that the form of the body corresponds to the form of the understanding and will. But this is not the place to describe the nature of these respective forms. In each form there are things innumerable; and these, in each of them, act as one, because they mutually correspond. It is from this that the mind (that is, the will and understanding) rules the body at its pleasure, thus as entirely as it rules its own self. From all this it follows that the interiors of the mind act as a one with the interiors of the body, and the exteriors of the mind with the exteriors of the body. The interiors of the mind, likewise the interiors of the body, will be considered further on, when degrees of life have been treated of.

137. Since the interiors of the mind make one with the interiors of the body, it follows that when the interiors of the mind turn themselves to the Lord as a sun, those of the body turn themselves in like manner; and because the exteriors of both, of mind as well as body, depend upon their interiors, they also do the same. For what the external does, it does from internals, the general deriving all it has from the particulars from which it is. From this it is evident that as an angel turns his face and body to the Lord as a sun, all the interiors of his mind and body are turned in the same direction. It is the same with man, if he has the Lord constantly before his eyes, which is the case if he is in love and wisdom. He then looks to the Lord not only with eyes and face, but also with all the mind and all the heart, that is, with all things of the will and understanding, together with all things of the body.

138. This turning to the Lord is an actual turning, a kind of elevation; for there is an uplifting into the heat and light of heaven, which takes place by the opening of the interiors; when these are opened, love and wisdom flow into the inte-

riors of the mind, and the heat and light of heaven into the interiors of the body. From this comes the uplifting, like a rising out of a cloud into clear air, or out of air into ether. Moreover, love and wisdom, with their heat and light, are the Lord with man; and he, as was said before, turns man to himself. It is the reverse with those who are not in love and wisdom, and still more with those who are opposed to love and wisdom. Their interiors, both of mind and body, are closed; and when closed, the exteriors react against the Lord, for such is their inherent nature. Consequently, such persons turn themselves backward from the Lord; and turning oneself backward is turning to hell.

139. This actual turning to the Lord is from love together with wisdom; not from love alone, nor from wisdom alone; for love alone is like *esse* [being] without its *existere* [taking form], since love has its form in wisdom; and wisdom without love is like *existere* without its *esse,* since wisdom has its form from love. Love is indeed possible without wisdom; but such love is man's, and not the Lord's. Wisdom alone is possible without love; but such wisdom, although from the Lord, has not the Lord in it; for it is like the light of winter, which is from the sun; still the sun's essence, which is heat, is not in it.

Every spirit, whatever his quality, turns in like manner to his ruling love

140. It shall first be explained what a spirit is, and what an angel is. Every man after death comes, in the first place, into the world of spirits, which is midway between heaven and hell, and there passes through his own times, that is, his own states, and becomes prepared, according to his life, either for heaven or for hell. So long as one stays in that world he is called a spirit. He who has been raised out of that world into heaven is called an angel; but he who has been cast down into hell is called either a satan or a devil. So long as these continue in the world of spirits, he who is preparing for heaven is called an angelic spirit; and he who is preparing for hell, an infernal spirit; meanwhile the angelic spirit is conjoined with heaven, and the infernal spirit with hell. All spirits in the world of spirits are adjoined to men; because men, in respect to the interiors of their minds, are in like manner between heaven and hell, and through these spirits they communicate with heaven or with hell according to their life. It is to be observed that the world of spirits is one thing, and the spiritual world another; the world of spirits is that which has just been spoken of; but the spiritual world includes that world, and heaven and hell.

141. Since the subject now under consideration is the turning of angels and spirits to their own loves by reason of these loves, something shall be said also about loves. The whole heaven is divided into societies according to all the differences of loves; in like manner hell, and in like manner the world of spirits. But heaven is divided into societies according to the differences of heavenly loves; hell into societies according to the differences of infernal loves; and the world of spirits, according to the differences of loves both heavenly and infernal. There are two loves which are the heads of all the rest, that is, to which all other loves are referable; the love which is the head of all heavenly loves, or to which they all relate, is love to the Lord; and the love which is the head of all infernal loves, or to which they all relate, is the love of rule springing from the love of self. These two loves are diametrically opposed to each other.

142. Since these two loves, love to the Lord and love of rule springing from love of self, are wholly opposed to each other, and since all who are in love to the Lord turn to the Lord as a sun (as was shown in the preceding article), it can be seen that all who are in the love of rule springing from love of self, turn their backs to the Lord. They thus face in opposite directions, because those who are in love to the Lord love nothing more than to be led by the Lord, and will that the Lord alone shall rule; while those who are in the love of rule springing from love of self, love nothing more than to be led by themselves, and will that themselves alone may rule.

This is called a love of rule springing from love of self, because there is a love of rule springing from a love of performing uses, which is a spiritual love, because it makes one with love towards the neighbor. Still this cannot be called a love of rule, but a love of performing duties.

143. Every spirit, of whatever quality, turns to his own ruling love, because love is the life of everyone (as was shown in chapter 1, n. 1–3); and life turns its receptacles, called members, organs, and viscera, thus the whole man, to that society which is in a love similar to itself, thus where its own love is.

144. Since the love of rule springing from love of self is wholly opposed to love to the Lord, the spirits who are in that love of rule turn the face backwards from the Lord, and therefore look with their eyes to the western quarters of the spiritual world; and being thus bodily in a reversed position, they have the east behind them, the north at their right, and the south at their left. They have the east behind them because they hate the Lord; they have the north at their right, because they love fallacies and falsities therefrom; and they have the south at their left, because they despise the light of wisdom. They may turn themselves round and round, and yet all things which they see about them appear similar to their love. All such are sensual-natural; and some are of such a nature as to imagine that they alone live, looking upon others as images. They believe themselves to be wise above all others, though in truth they are insane.

145. In the spiritual world ways are seen, laid out like ways in the natural world; some leading to heaven, and some to hell; but the ways leading to hell are not visible to those going to heaven, nor are the ways leading to heaven visible to those going to hell. There are countless ways of this kind; for there are ways which lead to every society of heaven and to every society of hell. Each spirit enters the way which leads to the society of his own love, nor does he see the ways leading in other directions. Thus it is that each spirit, as he turns himself to his ruling love, goes forward in it.

Divine love and Divine wisdom proceeding from the Lord as a sun and producing heat and light in heaven, are the proceeding Divine, which is the holy spirit

146. In the *Doctrine of the New Jerusalem Concerning the Lord* it has been shown that God is one in person and essence in whom there is a trinity, and that that God is the Lord; also, that the trinity in him is called father, son, and holy spirit; and that the Divine from which [the creative Divine] is called the father; the human Divine, the son; and the proceeding Divine, the holy spirit. This is called the "proceeding Divine," but no one knows why it is called *proceeding*. This is not known, because until now it has been unknown that the Lord appears before the angels as a sun, from which sun proceeds heat which in its essence is Divine love, and also light which in its essence is Divine wisdom. So long as these things were unknown, it could not be known that the proceeding Divine is not a Divine by itself; consequently the Athanasian doctrine of the trinity declares that there is one person of the Father, another of the Son, and another of the Holy Spirit. Now, however, when it is known that the Lord appears as a sun, a correct idea may be had of the proceeding Divine, which is called the Holy Spirit, that it is one with the Lord, but proceeds from him, as heat and light from a sun. For

the same reason angels are in Divine heat and Divine light just so far as they are in love and wisdom. Without knowing that the Lord appears as a sun in the spiritual world, and that his Divine thus proceeds, it can in no way be known what is meant by "proceeding," whether it means simply communicating those things which are the Father's and the Son's, or simply enlightening and teaching. But inasmuch as it has been known that God is one, and that he is omnipresent, it is not in accord with enlightened reason to recognize the proceeding Divine as a Divine per se, and to call it God, and thus divide God.

147. It has been shown above that God is not in space, and that he is thereby omnipresent; also that the Divine is the same everywhere, but that there is an apparent variety of it in angels and men from variety of reception. Now since the proceeding Divine from the Lord as a sun is in light and heat, and light and heat flow first into universal recipients, which in the world are called atmospheres, and these are the recipients of clouds, it can be seen that according as the interiors pertaining to the understanding of man or angel are veiled by such clouds, is he a receptacle of the proceeding Divine.

By clouds are meant spiritual clouds, which are thoughts. These, if from truths, are in accordance, but if from falsities, are at variance with Divine wisdom; consequently, in the spiritual world thoughts from truths, when presented to the sight, appear as shining white clouds, but thoughts from falsities as black clouds. From all this it can be seen that the proceeding Divine is indeed in every man, but is variously veiled by each.

148. As the Divine itself is present in angel and man by spiritual heat and light, those who are in the truths of Divine wisdom and in the goods of Divine love, when affected by these, and when from affection they think from them and about them, are said to grow warm with God; and this sometimes becomes so evident as to be perceived and felt, as

when a preacher speaks from zeal. These same are also said to be enlightened by God, because the Lord, by his proceeding Divine, not only kindles the will with spiritual heat, but also enlightens the understanding with spiritual light.

149. From the following passages in the Word it is plain that the Holy Spirit is the same as the Lord, and is truth itself, from which man has enlightenment:

> Jesus said, When the spirit of truth is come, he will guide you into all truth; he shall not speak of himself; but whatsoever he shall have heard, that shall he speak (John 16:13).
>
> He shall glorify Me; for he shall receive of Mine, and shall show it unto you (John 16:14, 15).
>
> That he will be with the disciples and in them (John 14:17; 15:26).
>
> Jesus said, The words that I speak unto you, they are spirit and they are life (John 6:63).

From these passages it is evident that the truth itself which proceeds from the Lord, is called the Holy Spirit; and because it is in light, it enlightens.

150. Enlightenment, which is attributed to the Holy Spirit, is indeed in man from the Lord, yet it is effected by spirits and angels as media. But the nature of that mediation cannot yet be described; only it may be said that angels and spirits can in no way enlighten man from themselves, because they, in like manner as man, are enlightened by the Lord; and as they are enlightened in like manner, it follows that all enlightenment is from the Lord alone. It is effected by angels or spirits as media, because the man when he is enlightened is placed in the midst of such angels and spirits as, more than others, receive enlightenment from the Lord alone.

The Lord created the universe and all things of it by means of the sun which is the first proceeding of Divine love and Divine wisdom

151. By "the Lord" is meant God from eternity, that is, Jehovah, who is called father and creator, because he is one with him, as has been shown in the *Doctrine of the New Jerusalem Concerning the Lord;* consequently in the following pages, where also creation is treated of, he is called the Lord.

152. That all things in the universe were created by Divine love and Divine wisdom was fully shown in chapter 1 (particularly in n. 52, 53); here now it is to be shown that this was done by means of the sun, which is the first proceeding of Divine love and Divine wisdom. No one who is capable of seeing effects from causes, and afterwards by causes effects in their order and sequence, can deny that the sun is the first of creation, for all the things that are in its world have perpetual existence from it; and because they have perpetual existence from it, their existence was derived from it. The one involves and is proof of the other; for all things are under the sun's view, since it is determined that they should be, and to hold under its view is to determine perpetually; therefore it is said that subsistence is perpetual existence. If, moreover, anything were to be withdrawn entirely from the sun's influx through the atmospheres, it would instantly be dissipated; for the atmospheres, which are purer and purer, and are rendered active in power by the sun, hold all things in connection. Since, then, the perpetual existence of the universe, and of everything pertaining to it, is from the sun, it is plain that the sun is the first of creation, from which [is all else]. The sun is spoken of as creating, but this means the Lord, by means of the sun; for the sun also was created by the Lord.

153. There are two suns through which all things were created by the Lord, the sun of the spiritual world and the sun of the natural world. All things were created by the Lord through the sun of the spiritual world, but not through the sun of the natural world, since the latter is far below the former; it is in middle distance; above it is the spiritual world and below it is the natural world. This sun of the natural world was created to render aid, as a kind of substitute; this aid will be spoken of in what follows.

154. The universe and all things thereof were created by the Lord, the sun of the spiritual world serving as a medium, because that sun is the first proceeding of Divine love and Divine wisdom, and from Divine love and Divine wisdom all things are (as was pointed out above, n. 52–82). In everything created, greatest as well as least, there are these three, end, cause and effect. A created thing in which these three are not, is impossible. In what is greatest, that is, in the universe, these three exist in the following order; in the sun, which is the first proceeding of Divine love and Divine wisdom, is the end of all things; in the spiritual world are the causes of all things; in the natural world are the effects of all things. How these three are in things first and in things last shall be shown in what follows. Since, then, no created thing is possible in which these three are not, it follows that the universe and all things of it were created by the Lord through the sun, wherein is the end of all things.

155. Creation itself cannot be brought within man's comprehension unless space and time are removed from thought; but if these are removed, it can be comprehended. Removing these if you can, or as much as you can, and keeping the mind in ideas abstracted from space and time, you will perceive that there is no difference between the maximum of space and the minimum of space; and then you cannot but have a similar idea of the creation of the universe as of the creation of the particulars therein; you will also perceive that diversity in created things springs from this, that there are infinite things in God-man, consequently things without limit in the sun which is the first proceeding from him; these countless things take form, as in an image, in the created universe.

From this it is that no one thing can anywhere be precisely the same as another. From this comes that variety of all things which is presented to sight, in the natural world, together with space, but in the spiritual world with appearance of space; and it is a variety both of generals and of particulars. These are the things that have been pointed out in chapter 1, where it is shown that in God-man infinite things are one distinctly (n. 17–22); that all things in the universe were created by Divine love and Divine wisdom (n. 52, 53); that all things in the created universe are recipients of the Divine love and of the Divine wisdom of God-man (n. 54–60); that the Divine is not in space (n. 7–10); that the Divine apart from space fills all spaces (n. 66–72); that the Divine is the same in things greatest and least (n. 77–82).

156. The creation of the universe, and of all things of it, cannot be said to have been wrought from space to space, or from time to time, thus progressively and successively, but from eternity and from infinity; not from eternity of time, because there is no such thing, but from eternity not of time, for this is the same with the Divine; nor from infinity of space, because again there is no such thing, but from infinity not of space, which also is the same with the Divine. These things, I know, transcend the ideas of thoughts that are in natural light, but they do not transcend the ideas of thoughts that are in spiritual light, for in these there is nothing of space and time. Neither do they wholly transcend ideas that are in natural light; for when it is said that infinity of space is not possible, this is affirmed by everyone from reason. It is the same with eternity, for this is infinity of time. If you say "to eternity," it is comprehensible from time; but "from eternity" is not comprehensible, unless time is removed.

The sun of the natural world is pure fire, consequently dead; nature also is dead, because it derives its origin from that sun

157. Creation itself cannot be ascribed in the least to the sun of the natural world, but must be wholly ascribed to the sun of the spiritual world; because the sun of the natural world is altogether dead; but the sun of the spiritual world is living; for it is the first proceeding of Divine love and Divine wisdom; and what is dead does not act at all from itself, but is acted upon; consequently to ascribe to it anything of creation would be like ascribing the work of an artificer to the tool which is moved by his hands. The sun of the natural world is pure fire from which everything of life has been withdrawn; but the sun of the spiritual world is fire in which is Divine life. The angelic idea of the fire of the sun of the natural world, and of the fire of the sun of the spiritual world, is this; that in the fire of the sun of the spiritual world the Divine life is within, but in the fire of the sun of the natural world it is without. From this it can be seen that the actuating power of the natural sun is not from itself, but from a living force proceeding from the sun of the spiritual world; consequently if the living force of that sun were withdrawn or taken away, the natural sun would have no vital power. For this reason the worship of the sun is the lowest of all the forms of God-worship, for it is wholly dead, as the sun itself is, and therefore in the Word it is called "abomination."

158. As the sun of the natural world is pure fire, and therefore dead, the heat proceeding from it is also dead, likewise the light proceeding from it is dead; so also are the atmospheres, which are called ether and air, and which receive in their bosom and carry down the heat and light of that sun; and as these are dead so are each and all things of the earth which are beneath the atmospheres, and are called soils, yet these, one and all, are encompassed by what is spiritual, proceeding and flowing forth from the sun of the spiritual world. Unless they had been so encompassed, the soils could not have been stirred into activity, and have produced forms of uses, which are plants, nor forms of life, which are animals; nor could have supplied the materials by which man begins and continues to exist.

159. Now since nature begins from that sun, and all that springs forth and continues to exist from it is called natural, it follows that nature, with each and every thing pertaining thereto, is dead. It appears in man and animal as if alive, because of the life which accompanies and actuates it.

160. Since these lowest things of nature which form the lands are dead, and are not changeable and varying according to states of affections and thoughts, as in the spiritual world, but unchangeable and fixed, therefore in nature there are spaces and spatial distances. There are such things, because creation has there terminated, and abides at rest. From this it is evident that spaces are a property of nature; and because in nature spaces are not appearances of spaces according to states of life, as they are in the spiritual world, these also may be called dead.

161. Since times in like manner are settled and constant, they also are a property of nature; for the length of a day is constantly twenty-four hours, and the length of a year is constantly three hundred and sixty-five days and a quarter. The very states of light and shade, and of heat and cold, which cause these periods to vary, are also regular in their return. The states which recur daily are morning, noon, evening, and night; those recurring yearly are spring, summer, autumn, and winter. Moreover, the annual states modify regularly the daily states. All these states are likewise dead because they are not states of life, as in the spiritual world; for in the spiritual world there is continuous light and there is continuous heat, the light corresponding to the state of wisdom, and the heat to the state of love with the angels; consequently the states of these are living.

162. From all this the folly of those who ascribe all things to nature can be seen. Those who have confirmed themselves in favor of nature have brought such a state on themselves that they are no longer willing to raise the mind above nature; consequently their minds are shut above and opened below.

Man thus becomes sensual-natural, that is, spiritually dead; and because he then thinks only from such things as he has imbibed from his bodily senses, or through the senses from the world, he at heart even denies God. Then because conjunction with heaven is broken, conjunction with hell takes place, the capacity to think and will alone remaining; the capacity to think, from rationality, and the capacity to will, from freedom; these two capacities every man has from the Lord, nor are they taken away. These two capacities devils have equally with angels; but devils devote them to insane thinking and evil doing, and angels to becoming wise and doing good.

Without a double sun, one living and the other dead, no creation is possible

163. The universe in general is divided into two worlds, the spiritual and the natural. In the spiritual world are angels and spirits, in the natural world men. In external appearance these two worlds are entirely alike, so alike that they cannot be distinguished; but as to internal appearance they are entirely unlike. The men themselves in the spiritual world, who (as was said above) are called angels and spirits, are spiritual, and, being spiritual, they think spiritually and speak spiritually. But the men of the natural world are natural, and therefore think naturally and speak naturally; and spiritual thought and speech have nothing in common with natural thought and speech. From this it is plain that these two worlds, the spiritual and the natural, are entirely distinct from each other, so that they can in no respect be together.

164. Now as these two worlds are so distinct, it is necessary that there should be two suns, one from which all spiritual things are, and another from which all natural things are. And as all spiritual things in their origin are living, and all natural things from their origin are dead, and these origins are suns, it follows

that the one sun is living and the other dead; also, that the dead sun itself was created by the Lord through the living sun.

165. A dead sun was created to this end, that in outmosts all things may be fixed, settled, and constant, and thus there may be forms of existence which shall be permanent and durable. In this and in no other way is creation founded. The terraqueous globe, in which, upon which, and about which things exist, is a kind of base and support; for it is the outmost work *[ultimum opus]* in which all things terminate, and upon which they rest. It is also a kind of matrix, out of which effects, which are ends of creation, are produced, as will be shown in what follows.

166. That all things were created by the Lord through the living sun, and nothing through the dead sun, can be seen from this, that what is living disposes what is dead in obedience to itself, and forms it for uses, which are its ends; but not the reverse. Only a person bereft of reason and who is ignorant of what life is, can think that all things are from nature, and that life even comes from nature. Nature cannot dispense life to anything, since nature in itself is wholly inert. For what is dead to act upon what is living, or for dead force to act upon living force, or, what is the same, for the natural to act upon the spiritual, is entirely contrary to order, therefore so to think is contrary to the light of sound reason. What is dead, that is, the natural, may indeed in many ways be perverted or changed by external accidents, but it cannot act upon life; on the contrary life acts into it, according to the induced change of form. It is the same with physical influx into the spiritual operations of the soul; this, it is known, does not occur, for it is not possible.

The end of creation has form in outmosts, which end is that all things may return to the creator and that there may be conjunction

167. In the first place, something shall be said about ends. There are three things that follow in order, called first end, middle end, and last end; they are also called end, cause, and effect. These three must be together in everything, that it may be anything. For a first end without a middle end, and at the same time a last end, is impossible; or, what is the same, an end alone, without a cause and an effect is impossible. Equally impossible is a cause alone without an end from which and an effect in which it is, or an effect alone, that is, an effect without its cause and end. That this is so may be comprehended if it be observed that an end without an effect, that is, separated from an effect, is a thing without existence, and therefore a mere term. For in order that an end may actually be an end it must be terminated, and it is terminated in its effect, wherein it is first called an end because it is an end. It appears as if the agent or the efficient exists by itself; but this so appears from its being in the effect; but if separated from the effect it would instantly vanish. From all this it is evident that these three, end, cause, and effect, must be in everything to make it anything.

168. It must be known further, that the end is everything in the cause, and also everything in the effect; from this it is that end, cause, and effect, are called first end, middle end, and last end. But that the end may be everything in the cause, there must be something from the end [in the cause] wherein the end shall be; and that the end may be everything in the effect, there must be something from the end through the cause [in the effect] wherein the end shall be. For the end cannot be in itself alone, but it must be in something having existence from it, in which it can dwell as to all that is its own, and by acting, come into effect, until it has permanent existence. That in which it has permanent existence is the last end, which is called effect.

169. These three, namely, end, cause, and effect, are in the created universe, both in its greatest and least parts. They are in the greatest and least parts of the created universe, because they are in God the creator, who is the Lord from eternity. But since he is infinite, and in the Infinite infinite things are one distinctly (as was shown above, n. 17–22), therefore also these three in him, and in his infinites, are one distinctly. From this it is that the universe which was created from his *Esse*, and which, regarded as to uses, is his image, possesses these three in each and all of its parts.

170. The universal end, that is, the end of all things of creation, is that there may be an eternal conjunction of the creator with the created universe; and this is not possible unless there are subjects wherein his Divine can be as in itself, thus in which it can dwell and abide. In order that these subjects may be dwelling places and mansions of him, they must be recipients of his love and wisdom as of themselves; such, therefore, as will elevate themselves to the creator as of themselves, and conjoin themselves with him. Without this ability to reciprocate no conjunction is possible. These subjects are men, who are able as of themselves to elevate and conjoin themselves. That men are such subjects, and that they are recipients of the Divine as of themselves, has been pointed out above many times. By means of this conjunction, the Lord is present in every work created by him; for everything has been created for man as its end; consequently the uses of all created things ascend by degrees from outmosts to man, and through man to God the creator from whom [are all things] (as was shown above, n. 65–68).

171. To this last end creation progresses continually, through these three, namely, end, cause, and effect, because these three are in the Lord the creator (as was said just above); and the Divine apart from space is in all space (n. 69–72); and is the same in things greatest and least (n. 77–82); from which it is evident that the created universe, in its general progression to its last end, is relatively the middle end. For out of the earth

forms of uses are continually raised by the Lord the creator, in their order up to man, who as to his body is also from the earth. Thereafter, man is elevated by the reception of love and wisdom from the Lord; and for this reception of love and wisdom, all means are provided; and he has been so made as to be able to receive, if he will. From what has now been said it can be seen, though as yet only in a general manner, that the end of creation takes form *[existat]* in outmost things; which end is, that all things may return to the creator, and that there may be conjunction.

172. That these three, end, cause, and effect, are in each and every thing created, can also be seen from this, that all effects, which are called last ends, become anew first ends in uninterrupted succession from the First, who is the Lord the creator, even to the last end, which is the conjunction of man with him. That all last ends become once more first ends is plain from this, that there can be nothing so inert and dead as to have no efficient power in it. Even out of sand there is such an exhalation as gives aid in producing and therefore in effecting something.

Chapter 3
[The Structure of Creation]

In the spiritual world there are atmospheres, waters, and lands, just as in the natural world; only the former are spiritual, while the latter are natural

173. It has been said in the preceding pages, and shown in the work *Heaven and Hell*, that the spiritual world is like the natural world, with the difference only that each and every thing of the spiritual world is spiritual, and each and every thing of the natural world is natural. As these two worlds are alike, there are in both, atmospheres, waters, and lands, which are the generals through and from which each and all things take their form *[existunt]* with infinite variety.

174. As regards the atmospheres, which are called ethers and airs, they are alike in both worlds, the spiritual and the natural, with the difference only that they are spiritual in the spiritual world, and natural in the natural world. The former are spiritual, because they have their form from the sun which is the first proceeding of the Divine love and Divine wisdom of the Lord, and from him receive within them the Divine fire which is love, and the Divine light which is wisdom, and carry these down to the heavens where the angels dwell, and cause the presence of that sun there in things greatest and least. The spiritual atmospheres are divided substances, that is, least forms, originating from the sun. As these each singly receive the sun, its fire, distributed among so many substances, that is, so many forms, and as it were enveloped by them, and tempered by these envelopments, becomes heat, adapted finally to the love of angels in heaven and of spirits under heaven. The same is true of the light of that sun. In this the natural atmospheres are like spiritual atmospheres, that they also are divided substances or least forms originating from the sun of the natural world; these also each singly receive the sun and store up its fire in themselves, and temper it, and carry it down as heat to the earth, where men dwell. The same is true of natural light.

175. The difference between spiritual and natural atmospheres is that spiritual atmospheres are receptacles of Divine fire and Divine light, thus of love and wisdom, for they contain these interiorly within them; while natural atmospheres are receptacles, not of Divine fire and Divine light, but of the fire and light of their own sun, which in itself is dead, as was shown above; consequently there is nothing interiorly in them from the sun of the spiritual world, although they are environed by spiritual atmospheres from that sun. That this is the difference between spiritual and natural atmospheres has been learned from the wisdom of angels.

176. That there are atmospheres in the spiritual, just as in the natural world, can be seen from this, that angels and spirits breathe, and also speak and hear just as men do in the natural world; and respiration, speech, and hearing are all effected by means of a lowest atmosphere, which is called air; it can be seen also from this, that angels and spirits, like men in the natural world, have sight, and sight is possible only by means of an atmosphere purer than air; also from this, that angels and spirits, like men in the natural world, think and are moved by affection, and thought and affection are not possible except by means of still purer atmospheres; and finally from this, that all parts of the bodies of angels and spirits, external as well as internal, are held together in connection by atmospheres, the external by air and the internal by ethers.

Without the surrounding pressure and action of these atmospheres the interior and exterior forms of the body would evidently dissolve away. Since angels are spiritual, and each and all things of their bodies are held together in connection, form, and order by means of atmospheres, it follows that these atmospheres are spiritual; they are spiritual, because they arise from the spiritual sun which is the first proceeding of the Lord's Divine love and Divine wisdom.

177. That there are also waters and lands in the spiritual as well as in the natural world, with the difference that these waters and lands are spiritual, has been said above and has been shown in the work *Heaven and Hell;* and because these are spiritual, they are moved and modified by the heat and light of the spiritual sun, the atmospheres therefrom serving as mediums, just as the waters and lands in the natural world are moved and modified by the heat and light of the sun of their world, its atmospheres serving as mediums.

178. Atmospheres, waters, and lands are here specified, because these three are generals, through and from which each and all things have their form *[existunt]* in infinite variety. The atmospheres are the active forces, the waters are the mediate forces, and the lands are the passive forces, from which all effects have existence. These three forces are such in their series solely by virtue of life that proceeds from the Lord as a sun, and that makes them active.

There are degrees of love and wisdom, consequently degrees of heat and light, also degrees of atmospheres

179. The things which follow cannot be comprehended unless it be known that there are degrees, also what they are, and what their nature is, because in every created thing, thus in every form, there are degrees. This chapter will therefore treat of degrees. That there are degrees of love and wisdom can be clearly seen from the fact that there are angels of the three heavens. The angels of the third heaven so far excel the angels of the second heaven in love and wisdom, and these, the angels of the lowest heaven, that they cannot be together. The degrees of love and wisdom distinguish and separate them. It is from this that angels of the lower heavens cannot ascend to angels of higher heavens, or if allowed to ascend, they do not see the higher angels or anything that is about them. They do not see them because the love and wisdom of the higher angels is of a higher degree, transcending the perception of the lower angels. For each angel is his own love and his own wisdom; and love together with wisdom in its form is a man, because God, who is love itself and wisdom itself, is a man. It has sometimes been permitted me to see angels of the lowest heaven who have ascended to the angels of the third heaven; and when they had made their way thither, I have heard them complaining that they did not see anyone, and all the while they were in the midst of the higher angels. Afterwards they were instructed that those angels were invisible to them because their love and wisdom were imperceptible to them, and that love and wisdom are what make an angel appear as a man.

180. That there must be degrees of love and wisdom is still more evident when the love and wisdom of angels are compared with the love and wisdom of men. It is well known that the wisdom of angels, when thus compared, is ineffable; also it will be seen in what follows that to men who are in natural love, this wisdom is incomprehensible. It appears ineffable and incomprehensible because it is of a higher degree.

181. Since there are degrees of love and wisdom, there are also degrees of heat and light. By heat and light are meant spiritual heat and light, such as angels in the heavens have, and such as men have as to the interiors of their minds; for men have a heat of love similar to that of the angels, and a similar light of wisdom. In the heavens, such and so much love as the angels have, such and so much is their heat; and the same is true of their light as compared with their wisdom; the reason is, that with them love is in the heat, and wisdom in the light (as was shown above).

It is the same with men on earth, with the difference, however, that angels feel that heat and see that light, but men do not, because they are in natural heat and light; and while they are in the natural heat and light spiritual heat is not felt except by a certain enjoyment of love, and spiritual light is not seen except by a perception of truth. Now since man, so long as he is in natural heat and light, knows nothing of the spiritual heat and light within him, and since knowledge of these can be obtained only through experience from the spiritual world, the heat and light in which the angels and their heavens are, shall here be especially spoken of From this and from no other source can enlightenment on this subject be had.

182. But degrees of spiritual heat cannot be described from experience, because love, to which spiritual heat corresponds, does not come thus under ideas of thought; but degrees of spiritual light can be described, because light pertains to thought, and therefore comes under ideas of thought. Yet degrees of spiritual heat can be comprehended by their relation to the degrees of light, for the two are in like degree. With respect then to spiritual light in which angels are, it has been granted me to see it with my eyes.

With angels of the higher heavens, the light is so glistening white as to be indescribable, even by comparison with the shining whiteness of snow, and so glowing as to be indescribable even by comparison with the beams of this world's sun. In a word, that light exceeds a thousand times the noonday light upon earth. But the light with angels of the lower heavens can be described in a measure by comparisons, although it still exceeds the most intense light of our world. The light of angels of the higher heavens is indescribable, because their light makes one with their wisdom; and because their wisdom, compared to the wisdom of men, is ineffable, thus also is their light. From these few things it can be seen that there must be degrees of light; and because wisdom and love are of like degrees, it follows that there must be like degrees of heat.

183. Since atmospheres are the receptacles and containers of heat and light, it follows that there are as many degrees of atmospheres as there are degrees of heat and light; also that there are as many as there are degrees of love and wisdom. That there are several atmospheres, and that these are distinct from each other by means of degrees, has been manifested to me by much experience in the spiritual world; especially from this, that angels of the lower heavens are not able to breathe in the region of higher angels, and appear to themselves to gasp for breath, as living creatures do when they are raised out of air into ether, or out of water into air. Moreover, spirits below the heavens appear in a kind of cloud. That there are several atmospheres, and that they are distinct from each other by means of degrees, may be seen above (n. 176).

Degrees are of a twofold kind, degrees of height and degrees of breadth

184. A knowledge of degrees is like a key to lay open the causes of things, and to give entrance into them. Without this knowledge, scarcely anything of cause can be known; for without it, the objects and subjects of both worlds seem to have but a single meaning, as if there were nothing in them beyond that which meets the eye; when yet compared to the things which lie hidden within, what is thus seen is as one to thousands, yea, to tens of thousands. The interiors which are not open to view can in no way be discovered except through a knowledge of degrees. For things exterior advance to things interior and through these to things inmost, by means of degrees; not by continuous degrees but by discrete degrees. "Continuous degrees" is a term applied to the gradual lessenings or decreasings from grosser to finer, or from denser to rarer; or rather, to growths and increasings from finer to grosser, or from rarer to denser; precisely like the gradations of light to shade, or of heat to cold. But discrete degrees are entirely different: they are like things prior, subsequent and final; or like end, cause, and effect.

These degrees are called discrete, because the prior is by itself; the subsequent by itself; and the final by itself; and yet taken together they make one. There are atmospheres, from highest to lowest, that is, from the sun to the earth, called ethers and airs, that are separated into such degrees; they are like simples, collections of simples, and again collections of these, which taken together are called a composite. Such degrees are discrete [or separate], because each has a distinct existence, and these degrees are what are meant by "degrees of height"; but the former degrees are continuous, because they increase continuously, and these degrees are what are meant by "degrees of breadth."

185. Each and all things that have existence in the spiritual world and in the natural world, have conjoint existence from discrete degrees and from continuous degrees together, that is, from degrees of height and from degrees of breadth. The dimension which consists of discrete degrees is called height, and the dimension that consists of continuous degrees is called breadth; their position relatively to the sight of the eye does not alter the designation. Without a knowledge of these degrees nothing can be known of how the three heavens differ from each other; nor can anything be known of the differences of love and wisdom of the angels there; nor of the differences of heat and light in which they are; nor of the differences of atmospheres

which environ and contain these. Nor without a knowledge of these degrees can anything be known of the differences among the interior powers of the minds of men, thus nothing of their state as regards reformation and regeneration; nor anything of the differences among the exterior powers of the bodies both of angels and men; and nothing whatever can be known of the distinction between spiritual and natural, thus nothing of correspondence. Nor, indeed, can anything be known of any difference between the life of men and that of beasts, or between the more perfect and the less perfect animals; neither of the differences among the forms of the vegetable kingdom, nor among the matters of the mineral kingdom.

From which it can be seen that they who are ignorant of these degrees are unable to see causes from anything of judgment; they see only effects, and from these judge of causes, which is done for the most part by an induction that is continuous with effects. But causes produce effects not continuously but discretely; for cause is one thing, and effect is another. The difference between the two is like the difference between prior and subsequent, or between that which forms and that which is formed.

186. That it may be still better comprehended what discrete degrees are, what their nature is, and how they differ from continuous degrees, the angelic heavens may serve as an example. There are three heavens, and these are separated by degrees of height; therefore the heavens are one below another, nor do they communicate with each other except by influx, which proceeds from the Lord through the heavens in their order to the lowest; and not contrariwise. Each heaven by itself, however, is divided not by degrees of height but by degrees of breadth.

Those who are in the middle, that is, at the center, are in the light of wisdom; but those who are around about, even to the boundaries, are in the shade of wisdom. Thus wisdom grows less and less even to ignorance, as light decreases to shade, which takes place continuously. It is the same with men. The interiors belonging to their minds are separated into as many degrees as the angelic heavens; and these degrees are one above another; therefore the interiors of men which belong to their minds are separated by discrete degrees, that is, degrees of height. Consequently a man may be in the lowest degree, then in a higher, and also in the highest degree, according to the degree of his wisdom; moreover, when he is in the lowest degree only, the higher degree is shut, but is opened as he receives wisdom from the Lord. There are also in a man, as in heaven, continuous degrees, that is degrees of breadth. A man is like the heavens because as regards the interiors of his mind, he is a heaven in least form, in the measure in which he is in love and wisdom from the Lord. That man as regards the interiors of his mind is a heaven in least form may be seen in the work *Heaven and Hell* (n. 51–58.)

187. From all this it can be seen, that one who knows nothing about discrete degrees, that is, degrees of height, can know nothing about the state of man as regards his reformation and regeneration, which are effected through the reception of love and wisdom of the Lord, and then through the opening of the interior degrees of his mind in their order. Nor can he know anything about influx from the Lord through the heavens nor anything about the order into which he was created. For if anyone thinks about these, not from discrete degrees or degrees of height but from continuous degrees or degrees of breadth, he is not able to perceive anything about them from causes, but only from effects; and to see from effects only is to see from fallacies, from which come errors, one after another; and these may be so multiplied by inductions that at length enormous falsities are called truths.

188. I am not aware that anything has been known hitherto about discrete degrees or degrees of height; only continuous degrees or degrees of breadth have been known; yet nothing of the real truth about cause can become known without a knowledge of degrees of both kinds. These degrees therefore shall be treated of throughout this chapter; for it is the object of this little work to uncover causes, that effects may be seen from them, and thus the darkness may be dispelled in which the man of the church is in respect to God and the Lord, and in respect to Divine things in general which are called spiritual things. This I may mention, that the angels are in grief for the darkness on the earth; saying that they see light hardly anywhere, and that men eagerly lay hold of fallacies and confirm them, thereby multiplying falsities upon falsities; and to confirm fallacies men search out, by means of reasonings from falsities and from truths falsified, such things as cannot be controverted, owing to the darkness in respect to causes and the ignorance respecting truths. The angels lament especially over confirmations respecting faith separate from charity and justification thereby; also over men's ideas about God, angels and spirits, and their ignorance of what love and wisdom are.

Degrees of height are homogeneous, and one is from the other in succession like end, cause, and effect

189. As degrees of breadth, that is continuous degrees, are like gradations from light to shade, from heat to cold, from hard to soft, from dense to rare, from thick to thin, and so forth; and as these degrees are known from sensuous and ocular experience, while degrees of height, or discrete degrees, are not, the latter kind shall be treated of especially in this chapter; for without a knowledge of these degrees, causes cannot be seen. It is known indeed that end, cause, and effect follow in order, like prior, subsequent, and final; also that the end begets the cause, and, through the cause, the effect, that the end may have form; also about these many other things are known; and yet to know these things, and not to see them in their applications to existing things is simply to know abstractions, which remain in the memory only so long as the mind is in analytical ideas from metaphysical thought. From this it is that although end, cause, and effect advance according to discrete degrees, little if anything is known in the world about these degrees. For a mere knowledge of abstractions is like an airy something which flies away; but when abstractions are applied to such things as are in the world, they become like what is seen with the eyes on earth, and remain in the memory.

190. All things which have existence in the world, of which threefold dimension is predicated, that is, which are called compounds, consist of degrees of height, that is, discrete degrees; as examples will make clear. It is known from ocular experience, that every muscle in the human body consists of minute fibers, and these put together into little bundles form larger fibers, called motor fibers, and groups of these form the compound called a muscle. It is the same with nerves; in these from minute fibers larger fibers are compacted, which appear as filaments, and these grouped together compose the nerve.

The same is true of the rest of the combinations, bundlings and groupings out of which the organs and viscera are made up; for these are compositions of fibers and vessels variously put together according to like degrees. It is the same also with each and every thing of the vegetable and mineral kingdoms. In woods there are combinations of filaments in threefold order. In metals and stones there are groupings of parts, also in threefold order. From all this the nature of discrete degrees can be seen, namely, that one is from the other, and through the second there is a third which is called the composite; and that each degree is discreted from the others.

191. From these examples a conclusion may be formed respecting those things that are not visible to the eye, for with those it is the same; for example, with the organic substances which are the receptacles and abodes of thoughts and affections in the brains; with atmospheres; with heat and light; and with love and wisdom. For atmospheres are receptacles of heat and light; and heat and light are receptacles of love and wisdom; consequently, as there are degrees of atmospheres, there are also like degrees of heat and light, and of love and wisdom; for the same principle applies to the latter as to the former.

192. That these degrees are homogeneous, that is, of the same character and nature, appears from what has just been said. The motor fibers of muscles, least, larger, and largest, are homogeneous. Woody filaments, from the least to the composite formed of these, are homogeneous. So likewise are parts of stones and metals of every kind. The organic substances which are receptacles and abodes of thoughts and affections, from the most simple to their general aggregate which is the brain, are homogeneous. The atmospheres, from pure ether to air, are homogeneous. The degrees of heat and light in series, following the degrees of atmospheres, are homogeneous, therefore the degrees of love and wisdom are also homogeneous. Things which are not of the same character and nature are heterogeneous, and do not harmonize with things homogeneous; thus they cannot form discrete degrees with them, but only with their own, which are of the same character and nature and with which they are homogeneous.

193. That these things in their order are like ends, causes, and effects, is evident; for the first, which is the least, effectuates its cause by means of the middle, and its effect by means of the last.

194. It should be known that each degree is made distinct from the others by coverings of its own, and that all the degrees together are made distinct by means of a general covering; also, that this general covering communicates with interiors and inmosts in their order. From this there is conjunction of all and unanimous action.

The first degree is the all in everything of the subsequent degrees

195. This is because the degrees of each subject and of each thing are homogeneous; and they are homogeneous because produced from the first degree. For their formation is such that the first, by bundlings or groupings, in a word, by aggregations of parts, produces the second, and through this the third; and discretes each from the other by a covering drawn around it; from which it is clear that the first degree is chief and singly supreme in the subsequent degrees; consequently that in all things of the subsequent degrees, the first is the all.

196. When it is said that degrees are such in respect to each other, the meaning is that substances are such in their degrees. This manner of speaking by degrees is abstract, that is, universal, which makes the statement applicable to every subject or thing which is in degrees of this kind.

197. This can be applied to all those things which have been enumerated in the preceding chapter, to the muscles, the nerves, the matters and parts of both the vegetable and mineral kingdoms, to the organic substances that are the subjects of thoughts and affections in man, to atmospheres, to heat and light, and to love and wisdom. In all these, the first is singly supreme in the subsequent things; yea, it is the sole thing in them, and because it is the sole thing in them, it is the all in them. That this is so is clear also from these well-known truths; that the end is the all of the cause, and through the cause is the all of the effect; and thus end, cause, and effect are called first, middle, and last end. Further, that the cause of the cause is also the cause of the thing caused; and that there is nothing essential in causes except the end, and nothing essential in movement

excepting effort *[conatus]*; also, that the substance that is substance in itself is the sole substance.

198. From all this it can clearly be seen that the Divine, which is substance in itself, that is, the one only and sole substance, is the substance from which is each and every thing that has been created; thus that God is the All in all things of the universe, according to what has been shown in chapter 1, as follows. Divine love and Divine wisdom are substance and form (n. 40–43); Divine love and Divine wisdom are substance and form in itself, therefore the very and the only (n. 44–46); all things in the universe were created by Divine love and Divine wisdom (n. 52–60); consequently the created universe is his image (n. 61–65); the Lord alone is heaven where angels are (n. 113–118).

All perfections increase and ascend along with degrees and according to them

199. That degrees are of two kinds, degrees of breadth and degrees of height, has been shown above (n. 184–188); also that degrees of breadth are like those of light verging to shade, or of wisdom verging to ignorance; but that degrees of height are like end, cause, and effect, or like prior, subsequent, and final. Of these latter degrees it is said that they ascend or descend, for they are of height; but of the former that they increase or decrease, for they are of breadth. These two kinds of degrees differ so much that they have nothing in common; they should therefore be perceived as distinct, and by no means be confounded.

200. All perfections increase and ascend along with degrees and according to them, because all predicates follow their subjects, and perfection and imperfection are general predicates; for they are predicated of life, of forces, and of forms.

Perfection of life is perfection of love and wisdom; and because the will and understanding are receptacles of love and wisdom, perfection of life is also perfection of will and understanding, consequently of affections and thoughts; and because spiritual heat is the container of love, and spiritual light is the container of wisdom, perfection of these may also be referred to perfection of life.

Perfection of forces is perfection of all things that are actuated and moved by life, in which, however, there is no life. Atmospheres as to their active powers are such forces; the interior and exterior organic substances with man, and with animals of every kind, are such forces; all things in the natural world that are endowed with active powers both immediately and mediately from its sun are such forces.

Perfection of forms and perfection of forces make one, for as the forces are, such are the forms; with the difference only, that forms are substances but forces are their activities; therefore like degrees of perfection belong to both. Forms that are not at the same time forces are also perfect according to degrees.

201. The perfection of life, forces and forms that increase or decrease according to degrees of breadth, that is, continuous degrees, will not be discussed here, because there is a knowledge of these degrees in the world; but only the perfections of life, forces and forms that ascend or descend according to degrees of height, that is, discrete degrees; because these degrees are not known in the world. Of the mode in which perfections ascend and descend according to these degrees little can be learned from things visible in the natural world, but this can be seen clearly from things visible in the spiritual world. From things visible in the natural world it is merely found that the more interiorly they are looked into the more do wonders present themselves; as, for instance, in the eyes, ears, tongue; in muscles, heart, lungs, liver, pancreas, kidneys, and other viscera;

also, in seeds, fruits, and flowers; and in metals, minerals, and stones. That wonders increase in all these the more interiorly they are looked into is well known; yet it has become little known thereby that the objects are interiorly more perfect according to degrees of height or discrete degrees. This has been concealed by ignorance of these degrees. But since these degrees stand out conspicuously in the spiritual world (for the whole of that world from highest to lowest is distinctly discreted into these degrees), from that world knowledge of these degrees can be drawn; and afterwards conclusions may be drawn therefrom respecting the perfection of forces and forms that are in similar degrees in the natural world.

202. In the spiritual world there are three heavens, arranged according to degrees of height. In the highest heavens are angels superior in every perfection to the angels in the middle heaven; and in the middle heaven are angels superior in every perfection to the angels in the lowest heaven. The degrees of perfections are such, that angels of the lowest heaven cannot attain to the first threshold of the perfections of the angels of the middle heaven, nor these to the first threshold of the perfections of the angels of the highest heaven.

This seems incredible, yet it is a truth. The reason is that they are consociated according to discrete, not according to continuous degrees. I have learned from observation that the difference between the affections and thoughts, and consequently the speech, of the angels of the higher and the lower heavens, is such that they have nothing in common; and that communication takes place only through correspondences, which have existence by immediate influx of the Lord into all the heavens, and by mediate influx through the highest heaven into the lowest. Such being the nature of these differences, they cannot be expressed in natural language, therefore not described; for the thoughts of angels, being spiritual, do not fall into natural ideas. They can be expressed and described only by angels themselves, in their own languages, words, and writings, and not in those that are human. This is why it is said that in the heavens things beyond description are heard and seen.

These differences may be in some measure comprehended when it is known that the thoughts of angels of the highest or third heaven are thoughts of ends; the thoughts of angels of the middle or second heaven thoughts of causes, and the thoughts of angels of the lowest or first heaven thoughts of effects. It must be noted, that it is one thing to think from ends, and another to think about ends; that it is one thing to think from causes, and another to think about causes; and that it is one thing to think from effects, and another to think about effects. Angels of the lower heavens think about causes and about ends, but angels of the higher heavens from causes and from ends; and to think from these is a mark of higher wisdom, but to think about these is the mark of lower wisdom. To think from ends is of wisdom, to think from causes is of intelligence, and to think from effects is of knowledge. From all this it is clear that all perfection ascends and descends along with degrees and according to them.

203. Since the interior things of man, which are of his will and understanding, are like the heavens in respect to degrees (for man, as to the interiors of his mind, is a heaven in least form), their perfections also are like those of the heavens. But these perfections are not apparent to anyone so long as he lives in the world, because he is then in the lowest degree; and from the lowest degree the higher degrees cannot be known; but they are known after death, because man then enters into that degree which corresponds to his love and wisdom, for he then becomes an angel, and thinks and speaks things ineffable to his natural man; for there is then an elevation of all things of his mind, not in a single, but in a threefold ratio. Degrees of height

are in threefold ratio, but degrees of breadth are in single ratio. But into degrees of height none ascend and are elevated except those who in the world have been in truths, and have applied them to life.

204. It seems as if things prior must be less perfect than things subsequent, that is, things simple than things composite; but things prior out of which things subsequent are formed, that is, things simple out of which things composite are formed, are the more perfect. The reason is that the prior or the simpler are more naked and less covered over with substances and matters devoid of life, and are, as it were, more Divine, consequently nearer to the spiritual sun where the Lord is; for perfection itself is in the Lord, and from him in that sun which is the first proceeding of his Divine love and Divine wisdom, and from that in those things which come immediately after; and thus in order down to things lowest, which are less perfect as they are further removed. Without such preeminent perfection in things prior and simple, neither man nor any kind of animal could have come into existence from seed, and afterwards continue to exist; nor could the seeds of trees and shrubs vegetate and bear fruit. For the more prior anything prior is, or the more simple anything simple is, the more exempt is it from injury, because it is more perfect.

In successive order the first degree makes the highest, and the third the lowest; but in simultaneous order the first degree makes the innermost, and the third the outermost

205. There is successive order and simultaneous order. The successive order of these degrees is from highest to lowest, or from top to bottom. The angelic heavens are in this order; the third heaven there is the highest, the second is the middle, and the first is the lowest; such is their relative situation. In like successive order are the states of love and wisdom with the

angels there, also states of heat and light, and of the spiritual atmospheres. In like order are all the perfections of the forms and forces there. When degrees of height, that is, discrete degrees, are in successive order, they may be compared to a column divided into three stories, through which ascent and descent are made. In the upper rooms are things most perfect and most beautiful; in the middle rooms, things less perfect and beautiful; in the lowest, things still less perfect and beautiful. But simultaneous order, which consists of like degrees, has another appearance. In it, the highest things of successive order, which are (as was said above) the most perfect and most beautiful, are in the inmost, the lower things are in the middle, and the lowest in the circumference. They are as if in a solid body composed of these three degrees: in the middle or center are the finest parts, round about this are parts less fine, and in the extremes which constitute the circumference are the parts composed of these and which are therefore grosser. It is like the column mentioned just above subsiding into a plane, the highest part of which forms the innermost of the plane, the middle forms the middle, and the lowest the outermost.

206. As the highest of successive order becomes the innermost of simultaneous order, and the lowest becomes the outermost, so in the Word, "higher" signifies inner, and "lower" signifies outer. "Upwards" and "downwards," and "high" and "deep" have a like meaning.

207. In every outmost there are discrete degrees in simultaneous order. The motor fibers in every muscle, the fibers in every nerve, also the fibers and the little vessels in all viscera and organs, are in such an order. Innermost in these are the most simple things, which are the most perfect; the outermost is a composite of these. There is a like order of these degrees in every seed and in every fruit, also in every metal and stone; their parts, of which the whole is composed, are of such a

nature. The innermost, the middle, and the outermost elements of the parts exist in these degrees, for they are successive compositions, that is, bundlings and massings together from simples that are their first substances or matters.

208. In a word, there are such degrees in every outmost, thus in every effect. For every outmost consists of things prior and these of their firsts. And every effect consists of a cause, and this of an end; and end is the all of cause, and cause is the all of effect (as was shown above); and end makes the inmost, cause the middle, and effect the outmost. The same is true of degrees of love and wisdom, and of heat and light, also of the organic forms of affections and thoughts in man (as will be seen in what follows). The series of these degrees in successive order and in simultaneous order has been treated of also in the *Doctrine of the New Jerusalem Concerning the Sacred Scripture* (n. 38, and elsewhere), where it is shown that there are like degrees in each and all things of the Word.

The outmost degree is the complex, container, and base of the prior degrees

209. The doctrine of degrees which is taught in this chapter, has hitherto been illustrated by various things which exist in both worlds; as by the degrees of the heavens where angels dwell, by the degrees of heat and light with them, and by the degrees of atmospheres, and by various things in the human body, and also in the animal and mineral kingdoms. But this doctrine has a wider range; it extends not only to natural, but also to civil, moral, and spiritual things, and to each and all their details. There are two reasons why the doctrine of degrees extends also to such things. First, in everything of which anything can be predicated there is the trine which is called end, cause, and effect, and these three are related to one another according to degrees of height. And secondly things civil, moral, and spiritual are not something abstract from substance, but are substances. For as love and wisdom are not abstract things, but substance (as was shown above, n. 40–43), so in like manner are all things that are called civil, moral, and spiritual.

These may be thought of abstractly from substances, yet in themselves they are not abstract; as for example, affection and thought, charity and faith, will and understanding; for it is the same with these as with love and wisdom, in that they are not possible outside of subjects which are substances, but are states of subjects, that is, substances. That they are changes of these, presenting variations, will be seen in what follows. By substance is also meant form, for substance is not possible apart from form.

210. From its being possible to think of will and understanding, of affection and thought, and of charity and faith, abstractly from the substances which are their subjects, and from their having been so thought of, it has come to pass, that a correct idea of these things, as being states of substances or forms, has perished. It is altogether as with sensations and actions, which are not things abstract from the organs of sensation and motion. Abstracted, that is, separate, from these they are mere figments of reason; for they are like sight apart from an eye, hearing apart from an ear, taste apart from a tongue, and so forth.

211. Since all things civil, moral, and spiritual advance through degrees, just as natural things do, not only through continuous but also through discrete degrees; and since the progressions of discrete degrees are like progressions of ends to causes, and of causes to effects, I have chosen to illustrate and confirm the present point, that the outmost degree is the complex, container, and base of prior degrees, by the things above mentioned, that is, by what pertains to love and wisdom, to will and understanding, to affection and thought, and to charity and faith.

212. That the outmost degree is the complex, container, and base of prior degrees, is clearly seen from progression of ends and causes to effects. That the effect is the complex, container, and base of causes and ends can be comprehended by enlightened reason; but it is not so clear that the end with all things thereof, and the cause with all things thereof, are actually in the effect, and that the effect is their full complex. That such is the case can be seen from what has been said above in this chapter, particularly from this, that one thing is from another in a threefold series, and that the effect is nothing else than the end in its outmost. And since the outmost is the complex, it follows that it is the container and also the base.

213. As regards love and wisdom: love is the end, wisdom the instrumental cause, and use is the effect; and use is the complex, container, and base of wisdom and love; and use is such a complex and such a container, that all things of love and all things of wisdom are actually in it; it is where they are all simultaneously present. But it should be borne in mind that all things of love and wisdom, which are homogeneous and concordant, are present in use, according to what is said and shown above (n. 189–194).

214. Affection, thought, and action are also in a series of like degrees, because all affection has relation to love, thought to wisdom, and action to use. Charity, faith, and good works are in a series of like degrees, for charity is of affection, faith of thought, and good works of action. Will, understanding, and doing are also in a series of like degrees; for will is of love and so of affection, understanding is of wisdom and so of faith, and doing is of use and so of work; as, then, all things of wisdom and love are present in use, so all things of thought and affection are present in action, all things of faith and charity in good works, and so forth; but all are homogeneous, that is, concordant.

215. That the outmost in each series, that is to say, use, action, work, and doing, is the complex and container of all things prior, has not yet been known. There seems to be nothing more in use, in action, in work, and in doing than such as there is in movement; yet all things prior are actually present in these, and so fully that nothing is lacking. They are contained therein like wine in its cask, or like furniture in a house. They are not apparent, because they are regarded only externally; and regarded externally they are simply activities and motions. It is as when the arms and hands are moved, and man is not conscious that a thousand motor fibers concur in every motion of them, and that to the thousand motor fibers correspond thousands of things of thought and affection, by which the motor fibers are excited. As these act deep within, they are not apparent to any bodily sense.

This much is known, that nothing is done in or through the body except from the will through the thought; and because both of these act, it must needs be that each and all things of the will and thought are present in the action. They cannot be separated; consequently from a man's deeds or works others judge of the thought of his will, which is called his intention. It has been made known to me that angels, from a man's deed or work alone, perceive and see everything of the will and thought of the doer; angels of the third heaven perceiving and seeing from his will the end for which he acts, and angels of the second heaven the cause through which the end operates. It is from this that works and deeds are so often commanded in the Word, and that it is said that a man is known by his works.

216. It is according to angelic wisdom that unless the will and understanding, that is, affection and thought, as well as charity and faith, clothe and wrap themselves in works or deeds, whenever possible, they are only like something airy which passes away, or like phantoms in air which perish; and that they first become permanent in man and a part of his life, when he practices and does them. The reason is that the outmost is the complex, container, and base of things prior. Such an airy nothing and such a phantom is faith separated from good works; such also are faith and charity without their exercise, with this difference only, that those who hold to faith and charity know what is good and can will to do it, but not so those who are in faith separated from charity.

The degrees of height are in fullness and in power in their outmost degree

217. In the preceding chapter it is shown that the outmost degree is the complex and container of prior degrees. From this it follows that prior degrees are in their fullness in their outmost degree, for they are in their effect, and every effect is the fullness of causes.

218. That these ascending and descending degrees, also called prior and subsequent, likewise degrees of height or discrete degrees, are in their power in their outmost degree, may be confirmed by all those things that have been adduced in the preceding chapters as confirmations from objects of sense and perception. Here, however, I choose to confirm them only by the conatus, forces and motions in dead and in living subjects. It is known that conatus does nothing of itself, but acts through forces corresponding to it, thereby producing motion; consequently that conatus is the all in forces, and through forces is the all in motion; and since motion is the outmost degree of conatus, through motion conatus exerts its power.

Conatus, force, and motion are no otherwise conjoined than according to degrees of height, conjunction of which is not by continuity, for they are discrete, but by correspondences. For conatus is not force, nor is force motion, but force is produced by conatus, because force is conatus made active, and through force motion is produced; consequently there is no power in conatus alone, nor in force alone, but in motion, which is their product. That this is so may still seem doubtful, because not illustrated by applications to sensible and perceptible things in nature; nevertheless, such is the progression of conatus, force, and motion into power.

219. But let application of this be made to living conatus, and to living force, and to living motion. Living conatus in man, who is a living subject, is his will united to his understanding; living forces in man are the interior constituents of his body, in all of which there are motor fibers interlacing in various ways; and living motion in man is action, which is produced through these forces by the will united to the understanding. For the interior things pertaining to the will and understanding make the first degree; the interior things pertaining to the body make the second degree; and the whole body, which is the complex of these, makes the third degree. That the interior things pertaining to the mind have no power except through forces in the body, also that forces have no power except through the action of the body itself, is well known.

These three do not act by what is continuous, but by what is discrete; and to act by what is discrete is to act by correspondences. The interiors of the mind correspond to the interiors of the body, and the interiors of the body correspond to the exteriors, through which actions come forth; consequently the two prior degrees have power through the exteriors of the body. It may seem as if conatus and forces in man have some power even when there is no action, as in sleep and in states of rest, but still at such times the determinations of conatus and forces are directed into the general motor organs of the body, which are the heart and the lungs; but when their action ceases the forces also cease, and, with the forces, the conatus.

220. Since the powers of the whole, that is, of the body, are determined chiefly into the arms and hands, which are outmosts, "arms" and "hands," in the Word, signify power, and the "right hand" signifies superior power. And such being the evolution and putting forth of degrees into power, the angels that are with man and in correspondence with all things belonging to him, know merely from such action as is effected through the hands, what a man is in respect to his understanding and will, also his charity and faith, thus in respect to the internal life pertaining to his mind and the external life derived therefrom in the body.

I have often wondered that the angels have such knowledge from the mere action of the body through the hands; but that it is so has been shown to me repeatedly by living experience, and it has been said that it is from this that inductions into the ministry are performed by the laying on of the hands, and that "touching with the hand" signifies communicating, with other like things. From all this the conclusion is formed that the all of charity and faith is in works, and that charity and faith without works are like rainbows about the sun, which vanish away and are dispersed by a cloud. On this account "works" and "doing works" are so often mentioned in the Word, and it is said that a man's salvation depends upon these; moreover, he that doeth is called a wise man, and he that doeth not is called a foolish man. But it should be remembered that by "works" here are meant uses actually done; for the all of charity and faith is in uses and according to uses. There is this correspondence of works with uses, because the correspondence is spiritual, but it is carried out through substances and matters, which are subjects.

221. Two arcana, which are brought within reach of the understanding by what precedes, may here be revealed. The first arcanum is that the Word is in its fullness and in its power in the sense of the letter. For there are three senses in the Word, according to the three degrees; the celestial sense, the spiritual sense, and the natural sense. Since these senses are in the Word according to the three degrees of height, and their conjunction is effected by correspondences, the outmost sense, which is the natural and is called the sense of the letter, is not only the complex, container, and base of the corresponding interior senses, but moreover in the outmost sense the Word is in its fullness and in its power. This is abundantly shown and proved in the *Doctrine of the New Jerusalem Concerning the Sacred Scripture* (n. 27–35, 36–49, 50–61, 62–69).

The second arcanum is that the Lord came into the world, and took upon him the human, in order to put himself into the power of subjugating the hells, and of reducing all things to order both in the heavens and on the earth. This human he put on over his former human. This human which he put on in the world was like the human of a man in the world. Yet both humans are Divine, and therefore infinitely transcend the finite humans of angels and men. And because he fully glorified the natural human even to its outmosts, he rose again with the whole body, differently from any man.

Through the assumption of this human the Lord put on Divine omnipotence not only for subjugating the hells and reducing the heavens to order, but also holding the hells in subjection to eternity and saving mankind. This power is meant by his "sitting at the right hand of the power and might of God." Because the Lord, by the assumption of a natural human, made himself Divine truth in outmosts, he is called "the Word," and it is said that "the Word was made flesh"; moreover, Divine truth in outmosts is the Word in the sense of the letter. This the Lord made himself by fulfilling all things of the Word concerning himself in Moses and the Prophets. For while every man is his own good and his own truth, and man is man on no other ground, the Lord, by the assumption of a natural human, is Divine Good itself and Divine truth itself, or what is the same, he is Divine love itself and Divine wisdom itself, both in firsts and in lasts. Consequently the Lord, since his advent into the world, appears as a sun in the angelic heavens, in stronger radiance and in greater splendor than before his advent. This is an arcanum which is brought within the range of the understanding by the doctrine of degrees. The Lord's omnipotence before his advent into the world will be treated of in what follows.

There are degrees of both kinds in the greatest and in the least of all created things

222. That the greatest and the least of all things consist of discrete and continuous degrees, that is, of degrees of height and of breadth, cannot be illustrated by examples from visible objects, because the least things are not visible to the eyes, and the greatest things which are visible seem undistinguished into degrees; consequently this matter does not allow of demonstration otherwise than by universals. And since angels are in wisdom from universals, and from that in knowledge of particulars, it is allowed to bring forward their statements concerning these things.

223. The statements of angels on this subject are as follows: there can be nothing so minute as not to have in it degrees of both kinds; for instance, there can be nothing so minute in any animal, or in any plant, or in any mineral, or in the ether or air, as not to have in it degrees of both kinds, and since ether and air are receptacles of heat and light, and spiritual heat and spiritual light are the receptacles of love and wisdom, there can be nothing of heat and light or of love and wisdom so minute as not to have in it degrees of both kinds. Angels also declare that the minutest thing of an affection and the minutest thing of a thought, nay, the minutest thing of an idea of thought, consists of degrees of both kinds, and that a minute thing not consisting of these degrees would be nothing; for it would have no form, thus no quality, nor any state which could be changed and varied, and by this means have existence. Angels confirm this by the truth, that infinite things in God the Creator, who is the Lord from eternity, are one distinguishly; and that there are infinite things in his infinites; and that in things infinitely infinite there are degrees of both kinds, which also in him are one distinguishly; and because these things are in him, and all things were created by him, and things created repeat in an image the things which are in him, it follows that there cannot be the least finite in which there are not such degrees. These degrees are equally in things least and greatest, because the Divine is the same in things greatest and in things least. That in God-man infinite things are one distinguishly, see above (n. 17–22); and that the Divine is the same in things greatest and in things least (n. 77–82); which positions are further illustrated (n. 155, 169, 171).

224. There cannot be the least thing of love and wisdom, or the least thing of affection and thought, or even the least thing of an idea of thought, in which there are not degrees of both kinds, for the reason that love and wisdom are substance and form (as shown above, n. 40–43), and the same is true of affection and thought; and because there can be no form in which these degrees are not (as was said above), it follows that in these there are like degrees; for to separate love and wisdom, or affection and thought, from substance in form, is to annihilate them, since they are not possible outside of their subjects; for they are states of their subjects perceived by man varyingly, which states present them to view.

225. The greatest things in which there are degrees of both kinds are the universe in its whole complex, the natural world in its complex, and the spiritual world in its complex; every empire and every kingdom in its complex; also, all civil, moral and spiritual concerns of these in their complex; the whole animal kingdom, the whole vegetable kingdom, and the whole mineral kingdom, each in its complex; all atmospheres of both worlds taken together, also their heats and lights. Likewise things less general, as man in his complex; every animal in its complex, every tree and every shrub in its complex; as also every stone and every metal in its complex. The forms of these are alike in this, that they consist of degrees of both kinds; the reason is that the Divine, by which they were created, is the same in things greatest and least (as was shown above, n. 77–82). The particulars and the veriest particulars of all these are like generals and the largest generals in this, that they are forms of both kinds of degrees.

226. On account of things greatest and least being forms of both kinds of degrees, there is connection between them from first to last; for likeness conjoins them. Still, there can be no least thing which is the same as any other; consequently all particulars are distinct from each other, likewise all veriest particulars. In any form or in different forms there can be no least thing the same as any other, for the reason that in greatest forms there are like degrees, and the greatest are made up of leasts. From there being such degrees in things greatest, and perpetual differences in accordance with these degrees, from top to bottom and from center to circumference, it follows that their lesser or least constituents, in which there are like degrees, can no one of them be the same as any other.

227. It is likewise a matter of angelic wisdom that from this similitude between generals and particulars, that is, between things greatest and least in respect to these degrees, comes the perfection of the created universe; for thereby one thing regards another as its like, with which it can be conjoined for every use, and can present every end in effect.

228. But these things may seem paradoxical, because they are not explained by application to visible things; yet things abstract, being universals, are often better comprehended than things applied, for these are of perpetual variety, and variety obscures.

229. Some contend that there can be a substance so simple as not to be a form from lesser forms, and out of that substance, through a process of massing, substantiated or composite things arise, and finally substances called material. But there can be no such absolutely simple substances. For what is substance without form? It is that of which nothing can be predicated; and out of mere being of which nothing can be predicated, no process of massing can make anything. That there are things innumerable in the first created substance of all things, which are things most minute and simple, will be seen in what follows, where forms are treated of.

In the Lord the three degrees of height are infinite and uncreate, but in man the three degrees are finite and created

230. In the Lord the three degrees of height are infinite and uncreate, because the Lord is love itself and wisdom itself (as has been already shown); and because the Lord is love itself and wisdom itself, he is also Use itself. For love has use for its end, and brings forth use by means of wisdom; for without use love and wisdom have no boundary or end, that is, no home of their own, consequently they cannot be said to have being and have form unless there be use in which they may be.

These three constitute the three degrees of height in subjects of life. These three are like first end, middle end which is called cause, and last end which is called effect. That end, cause and effect constitute the three degrees of height has been shown above and abundantly proved.

231. That in man there are these three degrees can be seen from the elevation of his mind even to the degrees of love and wisdom in which angels of the second and third heavens are; for all angels were born men; and man, as regards the interiors pertaining to his mind, is a heaven in least form; therefore there are in man, by creation, as many degrees of height as there are heavens. Moreover, man is an image and likeness of God; consequently these three degrees have been inscribed on man, because they are in God-man, that is, in the Lord.

That in the Lord these degrees are infinite and uncreate, and in man finite and created, can be seen from what was shown in chapter 1; namely, from this, that the Lord is love and wisdom in himself; and that man is a recipient of love and wisdom from the Lord; also, that of the Lord nothing but what is infinite can be predicated, and of man nothing but what is finite.

232. These three degrees with the angels are called celestial, spiritual, and natural; and for them the celestial degree is the degree of love, the spiritual the degree of wisdom, and the natural the degree of uses. These degrees are so called because the heavens are divided into two kingdoms, one called the celestial, the other the spiritual, to which is added a third kingdom wherein are men in the world, and this is the natural kingdom. Moreover, the angels of whom the celestial kingdom consists are in love; the angels of whom the spiritual kingdom consists are in wisdom; while men in the world are in uses; therefore these kingdoms are conjoined. How it is to be understood that men are in uses will be shown in the next chapter.

233. It has been told me from heaven, that in the Lord from eternity, who is Jehovah, before his assumption of a human in the world, the two prior degrees existed actually, and the third degree potentially, as they do also with angels; but that after the assumption of a human in the world, he put on over these the third degree, called the natural, thereby becoming man, like a man in the world; but with the difference, that in the Lord this degree, like the prior degrees, is infinite and uncreate, while in angel and in man they are all finite and created. For the Divine which, apart from space, had filled all spaces (n. 69–72), penetrated even to the outmosts of nature; yet before the assumption of the human, the Divine influx into the natural degree was mediate through the angelic heavens, but after the assumption it was immediate from himself. This is the reason why all churches in the world before his advent were representative of spiritual and celestial things, but after his advent became spiritual-natural and celestial-natural, and representative worship was abolished. This also was the reason why the sun of the angelic heaven, which, as was said above, is the first proceeding of his Divine love and Divine wisdom, after the assumption of the human shone out with greater effulgence and splendor than before the assumption. And this is what is meant by these words in Isaiah:

> In that day the light of the moon shall be as the light of the sun, and the light of the sun shall be sevenfold, as the light of seven days (Isa. 30:26).

This is said of the state of heaven and of the church after the Lord's coming into the world. Again, in Revelation:

> The countenance of the Son of man was as the sun shineth in his strength (Rev. 1:16);

and elsewhere (as in Isaiah 60:20; 2 Sam. 23:3, 4; Matt. 17:1, 2). The mediate enlightenment of men through the angelic heaven, which existed before the coming of the Lord, may be compared to the light of the moon, which is the mediate light of the sun; and because after his coming this was made immediate, it is said in Isaiah:

> That the light of the moon shall be as the light of the sun (Isa. 30:26);

and in David:

> In his days shall the righteous flourish, and abundance of peace until there is no longer any moon (Ps. 72:7).

This also is said of the Lord.

234. The reason why the Lord from eternity, that is, Jehovah, put on this third degree by the assumption of a human in the world, was that he could enter into this degree only by means of a nature like human nature, thus only by means of conception from his Divine and by birth from a virgin; for in this way he could put off a nature which, although a receptacle of the Divine, is in itself dead, and could put on the Divine. This is meant by the Lord's two states in the world, which are called the state of exinanition and the state of glorification, which are treated of in the *Doctrine of the New Jerusalem Concerning the Lord.*

235. Of the threefold ascent of the degrees of height this much has been said in general; but these degrees cannot here be discussed in detail, because (as was said in the preceding chapter) there must be these three degrees in things greatest and things least; this only need be said, that there are such degrees in each and all things of love, and therefrom in each and all things of wisdom, and from both of these in each and all things of use. In the Lord all these degrees are infinite; in angel and man they are finite. But how there are these three degrees in love, in wisdom, and in uses cannot be described and unfolded except in series.

These three degrees of height are in every man from birth, and can be opened successively; and, as they are opened, man is in the Lord and the Lord in man

236. That there are three degrees of height in every man has not until now become known for the reason that these degrees have not been recognized, and so long as they remained unnoticed, none but continuous degrees could be known; and when none but continuous degrees are known, it may be supposed that love and wisdom increase in man only by continuity. But it should be known, that in every man from his birth there are three degrees of height, or discrete degrees, one above or within another; and that each degree of height, or discrete degree, has also degrees of breadth, or continuous degrees, according to which it increases by continuity. For there are degrees of both kinds in things greatest and least of all things (as was shown above, n. 222–229); for no degree of one kind is possible without degrees of the other kind.

237. These three degrees of height are called natural, spiritual, and celestial (as was said above, n. 232). When man is born he comes first into the natural degree, and this grows in him, by continuity, according to his knowledges and the understanding acquired by means of knowledges even to the highest point of understanding, which is called the rational. Yet not by this means is the second degree opened, which is called the spiritual. That degree is opened by means of a love of uses in accordance with the things of the understanding, although by a spiritual love of uses, which is love towards the neighbor.

This degree may grow in like manner by continuous degrees to its height, and it grows by means of knowledges of truth and good, that is, by spiritual truths. Yet even by such truths the third degree which is called the celestial is not opened; for this degree is opened by means of the celestial love of use, which is love to the Lord; and love to the Lord is nothing else than committing to life the precepts of the Word, the sum of which is to flee from evils because they are hellish and devilish, and to do good because it is heavenly and Divine. In this manner these three degrees are successively opened in man.

238. So long as man lives in the world he knows nothing of the opening of these degrees within him, because he is then in the natural degree, which is the outmost, and from this he then thinks, wills, speaks, and acts; and the spiritual degree, which is interior, communicates with the natural degree, not by continuity but by correspondences, and communication by correspondences is not sensibly felt. But when man puts off the natural degree, which he does at death, he comes into that degree which has been opened within him in the world; he in whom the spiritual degree has been opened coming into that degree, and he within whom the celestial degree has been opened coming into that degree.

He who comes into the spiritual degree after death no longer thinks, wills, speaks, and acts naturally, but spiritually; and he who comes into the celestial degree thinks, wills, speaks, and acts according to that degree. And as there can be communication between the three degrees only by correspondences, the differences of love, wisdom, and use, as regards these degrees are such as to have no common ground by means of anything continuous. From all this it is plain that man has three degrees of height that may be successively opened in him.

239. Since there are in man three degrees of love and wisdom, and therefore of use, it follows that there must be in him three degrees of will, of understanding, and of result therefrom, thus of determination to use; for will is the receptacle of love, understanding the receptacle of wisdom, and result is use from these. From this it is evident that there are in every man a natural, a spiritual, and a celestial will and understanding, potentially by birth and actually when they are opened. In a word the mind of man, which consists of will and understanding, is from creation and therefore from birth, of three degrees, so that man has a natural mind, a spiritual mind, and a celestial mind, and can thereby be elevated into and possess angelic wisdom while he lives in the world; but it is only after death, and then only if he becomes an angel, that he enters into that wisdom, and his

speech then becomes ineffable and incomprehensible to the natural man. I knew a man of moderate learning in the world, whom I saw after death and spoke with in heaven, and I clearly perceived that he spoke like an angel, and that the things he said would be inconceivable to the natural man; and for the reason that in the world he had applied the precepts of the Word to life and had worshiped the Lord, and was therefore raised up by the Lord into the third degree of love and wisdom. It is important that this elevation of the human mind should be known about, for upon it depends the understanding of what follows.

240. There are in man from the Lord two capacities whereby he is distinguished from beasts. One of these is the ability to understand what is true and what is good; this is called rationality, and is a capacity of his understanding. The other is an ability to do what is true and good; this is called freedom, and is a capacity of his will. For man by virtue of his rationality is able to think whatever he pleases, either with or against God, either with or against the neighbor; he is also able to will and to do what he thinks; but when he sees evil and fears punishment, he is able, by virtue of his freedom, to abstain from doing it. By virtue of these two capacities man is man, and is distinguished from beasts. Man has these two capacities from the Lord, and they are from him every moment; nor are they taken away, for if they were, man's human would perish. In these two capacities the Lord is with every man, good and evil alike; they are the Lord's abode in the human race; from this it is that all men live forever, both the good and evil. But the Lord's abode in man is nearer as by the agency of these capacities man opens the higher degrees, for by the opening of these man comes into higher degree of love and wisdom, thus nearer to the Lord. From this it can be seen that as these degrees are opened, man is in the Lord and the Lord in him.

241. It is said above, that the three degrees of height are like end, cause, and effect, and that love, wisdom, and use follow in succession according to these degrees; therefore a few things shall be said here about love as being end, wisdom as being cause, and use as being effect. Whoever consults his reason, if it is enlightened, can see that the end of all things of man is his love; for what he loves, that he thinks, decides upon, and does, consequently that he has for his end.

Man can also see from his reason that wisdom is cause; since he, that is, his love, which is his end, searches in his understanding for its means through which to attain its end, thus consulting its wisdom, and these means constitute the instrumental cause. That use is effect is evident without explanation. But one man's love is not the same as another's, neither is one man's wisdom the same as another's; so it is with use. And since these three are homogeneous (as was shown above, n. 189–194), it follows that such as is the love in man, such is the wisdom and such is the use. Wisdom is here spoken of, but by it what pertains to man's understanding is meant.

Spiritual light flows in with man through three degrees, but not spiritual heat, except so far as man flees from evils as sins and looks to the Lord

242. It is evident from what has been shown above that from the sun of heaven, which is the first proceeding of Divine love and Divine wisdom (treated of in chapter 2), light and heat proceed—light from its wisdom, and heat from its love; also that light is the receptacle of wisdom, and heat of love; also that so far as man comes into wisdom he comes into that Divine light, and so far as he comes into love he comes into that Divine heat. From what has been shown above it is also evident that there are three degrees of light and three degrees of heat, that is, three degrees of wisdom and three degrees of love, and that these degrees have been formed in man in order that he may be a receptacle of the Divine love and the Divine wisdom, thus of the Lord. It is now to be shown that spiritual light flows in through these three degrees in man, but not spiritual heat, except so far as man shuns evils as sins and looks to the Lord—or, what is the same, that man is able to receive wisdom even to the third degree, but not love, unless he flees from evils as sins and looks to the Lord; or what is still the same, that man's understanding can be raised into wisdom, but not his will, except so far as he flees from evils as sins.

243. That the understanding can be raised into the light of heaven, that is, into angelic wisdom, while the will cannot be raised into the heat of heaven, that is, into angelic love, unless man flees from evils as sins and looks to the Lord, has been made plainly evident to me from experience in the spiritual world. I have frequently seen and perceived that simple spirits, who knew merely that God is and that the Lord was born a man, and who knew scarcely anything else, clearly apprehended the arcana of angelic wisdom almost as the angels do; and not these simple ones alone, but many also of the infernal crew. These, while they listened, understood, but not when they thought within themselves; for while they listened, light entered from above, and when they thought within themselves, no light could enter except that which corresponded to their heat or love; consequently when they had listened to and perceived these arcana, as soon as they turned their ears away they remembered nothing, those belonging to the infernal crew even rejecting these things with disgust and utterly denying them, because the fire of their love and its light, being delusive, induced darkness, by which the heavenly light entering from above was extinguished.

244. The same thing happens in the world. A man not altogether stupid, and who has not confirmed himself in falsities from the pride of self-intelligence, hearing others speak on some exalted matter, or reading something of the kind, if he is in any affection of knowing, understands these things and also retains them, and may afterwards confirm them. A bad man as well as a good man may do this. Even a bad man, though in heart he denies the Divine things pertaining to the church, can still understand them, and also speak of and preach them, and in writing learnedly prove them; but when left to his own thought, from his own infernal love he thinks against them and denies them.

From which it is obvious that the understanding can be in spiritual light even when the will is not in spiritual heat; and from this it also follows that the understanding does not lead the will, or that wisdom does not beget love, but only teaches and shows the way, teaching how a man ought to live, and showing the way in which he ought to go. It further follows that the will leads the understanding, and causes it to act as one with itself; also that whatever in the understanding agrees with the love which is in the will, the love calls wisdom. In what follows it will be seen that the will does nothing by itself apart from the understanding, but does all that it does in conjunction with the understanding; moreover, that it is the will that by influx takes the understanding into partnership with itself, and not the reverse.

245. The nature of the influx of light into the three degrees of life in man which belong to his mind, shall now be shown. The forms which are receptacles of heat and light, that is, of love and wisdom in man, and which (as was said) are in threefold order or of three degrees, are transparent from birth, transmitting spiritual light as crystal glass transmits natural light; consequently in respect to wisdom man can be raised even into the third degree. Nevertheless these forms are not opened except when spiritual heat conjoins itself to spiritual light, that is, love to wisdom; by such conjunction these transparent forms are opened according to degrees. It is the same with light and heat from the sun of the world in their action on plants on the earth. The light of winter, which is as bright as that of summer, opens nothing in seed or in tree, but when vernal heat conjoins itself to that light then the heat opens them. There is this similarity because spiritual light corresponds to natural light, and spiritual heat to natural heat.

246. This spiritual heat is obtained only by fleeing from evils as sins, and at the same time looking to the Lord; for so long as man is in evils he is also in the love of them, for he lusts after them; and the love of evil and the lust abide in a love contrary to spiritual love and affection; and such love or lust can be removed only by fleeing from evils as sins; and because man cannot flee from evils from himself, but only from the Lord, he must look to the Lord. So when he flees from evils from the Lord, the love of evil and its heat are removed, and the love of good and its heat are introduced in their stead, whereby a higher degree is opened; for the Lord flowing in from above opens that degree, and then conjoins love, that is, spiritual heat, to wisdom or spiritual light, from which conjunction man begins to flourish spiritually, like a tree in springtime.

247. By the influx of spiritual light into all three degrees of the mind man is distinguished from beasts; and, as contrasted with beasts, he can think analytically, and see both natural and spiritual truth; and when he sees them he can acknowledge them, and thus be reformed and regenerated. This capacity to receive spiritual light is what is meant by rationality (referred to above), which every man has from the Lord, and which is not taken away from him, for if it were taken away he could not be reformed. From this capacity, called rationality, man, unlike the beasts, is able not only to think but also to speak from thought; and afterwards from his other capacity, called freedom (also referred to above), he is able to do those things that he thinks from his understanding. As these two capacities, rationality and freedom, which are proper to man, have been treated of above (n. 240), no more will be said about them here.

Unless the higher degree, which is the spiritual, is opened in man, he becomes natural and sensual

248. It was shown above that there are three degrees of the human mind, called natural, spiritual, and celestial, and that these degrees may be opened successively in man; also, that the natural degree is first opened; afterwards, if man flees from evil as sins and looks to the Lord, the spiritual degree is opened; and lastly, the celestial. Since these degrees are opened successively according to man's life, it follows that the two higher degrees may remain unopened, and man then continues in the natural degree, which is the outmost. Moreover, it is known in the world that there is a natural and a spiritual man, or an external and an internal man; but it is not known that a natural man becomes spiritual by the opening of some higher degree in him, and that such opening is effected by a spiritual life, which is a life conformed to the Divine precepts; and that without a life conformed to these man remains natural.

249. There are three kinds of natural men; the first consists of those who know nothing of the Divine precepts; the second, of those who know that there are such precepts, but give no thought to a life according to them; and the third, of those who despise and deny these precepts. In respect to the first class, which consists of those who know nothing of the Divine precepts, since they cannot be taught by themselves, they must needs remain natural. Every man is taught respecting the Divine precepts, not by immediate revelations, but by others who know them from religion, on which subject see the *Doctrine of the New Jerusalem Concerning the Sacred Scriptures*

(n. 114–118). Those of the second class, who know that there are Divine precepts but give no thought to a life according to them, also remain natural, and care about no other concerns than those of the world and the body. These after death become mere menials and servants, according to the uses which they are able to perform for those who are spiritual; for the natural man is a menial and servant, and the spiritual man is a master and lord. Those of the third class, who despise and deny the Divine precepts, not only remain natural, but also become sensual in the measure of their contempt and denial. Sensual men are the lowest natural men, who are incapable of thinking above the appearances and fallacies of the bodily senses. After death they are in hell.

250. As it is unknown in the world what the spiritual man is, and what the natural, and as by many he who is merely natural is called spiritual, and conversely, these subjects shall be separately discussed, as follows:

(1) What the natural man is, and what the spiritual man.

(2) The character of the natural man in whom the spiritual degree is opened.

(3) The character of the natural man in whom the spiritual degree is not opened and yet not closed.

(4) The character of the natural man in whom the spiritual degree is entirely closed.

(5) Lastly, the nature of the difference between the life of a man merely natural and the life of a beast.

251. (1) *What the natural man is, and what the spiritual man.* Man is not man from face and body, but from understanding and will; therefore by the natural man and the spiritual man is meant that man's understanding and will are either natural or spiritual. The natural man in respect to his understanding and will is like the natural world, and may be called a world or

microcosm; and the spiritual man in respect to his understanding and will is like the spiritual world, and may be called a spiritual world or heaven. From which it is evident that as the natural man is in a kind of image a natural world, so he loves those things which are of the natural world; and that as the spiritual man is in a kind of image a spiritual world, so he loves those things which are of that world, or of heaven. The spiritual man indeed loves the natural world also but not otherwise than as a master loves his servant through whom he performs uses. Moreover, according to uses the natural man becomes like the spiritual, which is the case when the natural man feels from the spiritual the delight of use; such a natural man may be called spiritual-natural.

The spiritual man loves spiritual truths; he not only loves to know and understand them, but also wills them; while the natural man loves to speak of those truths and also do them. Doing truths is performing uses. This subordination is from the conjunction of the spiritual world and the natural world; for whatever appears and is done in the natural world derives its cause from the spiritual world. From all this it can be seen that the spiritual man is altogether distinct from the natural, and that there is no other communication between them than such as there is between cause and effect.

252. (2) *The character of the natural man in whom the spiritual degree is opened.* This is obvious from what has been said above; to which it may be added, that a natural man is a complete man when the spiritual degree is opened in him, for he is then consociated with angels in heaven and at the same time with men in the world, and in regard to both, lives under the Lord's guidance. For the spiritual man imbibes commands from the Lord through the Word, and executes them through the natural man. The natural man who has the spiritual degree opened does not know that he thinks and acts from his spiritual man, for it seems as if he did this from himself, when yet he does not do it from himself but from the Lord. Nor does the natural man whose spiritual degree has been opened know that by means of his spiritual man he is in heaven, when yet his spiritual man is in the midst of angels of heaven, and sometimes is even visible to them; but because he draws himself back to his natural man, after a brief stay there he disappears. Nor does the natural man in whom the spiritual degree has been opened know that his spiritual mind is being filled by the Lord with thousands of arcana of wisdom, and with thousands of delights of love, and that he is to come into these after death, when he becomes an angel. The natural man does not know these things because communication between the natural man and the spiritual man is effected by correspondences; and communication by correspondences is perceived in the understanding only by the fact that truths are seen in light, and is perceived in the will only by the fact that uses are performed from affection.

253. (3) *The character of the natural man in whom the spiritual degree is not opened, and yet not closed.* The spiritual degree is not opened, and yet not closed, in the case of those who have led somewhat of a life of charity and yet have known little of genuine truth. The reason is, that this degree is opened by conjunction of love and wisdom, or of heat with light; love alone or spiritual heat alone not opening it, nor wisdom alone or spiritual light alone, but both in conjunction.

Consequently, when genuine truths, out of which wisdom or light arises, are unknown, love is inadequate to open that degree; it only keeps it in the possibility of being opened; this is what is meant by its not being closed. Something like this is seen in the vegetable kingdom, in that heat alone does not cause seeds and trees to vegetate, but heat in conjunction with light effects this. It is to be known that all truths are of spiritual light and all goods are of spiritual heat, and that good opens the spiritual degree by means of truths; for good, by means of truths, effects use, and uses are goods of love, which derive their essence from a conjunction of good and truth.

The lot, after death, of those in whom the spiritual degree is not opened and yet not closed, is that since they are still natural and not spiritual, they are in the lowest parts of heaven, where they sometimes suffer hard times; or they are in the outskirts in some higher heaven, where they are as it were in the light of evening; for (as was said above) in heaven and in every society there the light decreases from the middle to the outskirts, and those who above others are in Divine truths are in the middle, while those who are in few truths are in the outskirts.

Those are in few truths who from religion know only that there is a God, and that the Lord suffered for them, and that charity and faith are essentials of the church, not troubling themselves to know what faith is or what charity is; when yet faith in its essence is truth, and truth is manifold, and charity is all the work of his calling which man does from the Lord; he does this from the Lord when he flees from evils as sins. It is just as was said above, that the end is the all of the cause, and the effect the all of the end by means of the cause; the end is charity or good, the cause is faith or truth, and effects are good works or uses; from which it is plain that from charity no more can be carried into works than the measure in which charity is conjoined with the truths which are called truths of faith. By means of these truths charity enters into works and qualifies them.

254. (4) *The character of the natural man in whom the spiritual degree is entirely closed.* The spiritual degree is closed in those who are in evils as to life, and still more in those who from evils are in falsities. It is the same as with the fibril of a nerve, which contracts at the slightest touch of anything heterogeneous; so every motive fiber of a muscle, yea, the muscle itself, and even the whole body shrinks from the touch of whatever is hard or cold. So also the substances or forms of the spiritual degree in man shrink from evils and their falsities, because these are heterogeneous. For the spiritual degree, being in the form of heaven, admits nothing but goods, and truths that are from good; these are homogeneous to it; but evils, and falsities that are from evil, are heterogeneous to it. This degree is contracted, and by contraction closed, especially in those who in the world are in love of ruling from love of self, because this love is opposed to love to the Lord. It is also closed, but not so much, in those who from love of the world are in the insane greed of possessing the goods of others.

These loves shut the spiritual degree, because they are the origins of evils. The contraction or closing of this degree is like the twisting back of a spiral in the opposite direction; for which reason, that degree after it is closed, turns back the light of heaven; consequently there is thick darkness there instead of heavenly light, and truth which is in the light of heaven becomes nauseous. In such persons, not only does the spiritual degree itself become closed, but also the higher region of the natural degree which is called the rational, until at last the lowest region of the natural degree, which is called the sensual, alone stands open; this being nearest to the world and to the outward senses of the body, from which such a man afterwards thinks, speaks, and reasons.

The natural man who has become sensual through evils and their falsities, in the spiritual world in the light of heaven does not appear as a man but as a monster, even with nose drawn back (the nose is drawn in because the nose corresponds to the perception of truth); moreover, he cannot bear a ray of heavenly light. Such have in their caverns no other light than what resembles the light from live coals or from burning charcoal. From all this it is evident who and of what character are those in whom the spiritual degree is closed.

255. (5) *The nature of the difference between the life of a natural man and the life of a beast.* This difference will be particularly discussed in what follows, where life will be treated of. Here it may be said only that the difference is that man has three degrees of mind, that is, three degrees of understanding and will, which degrees can be opened successively; and as these are transparent, man can be raised as to his understanding into the light of heaven and see truths, not only civil and moral, but also spiritual, and from many truths seen can form conclusions about truths in their order, and thus perfect the understanding to eternity. But beasts do not have the two higher degrees, but only the natural degrees, and these apart from the higher degrees have no capacity to think on any subject, civil, moral, or spiritual. And since the natural degrees of beasts are incapable of being opened, and thereby raised into higher light, they are unable to think in successive order, but only in simultaneous order, which is not thinking, but acting from a knowledge corresponding to their love. And because they are unable to think analytically, and to view a lower thought from any higher thought, they are unable to speak, but are able only to utter sounds in accordance with the knowledge pertaining to their love. Yet the sensual man, who is in the lowest sense natural, differs from the beast only in this, that he can fill his memory with knowledges, and think and speak therefrom; this power he gets from a capacity proper to every man, of being able to understand truth if he chooses; it is this capacity that makes the difference. Nevertheless many, by abuse of this capacity, have made themselves lower than beasts.

The natural degree of the human mind regarded in itself is continuous, but by correspondence with the two higher degrees it appears when it is elevated as if it were discrete

256. Although this is hardly comprehensible by those who have as yet no knowledge of degrees of height, it must nevertheless be revealed, because it is a part of angelic wisdom; and while the natural man is unable to think about this wisdom in the same way as angels do, nevertheless it can be comprehended by his understanding, when it has been raised into the degree of light in which angels are; for his understanding can be elevated even to that extent, and enlightened according to its elevation. But this enlightenment of the natural mind does not ascend by discrete degrees; but increases in a continuous degree, and as it increases, that mind is enlightened from within by the light of the two higher degrees. How this occurs can be comprehended from a perception of degrees of height, as being one above another, while the natural degree, which is the lowest, is a kind of general covering to the two higher degrees.

Then, as the natural degree is raised up towards a degree of the higher kind, the higher acts from within upon the outer natural and illuminates it. This illumination is effected, indeed, from within, by the light of the higher degrees, but the natural degree which envelops and surrounds the higher receives it by continuity, thus more lucidly and purely in proportion to its ascent; that is, from within, by the light of the higher degrees, the natural degree is enlightened discretely, but in itself is enlightened continuously. From this it is evident that so long as man lives in the world, and is thereby in the natural degree, he cannot be elevated into very wisdom, such as the angels have, but only into higher light, even up to angels, and can receive enlightenment from their light that flows in from within and illuminates. But these things cannot as yet be more clearly described; they can be better comprehended from effects; for effects present causes in themselves in clear light, and thus illustrate them, when there is some previous knowledge of causes.

257. The effects are these: (1) The natural mind may be raised up to the light of heaven in which angels are, and may perceive

naturally, thus not so fully, what the angels perceive spiritually; nevertheless, man's natural mind cannot be raised into angelic light itself.

(2) By means of his natural mind, raised to the light of heaven, man can think, yea, speak with angels; but the thought and speech of the angels then flow into the natural thought and speech of the man, and not conversely; so that angels speak with man in a natural language, which is the man's mother tongue.

(3) This is effected by a spiritual influx into what is natural, and not by any natural influx into what is spiritual.

(4) Human wisdom, which so long as man lives in the natural world is natural, can by no means be raised into angelic wisdom, but only into some image of it. The reason is that elevation of the natural mind is effected by continuity, as from shade to light, or from grosser to purer. Still the man in whom the spiritual degree has been opened comes into that wisdom when he dies; and he may also come into it by a suspension of bodily sensations, and then by an influx from above into the spiritual parts of his mind.

(5) Man's natural mind consists of spiritual substances together with natural substances; thought comes from its spiritual substances, not from its natural substances; these recede when the man dies, while its spiritual substances do not. Consequently, after death, when man becomes a spirit or angel, the same mind remains in a form like that which it had in the world.

(6) The natural substances of that mind, which recede (as was said) by death, constitute the cutaneous covering of the spiritual body which spirits and angels have. By means of such covering, which is taken from the natural world, their spiritual bodies maintain existence; for the natural is the outmost container; consequently there is no spirit or angel who was not born a man. These arcana of angelic wisdom are here adduced that the quality

of the natural mind in man may be known, which subject is further treated of in what follows.

258. Every man is born into a capacity to understand truths even to the inmost degree in which the angels of the third heaven are; for the human understanding, rising up by continuity around the two higher degrees, receives the light of their wisdom, in the manner stated above (n. 256). Therefore man has the ability to become rational according to his elevation; if raised to the third degree he becomes rational from that degree, if raised to the second degree he becomes rational from that degree, if not raised he is rational in the first degree. It is said that he becomes rational from those degrees, because the natural degree is the general receptacle of their light. The reason why man does not become rational to the height that he might is that love, which is of the will, cannot be raised in the same manner as wisdom, which is of the understanding. Love, which is of the will, is raised only by fleeing from evils as sins, and then by goods of charity, which are uses, which the man thereafter performs from the Lord. Consequently, when love, which is of the will, is not at the same time raised, wisdom, which is of the understanding, however it may have ascended, falls back again down to its own love. Therefore, if man's love is not at the same time raised into the spiritual degree, he is rational only in the lowest degree. From all this it can be seen that man's rational is in appearance as if it were of three degrees, a rational from the celestial, a rational from the spiritual, and a rational from the natural; also that rationality, which is the capacity whereby man is elevated, is still in man whether he be elevated or not.

259. It has been said that every man is born into that capacity, namely, rationality, but by this is meant every man whose externals have not been injured by some accident, either in the womb, or by some disease after birth, or by a wound inflicted on the head, or in consequence of some insane love bursting forth, and breaking down restraints. In such the rational cannot be elevated; for life, which is of the will and understanding, has in such no bounds in which it can terminate, so disposed that it can produce outmost acts according to order; for life acts in accordance with outmost determinations, though not from them. That there can be no rationality with infants and children, may be seen below (n. 266, at the end).

The natural mind, since it is the covering and container of the higher degrees of the human mind, is reactive; and if the higher degrees are not opened it acts against them, but if they are opened it acts with them

260. It has been shown in the preceding chapter that as the natural mind is in the outmost degree, it envelops and encloses the spiritual mind and the celestial mind, which, in respect to degrees, are above it. It is now to be shown that the natural mind reacts against the higher or interior minds. It reacts because it covers, includes, and contains them, and this cannot be done without reaction; for unless it reacted, the interior or enclosed parts would become loosened and press outward and thus fall apart, just as the viscera, which are the interiors of the body, would push forth and fall asunder if the coverings which are about the body did not react against them; so, too, unless the membrane investing the motor fibers of a muscle reacted against the force of these fibers in their activities, not only would action cease, but all the inner tissues would be let loose. It is the same with every outmost degree of the degrees of height; consequently with the natural mind with respect to higher degrees; for, as was said above, there are three degrees of the human mind, the natural, the spiritual, and the celestial, and the natural mind is in the outmost degree. Another reason why the natural mind reacts against the spiritual mind is that the natural mind consists not only of substances of the spiritual

world but also of substances of the natural world (as was said above, n. 257), and substances of the natural world of their very nature react against the substances of the spiritual world; for substances of the natural world are in themselves dead, and are acted upon from without by substances of the spiritual world; and substances which are dead, and which are acted upon from without, by their nature resist, and thus by their nature react. From all this it can be seen that the natural man reacts against the spiritual man, and that there is combat. It is the same thing whether the terms "natural and spiritual man" or "natural and spiritual mind" are used.

261. From this it is obvious that when the spiritual mind is closed the natural mind continually acts against the things of the spiritual mind, fearing lest anything should flow in therefrom to disturb its own states. Everything that flows in through the spiritual mind is from heaven, for the spiritual mind in its form is a heaven; while everything that flows into the natural mind is from the world, for the natural mind in its form is a world. From which it follows that when the spiritual mind is closed, the natural mind reacts against all things of heaven, giving them no admission except so far as they are serviceable to it as means for acquiring and possessing the things of the world. And when the things of heaven are made to serve the natural mind as means to its own ends, then those means, though they seem to be heavenly, are made natural; for the end qualifies them, and they become like the knowledges of the natural man, in which interiorly there is nothing of life. But as things heavenly cannot be so joined to things natural that the two act as one, they separate, and, with men merely natural, things heavenly arrange themselves from without, in a circuit about the natural things which are within. From this it is that a merely natural man can speak and preach about heavenly things, and even simulate them in his actions, though inwardly

he thinks against them; the latter he does when alone, the former when in company. But of these things more in what follows.

262. By virtue of the reaction which is in him from birth the natural mind, or man, when he loves himself and the world above all things, acts against the things that are of the spiritual mind or man. Then also he has a sense of enjoyment in evils of every kind, as adultery, fraud, revenge, blasphemy, and other like things; he then also acknowledges nature as the creator of the universe; and confirms all things by means of his rational faculty; and after confirmation he either perverts or suffocates or repels the goods and truths of heaven and the church, and at length either shuns them or turns his back upon them or hates them. This he does in his spirit, and in the body just so far as he dares to speak with others from his spirit without fear of the loss of reputation as a means to honor and gain. When man is such, he gradually shuts up the spiritual mind closer and closer. Confirmations of evil by means of falsities especially close it up; therefore evil and falsity when confirmed cannot be uprooted after death; they are only uprooted by means of repentance in the world.

263. But when the spiritual mind is open the state of the natural mind is wholly different. Then the natural mind is arranged in compliance with the spiritual mind, and is subordinated to it. For the spiritual mind acts upon the natural mind from above or within, and removes the things therein that react, and adapts to itself those that act in harmony with itself, whereby the excessive reaction is gradually taken away. It is to be noted, that in things greatest and least of the universe, both living and dead, there is action and reaction, from which comes an equilibrium of all things; this is destroyed when action overcomes reaction, or the reverse. It is the same with the natural and with the spiritual mind. When the natural mind

acts from the enjoyments of its love and the pleasures of its thought, which are in themselves evils and falsities, the reaction of the natural mind removes those things which are of the spiritual mind and blocks the doors lest they enter, and it makes action to come from such things as agree with its reaction.

The result is an action and reaction of the natural mind opposite to the action and reaction of the spiritual mind, whereby there is a closing of the spiritual mind like the twisting back of a spiral. But when the spiritual mind is opened, the action and reaction of the natural mind are inverted; for the spiritual mind acts from above or within, and at the same time it acts from below or from without, through those things in the natural mind which are arranged in compliance with it; and it twists back the spiral in which the action and reaction of the natural mind lie. For the natural mind is by birth in opposition to the things belonging to the spiritual mind; an opposition derived, as is well known, from parents by heredity. Such is the change of state which is called reformation and regeneration. The state of the natural mind before reformation may be compared to a spiral twisting or bending itself downward; but after reformation it may be compared to a spiral twisting or bending itself upwards; therefore man before reformation looks downwards to hell, but after reformation looks upwards to heaven.

The origin of evil is from the abuse of the capacities proper to man that are called rationality and freedom

264. By rationality is meant the capacity to understand what is true and thereby what is false, also to understand what is good and thereby what is evil; and by freedom is meant the capacity to think, will, and do these things freely. From what precedes it is evident, and it will become more evident from what follows, that every man from creation, consequently from

birth, has these two capacities, and that they are from the Lord; that they are not taken away from man; that from them is the appearance that man thinks, speaks, wills, and acts as from himself; that the Lord dwells in these capacities in every man, that man by virtue of that conjunction lives to eternity; that man by means of these capacities can be reformed and regenerated, but not without them; finally, that by them man is distinguished from beasts.

265. That the origin of evil is from the abuse of these capacities will be explained in the following order:

(1) A bad man equally with a good man enjoys these two capacities.

(2) A bad man abuses these capacities to confirm evils and falsities, but a good man uses them to confirm goods and truths.

(3) Evils and falsities confirmed in man are permanent, and come to be of his love, consequently of his life.

(4) Such things as have come to be of the love and life are engendered in offspring.

(5) All evils, both engendered and acquired, have their seat in the natural mind.

266. (1) *A bad man, equally with a good man enjoys these two capacities.* It was shown in the preceding chapter that the natural mind, as regards the understanding, can be elevated even to the light in which angels of the third heaven are, and can see truths, acknowledge them, and then give expression to them. From this it is plain that since the natural mind can be elevated, a bad man equally with a good man enjoys the capacity called rationality; and because the natural mind can be elevated to such an extent, it follows that a bad man can also think and speak about heavenly truths. Moreover, that he is able to will and to do them, even though he does not will and do them, both reason and experience affirm. Reason affirms it: for who cannot will and do what he thinks? His not willing and doing it is because he does not love to will and do it. This ability to will and to do is the freedom which every man has from the Lord; but his not willing and doing good when he can, is from a love of evil, which opposes; but this love he is able to resist, and many do resist it. Experience in the spiritual world has often corroborated this. I have listened to evil spirits who inwardly were devils, and who in the world had rejected the truths of heaven and the church. When the affection for knowing, in which every man is from childhood, was excited in them by the glory that, like the brightness of fire, surrounds each love, they perceived the arcana of angelic wisdom just as clearly as good spirits do who inwardly were angels.

Those diabolical spirits even declared that they were able to will and act according to those arcana, but did not wish to. When told that they might will them, if only they would flee from evils as sins, they said that they could even do that, but did not wish to. From this it was evident that the wicked equally with the good have the capacity called freedom. Let anyone look within himself, and he will observe that it is so. Man has the power to will, because the Lord, from whom that capacity comes, continually gives the power; for, as was said above, the Lord dwells in every man in both of these capacities, and therefore in the capacity, that is, in the power, of being able to will. As to the capacity to understand, called rationality, this man does not have until his natural mind reaches maturity; until then it is like seed in unripe fruit, which cannot be opened in the soil and grow up into a shrub. Neither does this capacity exist in those mentioned above (n. 259).

267. (2) *A bad man abuses these capacities to confirm evils and falsities, but a good man uses them to confirm goods and truths.* From the intellectual capacity called rationality, and from the voluntary capacity called freedom, man derives the ability to confirm whatever he wishes; for the natural man is able to raise his understanding into higher light to any extent he desires; but one who is in evils and in falsities therefrom raises it no higher than into the upper regions of his natural mind, and rarely as far as the border of the spiritual mind; for the reason that he is in the delights of the love of his natural mind, and when he raises the understanding above that mind, the delight of his love perishes; and if it is raised still higher, and sees truths which are opposed to the delights of his life or to the principles of his self-intelligence, he either falsifies those truths or passes them by and contemptuously leaves them behind, or retains them in the memory as means to serve his life's love, or the pride of his self-intelligence. That the natural man is able to confirm whatever he wishes is plainly evident from the multitude of heresies in the Christian world, each of which is confirmed by its adherents.

Who does not know that evils and falsities of every kind can be confirmed? It is possible to confirm, and by the wicked it is confirmed within themselves, that there is no God, and that nature is everything and created herself; that religion is only a means for keeping simple minds in bondage; that human prudence does everything, and Divine providence nothing except sustaining the universe in the order in which it was created; also that murders, adulteries, thefts, frauds, and revenge are allowable, as held by Machiavelli and his followers.

These and many like things the natural man is able to confirm, and even to fill volumes with the confirmations; and when such falsities are confirmed they appear in their delusive light, but truths in such obscurity as to be seen only as phantoms of the night. In a word, take what is most false and present it as a proposition, and ask an ingenious person to prove it, and he will do so to the complete extinction of the light of truth; but set aside his confirmations, return and view the proposition itself from your own rationality, and you will see its falsity in all its deformity. From all this it can be seen that man is able to abuse these two capacities, which he has from the Lord, to confirm evils and falsities of every kind. This no beast can do, because no beast enjoys these capacities. Consequently, a beast is born into all the order of its life, and into all the knowledge of its natural love, but man is not.

268. (3) *Evils and falsities confirmed in man are permanent, and come to be of his love and life.* Confirming evil and falsity is nothing else than putting away good and truth, and if persisted in, it is their rejection; for evil removes and rejects good, and falsity truth. For this reason confirming evil and falsity is a closing up of heaven, for every good and truth flows in from the Lord through heaven, and when heaven is closed, man is in hell, and in a society there in which a like evil prevails and a like falsity; from which hell he cannot afterwards be delivered.

It has been granted me to speak with some who ages ago confirmed themselves in the falsities of their religion, and I saw that they remained in the same falsities, in the same way as they were in them in the world. The reason is, that all things in which a man confirms himself come to be of his love and life. They come to be of his love because they come to be of his will and understanding; and will and understanding constitute the life of everyone; and when they come to be of man's life, they come to be not only of his whole mind but also of his whole body. From this it is evident that a man who has confirmed himself in evils and falsities is such from head to foot, and when he is wholly such, by no turning or twisting back can he be reduced to an opposite state, and thus withdrawn from hell. From all this, and from what precedes in this chapter, it can be seen what the origin of evil is.

269. (4) *Such things as have come to be of the love, and consequently of the life, are engendered in offspring.* It is known that man is born into evil, and that he derives it by inheritance from parents; though by some it is believed that he inherits it not from his parents, but through parents from Adam; this, however, is an error. He derives it from the father, from whom he has a soul that is clothed with a body in the mother. For the seed, which is from the father, is the first receptacle of life, but such a receptacle as it was with the father; for the seed is in the form of his love, and each one's love is, in things greatest and least, similar to itself; and there is in the seed a conatus to the human form, and by successive steps it goes forth into that form. From this it follows that evils called hereditary are from fathers, thus from grandfathers and great-grandfathers, successively transmitted to offspring.

This may be learned also from observation, for as regards affections, there is a resemblance of races to their first progenitor, and a stronger resemblance in families, and a still stronger resemblance in households; and this resemblance is such that generations are distinguishable not only by the disposition, but even by the face. But of this ingeneration of the love of evil by parents in offspring more will be said in what follows, where the correspondence of the mind, that is, of the will and understanding, with the body and its members and organs will be fully treated of.

Here these few things only are brought forward, that it may be known that evils are derived from parents successively, and that they increase through the accumulations of one parent after another, until man by birth is nothing but evil; also that the malignity of evil increases according to the degree in which the spiritual mind is closed up, for in this manner the natural mind also is closed above; finally, that there is no recovery from this in posterity except through their fleeing from evils as sins by the help of the Lord. In this and in no other way is the spiritual mind opened, and by means of such opening the natural mind is brought back into correspondent form.

270. (5) *All evils and their falsities, both engendered and acquired, have their seat in the natural mind.* Evils and their falsities have their seat in the natural mind, because that mind is, in form or image, a world; while the spiritual mind in its form or image is a heaven, and in heaven evil cannot be entertained. The spiritual mind, therefore, is not opened from birth, but is only in the capability of being opened. Moreover, the natural mind derives its form in part from substances of the natural world; but the spiritual mind from substances of the spiritual world only; and this mind is preserved in its integrity by the Lord, in order that man may be capable of becoming a man; for man is born an animal, but he becomes a man. The natural mind, with all its belongings, is coiled into gyres from right to left, but the spiritual mind into gyres from left to right; the two thus curving in directions contrary to each other—a proof that evil has its seat in the natural mind, and that of itself it acts against the spiritual mind. Moreover, the gyration from right to left is turned downward, thus towards hell, but the gyration from left to right tends upward, thus toward heaven. This was made evident to me by the fact that an evil spirit can gyrate his body only from right to left, not from left to right; while a good spirit can gyrate his body from right to left only with difficulty, but with ease from left to right. Gyration follows the flow of the interiors, which belong to the mind.

Evils and falsities are in complete opposition to goods and truths, because evils and falsities are diabolical and infernal, while goods and truths are divine and heavenly

271. That evil and good are opposites, also the falsity of evil and the truth of good, everyone acknowledges when he hears

it. Still those who are in evil do not feel, and therefore do not perceive, otherwise than that evil is good; for evil gives enjoyment to their senses, especially sight and hearing, and from that gives enjoyment also to their thoughts, and thus their perceptions. While, therefore, the evil acknowledge that evil and good are opposites, still, when they are in evil, they declare from their enjoyment of it that evil is good, and good evil. For example, one who abuses his freedom to think and to do what is evil calls that freedom, while its opposite, namely, to think the good which in itself is good, he calls bondage; when, in fact, the latter is to be truly free, and the former to be in bondage.

He who loves adulteries calls it freedom to commit adultery, but not to be allowed to commit adultery he calls bondage; for in lasciviousness he has a sense of enjoyment, but of the contrary in chastity. He who is in the love of ruling from love of self feels in that love an enjoyment of life surpassing other enjoyments of every kind; consequently, everything belonging to that love he calls good, and everything contrary to it he declares to be evil; when yet the reverse is true.

It is the same with every other evil. While everyone, therefore, acknowledges that evil and good are opposites, those who are in evils cherish a reverse conception of such opposition, and only those who are in good have a right conception of it. No one so long as he is in evil can see good, but he who is in good can see evil. Evil is below as in a cave, good is above as on a mountain.

272. Now as many do not know what the nature of evil is, and that it is entirely opposite to good, and as this knowledge is important, the subject shall be considered in the following order:

(1) The natural mind that is in evils and in falsities therefrom is a form and image of hell.

(2) The natural mind that is a form and image of hell descends through three degrees.

(3) The three degrees of the natural mind that is a form and image of hell are opposite to the three degrees of the spiritual mind which is a form and image of heaven.

(4) The natural mind that is a hell is in every respect opposed to the spiritual mind that is a heaven.

273. (1) *The natural mind that is in evils and in falsities therefrom is a form and image of hell.* The nature of the natural mind in man in its substantial form cannot here be described, that is, its nature in its own form woven out of the substances of both worlds, in the brains where that mind in its first principles, has its seat. The universal idea of that form will be given in what follows, where the correspondence of the mind and body is to be treated of. Here somewhat only shall be said of its form as regards the states and their changes, whereby perceptions, thoughts, intentions, volitions, and their belongings are manifested; for, as regards these states and changes, the natural mind that is in evils and their falsities is a form and image of hell. Such a form supposes a substantial form as a subject; for without a substantial form as a subject, changes of state are impossible, just as sight is impossible without an eye, or hearing without an ear. In regard, then, to the form or image wherein the natural mind images hell, that form or image is such that the reigning love with its lusts, which is the universal state of that mind, is like what the devil is in hell; and the thoughts of the false arising out of that reigning love are, as it were, the devil's crew. By "the devil" and by "his crew" nothing else is meant in the Word. Moreover, the case is similar, since in hell there is a love of ruling from love of self, a reigning love, called there the "devil"; and the affections of the false, with the thoughts arising out of that love, are called "his crew."

It is the same in every society of hell, with differences resembling the differences of species in a genus. And the natural mind that is in evils and in falsities therefrom is in a similar form; consequently, a natural man who is of this character comes, after death, into a society of hell similar to himself, and then, in each and every particular, he acts in unison with it; for he thus enters into his own form, that is, into the states of his own mind. There is also another love, called "satan," subordinate to the former love that is called the devil; it is the love of possessing the goods of others by every evil device. Cunning villainies and subtleties are its crew. Those who are in this hell are generally called satans; those in the former, devils; and such of them as do not act in a clandestine way there do not disown their name. From this it is that the hells, as a whole, are called the devil and satan.

The two hells are generically divided in accordance with these two loves, because all the heavens are divided into two kingdoms, the celestial and the spiritual, in accordance with two loves; and the devil-hell corresponds, by opposites, to the celestial kingdom, and the satan-hell corresponds, by opposites, to the spiritual kingdom. That the heavens are divided into two kingdoms, the celestial and the spiritual, may be seen in the work *Heaven and Hell* (n. 20–28). The reason why a natural mind of such a character is in form a hell, is that every spiritual form is like itself both in what is greatest and in what is least; therefore every angel is, in lesser form, a heaven, as is also shown in the work *Heaven and Hell* (n. 51–58); from which it follows that every man or spirit who is a devil or a satan is, in lesser form, a hell.

274. (2) *The natural mind that is a form or image of hell descends through three degrees.* It may be seen above (n. 222–229) that both in the greatest and in the least of all things there are degrees of two kinds, namely, degrees of height and degrees of breadth. This is also true of the natural mind in its greatest and its least parts. Degrees of height are what are now referred to.

The natural mind, by its two capacities called rationality and freedom, is in such a state as to be capable of ascending through three degrees, or of descending through three degrees; it ascends by goods and truths, and descends by evils and falsities. When it ascends, the lower degrees which tend to hell are shut, and when it descends, the higher degrees which tend to heaven are shut; for the reason that they are in reaction. These three degrees, higher and lower, are neither open nor shut in man in earliest infancy, for he is then ignorant both of good and truth and of evil and falsity; but as he lets himself into one or the other, the degrees are opened and shut on the one side or the other.

When they are opened towards hell, the reigning love, which is of the will, obtains the highest or inmost place; the thought of the false, which is of the understanding from that love, obtains the second or middle place; and the result of the love through the thought, or of the will through the understanding, obtains the lowest place.

The same is true here as of degrees of height treated of above; they stand in order as end, cause, and effect, or as first end, middle end, and last end. The descent of these degrees is towards the body, consequently in the descent they wax grosser, and become material and corporeal. If truths from the Word are received in the second degree to form it, these truths are falsified by the first degree, which is the love of evil, and become servants and slaves. From this it can be seen what the truths of the church from the Word become with those who are in the love of evil, or whose natural mind is in form a hell, namely, that they are profaned because they serve the devil as means; for the love of evil reigning in the natural mind that is a hell, is the devil, as was said above.

275. (3) *The three degrees of the natural mind that is a form and image of hell, are opposite to the three degrees of the spiritual mind which is a form and image of heaven.* It has been shown above that there are three degrees of the mind, called natural, spiritual, and celestial, and that the human mind, made up of these degrees, looks towards heaven, and turns itself about in that direction. From this it can be seen that the natural mind, looking downwards and turning itself about towards hell, is made up in like manner of three degrees, and that each degree of it is opposite to a degree of that mind which is a heaven.

That this is so has been made very clear to me by things seen in the spiritual world; namely, that there are three heavens, and these distinct according to three degrees of height; that there are three hells, and these also distinct according to three degrees of height or depth; that the hells are opposed to the heavens in each and every particular; also that the lowest hell is opposite to the highest heaven, and the middle hell to the middle heaven, and the uppermost hell to the lowest heaven. It is the same with the natural mind that is in the form of hell; for spiritual forms are like themselves in things greatest and least.

The heavens and hells are thus opposite, because their loves are opposed. In the heavens, love to the Lord, and consequent love to the neighbor, constitute the inmost degree; in the hells, love of self and love of the world constitute the inmost degree. In the heavens, wisdom and intelligence, springing from their loves, constitute the middle degree; in the hells folly and insanity, springing from their loves and appearing like wisdom and intelligence, constitute the middle degree. In the heavens, the results from the two other degrees, either laid up in the memory as knowledges, or determined into actions in the body, constitute the lowest degree; in the hells, the results from the two other degrees, which have become either knowledges or acts, constitute the outermost degree. How the goods and truths

of heaven are turned, in the hells, into evils and falsities, thus
into what is opposite, may be seen from this experience: I heard
that a certain Divine truth flowed down out of heaven into
hell, and that in its descent by degrees it was converted on the
way into what is false, until at the lowest hell, it became the
exact opposite of that truth; from which it was manifest that
the hells according to degrees are in opposition to the heavens
in regard to all goods and truths, these becoming evils and
falsities by influx into forms turned the reverse way; for all
inflowing, it is well known, is perceived and felt according to
recipient forms and their states.

This conversion into the opposite was made further evident
to me from this experience: it was granted me to see the hells
as they are placed relatively to the heavens; and those who
were there appeared inverted, the head downward and the feet
upward; but it was said that they nevertheless appear to
themselves to be upright on their feet; comparatively like the
antipodes. By these evidences from experience, it can be seen
that the three degrees of the natural mind, which is a hell in
form and image, are opposite to the three degrees of the
spiritual mind which is a heaven in form and image.

276. (4) *The natural mind that is a hell is in complete opposition to the spiritual mind which is a heaven.* When the loves are
opposite all things of perception become opposites; for out of
love, which makes the very life of man, everything else flows
like streams from their source; the things not from that source
separating in the natural mind from those which are. Whatever
springs from man's reigning love is in the middle, and other
things are at the sides. If these latter are truths of the church
from the Word, they are transferred from the middle further
away to the sides, and are finally exterminated; and then the
man, that is, the natural mind, perceives evil as good, and sees
falsity as truth; and conversely. This is why he believes perfidy

to be wisdom, insanity to be intelligence, cunning to be prudence, and evil devices to be ingenuity; moreover, he makes nothing of Divine and heavenly things pertaining to the church and worship, while he regards bodily and worldly things as of the greatest worth. He thus inverts the state of his life, making what is of the head to be of the sole of the foot, and trampling upon it; and making what is of the sole of the foot to be of the head. Thus from being alive he becomes dead. One is said to be alive whose mind is a heaven, and one is said to be dead whose mind is a hell.

All things of the three degrees of the natural mind are included in the deeds that are done by the acts of the body

277. By the knowledge of degrees, which is set forth in this chapter, the following arcanum is disclosed: all things of the mind, that is, of the will and understanding of man, are in his acts or deeds, included therein very much as things visible and invisible are in a seed or fruit or egg. Acts or deeds by themselves appear outwardly as these do, but in their internals there are things innumerable, such as the concurring forces of the motor fibers of the whole body and all things of the mind that excite and determine these forces, all of which, as shown above, are of three degrees. And since all things of the mind are in these, so also are things of the will, that is, all the affections of man's love, which make the first degree; all things of the understanding, that is, all thoughts from his perception, which makes the second degree; and all things of the memory, that is, all ideas of the thought nearest to speech, taken from the memory, which compose the third degree. Out of these things determined into act, deeds come forth, in which, seen in external form, prior things are not visible although they are actually therein. That the outmost is the complex, container, and base of things prior may be seen above (n. 209–216); and that degrees of height are in fullness in their outmost (n. 217–221).

278. The acts of the body when viewed by the eye, appear thus simple and uniform, as seeds, fruits, and eggs do, in external form, or as nuts and almonds in their shells, yet they contain in themselves all the prior things from which they exist, because every outmost is sheathed about and is thereby rendered distinct from things prior. So is each degree enveloped by a covering, and thereby separated from other degrees; consequently things of the first degree are not perceived by the second, nor those of the second by the third. For example: The love of the will, which is the first degree of the mind, is not perceived in the wisdom of the understanding, which is the second degree of the mind, except by a certain enjoyment in thinking of the matter. Again, the first degree, which is, as just said, the love of the will, is not perceived in the knowledge of the memory, which is the third degree, except by a certain pleasure in knowing and speaking. From all this it follows that every deed, or bodily act, includes all these things, although externally it appears simple, and as if it were a single thing.

279. This is corroborated by the following: The angels who are with man perceive separately the things that are from the mind in the act, the spiritual angels perceiving those things therein that are from the understanding, and the celestial angels those things therein that are from the will. This appears incredible, but it is true. It should be known, however, that the things of the mind pertaining to any subject that is under consideration, or before the mind, are in the middle, and the rest are round about these according to their affinities therewith. The angels declare that a man's character is perceived from a single deed, but in a likeness of his love, which varies according to its determinations into affections, and into thoughts therefrom. In a word, before the angels every act or deed of a spiritual man is like a palatable fruit, useful and beautiful, which when opened and eaten yields flavor, use, and delight. That the angels have such a perception of the acts and deeds of men may also be seen above (n. 220).

280. It is the same with man's speech. The angels recognize a man's love from his tone in speaking, his wisdom from his articulation, and his knowledge from the meaning of the words. They declare, moreover, that these three are in every word, because the word is a kind of resultant, involving tone, articulation, and meaning. It was told me by angels of the third heaven that from each successive word that a man speaks in discourse they perceive the general state of his disposition, and also some particular states. That in each single word of the Word there is something spiritual from the Divine wisdom, and something celestial from the Divine love, and that these are perceived by angels when the Word is devoutly read by man, has been abundantly shown in the *Doctrine of the New Jerusalem Concerning the Sacred Scripture.*

281. The conclusion is, that in the deeds of a man whose natural mind descends through three degrees into hell, there are all his evils and his falsities of evil; and that in the deeds of a man whose natural mind ascends into heaven there are all his goods and truths; and that both are perceived by the angels from the mere speech and act of man. From this it is said in the Word that a man "shall be judged according to his deeds," and that he shall render an account of his words.

Chapter 4
[The Method of Creation]

The Lord from eternity, who is Jehovah, created the universe and all things thereof from himself, and not from nothing

282. It is known throughout the world, and acknowledged by every wise man from interior perception, that God, who is the creator of the universe, is one; and it is known from the Word that God the creator of the universe is called "Jehovah," which is from the verb "to be," because he alone "is." That the Lord from eternity is that Jehovah is shown by many statements from the Word in the *Doctrine of the New Jerusalem Concerning the Lord.* Jehovah is called the Lord from eternity, since Jehovah assumed a human that he might save men from hell; he then commanded his disciples to call him Lord. Therefore in the New Testament Jehovah is called "the Lord"; as can be seen from this:

> Thou shalt love Jehovah thy God with all thy heart and with all thy soul (Deut. 6:5);

but in the New Testament:

> Thou shalt love the Lord thy God with all thy heart and with all thy soul (Matt. 22:35).

It is the same in other passages in the Gospels, taken from the Old Testament.

283. Everyone who thinks from clear reason sees that the universe was not created out of nothing, for he sees that not anything can be made out of nothing; since nothing is nothing, and to make anything out of nothing is a contradiction, and a contradiction is contrary to the light of truth, which is from divine wisdom; and whatever is not from divine wisdom is not from divine omnipotence.

Everyone who thinks from clear reason sees also that all things have been created out of a substance that is substance in itself, for that is *esse* itself, out of which everything that is can take form; and since God alone is substance in itself, and therefore *esse* itself, it is evident that from this source alone is the formation of things. Many have seen this, because reason causes them to see it; and yet they have not dared to confirm it, fearing lest they might thereby be led to think that the created universe is God, because from God, or that nature is from itself, and consequently that the inmost of nature is what is called God.

For this reason, although many have seen that the formation of all things is from God alone and out of his *esse,* yet they have not dared to go beyond their first thought on the subject, lest their understanding should become entangled in a so-called Gordian knot, beyond the possibility of release. Such release would be impossible, because their thought of God, and of the creation of the universe by God, has been in accordance with time and space, which are properties of nature; and from nature no one can have any perception of God and of the creation of the universe; but everyone whose understanding is in any interior light can have a perception of nature and of its creation out of God, because God is not in time and space. That the Divine is not in space may be seen above (n. 7–10); that the Divine apart from space fills all the spaces of the universe (n. 69–72); and that the Divine apart from time is in all time (n. 73–76). In what follows it will be seen that although God has created the universe and all things thereof out of himself, yet there is nothing whatever in the created universe that is God; and other things besides, which will place this matter in its proper light.

284. Chapter 1 of this work treated of God, that he is Divine love and Divine wisdom; that he is life, and that he is substance and form, which is the very and only *esse*. Chapter 2 treated of the spiritual sun and its world, and of the natural sun and its world, and of the creation of the universe with all things thereof from God by means of these two suns. Chapter 3 treated of degrees in which are each and all things that have been created. Chapter 4 will now treat of the creation of the universe from God. All these subjects are now explained, because the angels have lamented before the Lord, that when they look upon the world they see nothing but darkness, and among men no knowledge of God, of heaven, or of the creation of nature for their wisdom to rest upon.

The Lord from eternity, that is, Jehovah, could not have created the universe and all things thereof unless he were a man

285. Those who have a corporeal natural idea of God as a man, are wholly unable to comprehend how God as a man could have created the universe and all things thereof; for they think within themselves, How can God as a man wander all over the universe from space to space, and create? Or how can he, from his place, speak the word, and as soon as it is spoken, creation follow? When it is said that God is a man, such ideas present themselves to those whose conception of the God-man is like their conception of a man in the world, and who think of God from nature and its properties, which are time and space. But those whose conception of God-man is not drawn from their conception of a man in the world, nor from nature and its space and time, clearly perceive that unless God were a man the universe could not have been created. Bring your thought into the angelic idea of God as being a man, putting away, as much as you can, the idea of space, and you will come near in thought to the truth. In fact, some of the learned have a perception of spirits and angels as not in space, because they have a perception of the spiritual as apart from space. For the spiritual is like thought, which although it is in man, man is nevertheless able by means of it to be present as it were elsewhere, in any place however remote. Such is the state of spirits and angels, who are men even as regards their bodies. In whatever place their thought is, there they appear, because in the spiritual world spaces and distances are appearances, and make one with the thought that is from their affection.

From all this it can be seen that God, who appears as a sun far above the spiritual world, and to whom there can belong no appearance of space, is not to be thought of from space. And it can then be comprehended that he created the universe out of himself, and not out of nothing; also that his Human Body cannot be thought great or small, that is, of any one stature, because this also pertains to space; consequently that in things first and last, and in things greatest and least, he is the same; and still further, that the Human is the inmost in every created thing, though apart from space. That the Divine is the same in things greatest and least may be seen above (n. 77–82); and that the Divine apart from space fills all spaces (n. 69–72). And because the Divine is not in space, it is not continuous *[nec est continuum]*, as the inmost of nature is.

286. That God unless he were a man could not have created the universe and all things thereof, may be clearly apprehended by any intelligent person from this, that he cannot deny that in God there is love and wisdom, mercy and clemency, and also goodness itself and truth itself, inasmuch as these are from God. And because he cannot deny this, neither can he deny that God is a man; for abstractly from man not one of these is possible; for man is their subject, and to separate them from their subject is to say that they are not. Think of wisdom, and place it outside of man—is it anything? Can you conceive of it as something ethereal, or as something flaming? You cannot, unless perchance you conceive of it as being within these; and if within these, it must be wisdom in a form such as man has; it must be wholly in the form of man, not one thing can be lacking if wisdom is to be in that form. In a word, the form of wisdom is man; and because man is the form of wisdom, he is also the form of love, mercy, clemency, good and truth, because these make one with wisdom. That love and wisdom are not possible except in a form, see above (n. 40–43).

287. That love and wisdom are man is further evident from the fact that the angels of heaven are men in beauty in the measure in which they are in love and its wisdom from the Lord. The same is evident from what is said of Adam in the Word, that he was created into the likeness and into the image of God (Gen. 1:26), because into the form of love and wisdom. Every man on earth is born into the human form as regards his body, for the reason that his spirit, which is also called his soul, is a man; and this is a man because it is receptive of love and wisdom from the Lord; and so far as these are received by the spirit or soul of man, so far it becomes a man after the death of the material body which it had drawn about it; and so far as these are not received it becomes a monster, which derives something of manhood from the ability to receive.

288. Because God is a man, the whole angelic heaven in the aggregate resembles a single man, and is divided into regions and provinces according to the members, viscera, and organs of man. Thus there are societies of heaven which constitute the province of all things of the brain, of all things of the facial organs, and of all things of the viscera of the body; and these provinces are distinct from each other, just as those organs are in man; moreover, the angels know in what province of man they are. The whole heaven is in this image, because God is a man. God is also heaven, because the angels, who constitute

heaven, are recipients of love and wisdom from the Lord, and recipients are images. That heaven is in the form of all things of man is shown in the *Arcana Coelestia,* at the end of various chapters.

289. All this makes evident how empty are the ideas of those who think of God as something else than a man, and of the Divine attributes as not being in God as a man, since these separated from man are mere figments of reason. That God is very man, from whom every man is a man according to his reception of love and wisdom, may be seen above (n. 11–13). This truth is here corroborated on account of what follows, that the creation of the universe by God, because he is a man, may be perceived.

The Lord from eternity, that is, Jehovah, brought forth from himself the sun of the spiritual world, and from that created the universe and all things thereof

290. The sun of the spiritual world was treated of in chapter 2 of this work, and the following propositions were there established: Divine love and Divine wisdom appear in the spiritual world as a sun (n. 83–88). Spiritual heat and spiritual light go forth from that sun (n. 89–92). That sun is not God, but is a proceeding from the Divine love and Divine wisdom of God-man; so also are the heat and light from that sun (n. 93–98). The sun of the spiritual world is at a middle altitude, and appears far off from the angels like the sun of the natural world from men (n. 103–107). In the spiritual world the east is where the Lord appears as a sun, and from that the other quarters are determined (n. 119–123, 124–128). Angels turn their faces constantly to the Lord as a sun (n. 129–134, 135–139). The Lord created the universe and all things thereof by means of the sun, which is the first proceeding of Divine love and Divine wisdom (n. 151–156). The sun of the natural world is mere fire, and nature, which derives its origin from that sun, is consequently dead; and the sun of the natural world was created in order that the work of creation might be completed and finished (n. 157–162). Without a double sun, one living and the other dead, no creation is possible (n. 163–166).

291. This also, among other things, is shown in chapter 2: that the spiritual sun is not the Lord, but is a proceeding from his Divine love and his Divine wisdom. It is called a *proceeding* because the sun was brought forth out of Divine love and Divine wisdom which are in themselves substance and form, and it is by means of this that the Divine proceeds. But as human reason is such as to be unwilling to yield assent unless it sees a thing from its cause, and therefore has some perception of how it is—thus in the present case, how the sun of the spiritual world, which is not the Lord, but a proceeding from him, was brought forth—something shall be said on this subject. In regard to this matter I have conversed much with the angels. They said that they have a clear perception of it in their own spiritual light, but that they cannot easily present it to man, in his natural light, owing to the difference between the two kinds of light and the consequent difference of thought. The matter, however, may be likened, they said, to the sphere of affections and of thoughts therefrom which encompasses each angel, whereby his presence is made evident to others near and far. But that encompassing sphere, they said, is not the angel himself; it is from each and every thing of his body, wherefrom substances are constantly flowing out like a stream, and what flows out surrounds him; also that these substances, contiguous to his body, as they are constantly moved by his life's two fountains of motion, the heart and the lungs, arouse the same activities in the atmospheres, and thereby produce a perception as of his presence with others; therefore that it is not a separate sphere of affections and of thoughts therefrom that goes forth and is continuous from him, although it is so called, since the affections are mere states of the mind's forms in the angel. They said, moreover, that there is such a sphere about every angel, because there is one about the Lord, and that the sphere about the Lord is in like manner from him, and that that sphere is their sun, that is, the sun of the spiritual world.

292. A perception has often been granted me of such a sphere around each angel and spirit, and also a general sphere around many in a society. I have also been permitted to see it under various appearances, in heaven sometimes appearing like a thin flame, in hell like gross fire, also sometimes in heaven like a thin and shining white cloud, and in hell like a thick and black cloud. It has also been granted me to perceive these spheres as various kinds of odors and stenches. By these experiences I was convinced that a sphere, consisting of substances set free and separated from their bodies, encompasses everyone in heaven and everyone in hell.

293. It was also perceived that a sphere flows forth, not only from angels and spirits but also from each and all things that appear in the spiritual world—from trees and from their fruits, from shrubs and from their flowers, from herbs, and from grasses, even from the soils and from their very particles.

From which it was patent that both in the case of things living and things dead this is a universal law, that each thing is encompassed by something like that which is within it, and that this is continually exhaled from it. It is known, from the observation of many learned men, that it is the same in the natural world—that is, that there is a wave of effluvia constantly flowing forth out of man, also out of every animal, likewise out of tree, fruit, shrub, flower, and even out of metal and stone. This the natural world derives from the spiritual, and the spiritual world from the Divine.

294. Because those things that constitute the sun of the spiritual world are from the Lord, but are not the Lord, they are not life in itself, but are devoid of life in itself; just as those things that flow forth from angel or man, and constitute spheres around him are not the angel or the man, but are from him, and devoid of his life. These spheres make one with the angel or man no otherwise than that they are concordant; and this they are because taken from the forms of their bodies, which in them were forms of their life. This is an arcanum which angels, with their spiritual ideas, are able to see in thought and also express in speech, but men with their natural ideas are not; because a thousand spiritual ideas make one natural idea, and one natural idea cannot be resolved by man into any spiritual idea, much less into so many. The reason is that these ideas differ according to degrees of height, which were treated of in chapter 3.

295. That there is such a difference between the thoughts of angels and the thoughts of men was made known to me by this experience: the angels were asked to think spiritually on some subject, and afterwards to tell me what they had thought. This they did; but when they wished to tell me they could not, and said that these things could not be expressed in words. It was the same with their spiritual language and their spiritual writing; there was not a word of spiritual language that was like any word of natural language; nor was there anything of spiritual writing like natural writing, except the letters, each of which contained an entire meaning. But what is wonderful, they said that they seemed to themselves to think, speak, and write in the spiritual state in the same manner that man does in the natural state, when yet there is no similarity. From this it was plain that the natural and the spiritual differ according to

degrees of height, and that they communicate with each other only by correspondences.

There are in the Lord three things that are the Lord, the Divine of love, the Divine of wisdom, and the Divine of use; and these three are presented in appearance outside of the sun of the spiritual world, the Divine of love by heat, the Divine of wisdom by light and the Divine of use by the atmosphere which is their container

296. That heat and light go forth out of the sun of the spiritual world, heat out of the Lord's Divine love, and light out of his Divine wisdom, may be seen above (n. 89–92, 99–102, 146–150). Now it will be shown that the third which goes forth out of that sun is the atmosphere, which is the container of heat and light, and that this goes forth out of the Lord's Divine which is called Use.

297. Anyone who thinks with any enlightenment can see that love has use for an end and intends it, and brings it forth by means of wisdom; for love can bring forth no use of itself, but only by wisdom as a medium. What, in fact, is love unless there be something loved? That something is use; and because use is that which is loved, and is brought forth by means of wisdom, it follows that use is the container of wisdom and love. That these three, love, wisdom, and use, follow in order according to degrees of height, and that the outmost degree is the complex, container, and base of the prior degrees has been shown (n. 209–216, and elsewhere). From all this it can be seen that these three, the Divine of Love, the Divine of Wisdom, and the Divine of Use, are in the Lord, and are the Lord in essence.

298. That man, as regards both his exteriors and his interiors, is a form of all uses, and that all the uses in the created universe correspond to those uses in him, will be fully shown in what follows; it need only be mentioned here, that it may be known that God as a man is the form itself of all uses, from which form all uses in the created universe derive their origin, thus that the created universe, viewed as to uses, is an image of him. Those things are called uses which from God-man, that is, from the Lord, are by creation in order; but those things which are from what is man's own are not called uses; since what is man's own is hell, and whatever is therefrom is contrary to order.

299. Now since these three, love, wisdom, and use, are in the Lord, and are the Lord; and since the Lord is everywhere, for he is omnipresent; and since the Lord cannot make himself present, such as he is in himself and such as he is in his own sun, to any angel or man, he therefore presents himself by means of such things as can be received, presenting himself, as to love by heat, as to wisdom by light, and as to use by an atmosphere. The Lord presents himself as to use by an atmosphere, because an atmosphere is a container of heat and light, as use is the container of love and wisdom. For light and heat going forth from the Divine Sun cannot go forth in nothing, that is, in vacuum, but must go forth in a container which is a subject. This container we call an atmosphere; and this encompasses the sun, receiving the sun in its bosom, and bearing it to heaven where angels are, and then to the world where men are, thus making the Lord's presence everywhere manifest.

300. That there are atmospheres in the angelic world, as well as in the natural world, has been shown above (n. 173–178, 179–183). It was there declared that the atmospheres of the spiritual world are spiritual, and the atmospheres of the natural world are natural. It can now be seen, from the origin of the spiritual atmosphere most closely encompassing the spiritual sun, that everything belonging to it is in its essence such as the sun is in its essence. The angels, by means of their spiritual ideas, which are apart from space, elucidate this truth as

follows: There is only one substance from which all things are, and the sun of the spiritual world is that substance; and since the Divine is not in space, and is the same in things greatest and least, this is also true of that sun which is the first going forth of God-man; furthermore, this one only substance, which is the sun, going forth by means of atmospheres according to continuous degrees or degrees of breadth, and at the same time according to discrete degrees or degrees of height, presents the varieties of all things in the created universe. The angels declared that these things are totally incomprehensible, unless spaces be removed from the ideas; and if not removed, appearances must needs induce fallacies. But so long as the thought is held that God is the very *esse* from which all things are, fallacies cannot enter.

301. It is evident, moreover, from angelic ideas, which are apart from space, that in the created universe nothing lives except God-man, that is, the Lord, neither is anything moved except by life from him, nor has being except through the sun from him; so that it is a truth, that in God we live, and move, and have our being.

The atmospheres, of which there are three both in the spiritual and in the natural world, in their outmosts close into substances and matters such as are in lands

302. It has been shown in chapter 3 (n. 173–176), that there are three atmospheres both in the spiritual and in the natural world, which are distinct from each other according to degrees of height, and which, in their progress toward lower things, decrease [in activity] according to degrees of breadth. And since atmospheres in their progress toward lower things decrease [in activity], it follows that they constantly become more compressed and inert, and finally, in outmosts, become so compressed and inert as to be no longer atmospheres, but substances

at rest, and in the natural world, fixed like those in the lands that are called matters. As such is the origin of substances and matters, it follows, first, that these substances and matters also are of three degrees; secondly, that they are held together in mutual connection by encompassing atmospheres; thirdly, that they are fitted for the production of all uses in their forms.

303. That such substances or matters as are in earths, were brought forth by the sun through its atmospheres anyone will readily acknowledge who reflects that there are continual mediations from the first to outmosts, and that nothing can take form except from what is prior to itself, and so finally from the first. The first is the sun of the spiritual world, and the first of that sun is God-man, or the Lord. Now as atmospheres are those prior things, whereby the spiritual sun manifests itself in outmosts, and as these prior things continually decrease in activity and expansion down to the outmosts, it follows that when their activity and expansion come to an end in outmosts they become substances, and matters such as are in lands, which retain within them, from the atmospheres out of which they originated, an effort and conatus to bring forth uses. Those who do not evolve the creation of the universe and all things thereof by continuous mediations from the first [being], can but hold hypotheses, disjoined and divorced from their causes, which, when surveyed by a mind with an interior perception of things, do not appear like a house, but like heaps of rubbish.

304. From this universal origin of all things in the created universe, every particular thereof has a similar order; in that these also go forth from their first to outmosts which are relatively in a state of rest, that they may terminate and become permanent. Thus in the human body fibers proceed from their first forms until at last they become tendons; also fibers with vessels proceed from their first forms until they

become cartilages and bones; upon these they may rest and
become permanent. Because of such a progression of fibers
and vessels in man from firsts to outmosts, there is a similar
progression of their states, which are sensations, thoughts, and
affections. These, also, from their firsts, where they are in
light, proceed through to outmosts, where they are in shade;
or from their firsts, where they are in heat, to outmosts
where they are not in heat. With such a progression of these
there is also a like progression of love and of all things thereof, and of wisdom and all things thereof. In a word, such is
the progression of all things in the created universe. This is
the same as was shown above (n. 222–229), that there are
degrees of both kinds in the greatest and least of all created
things.

There are degrees of both kinds even in the least things of
all, because the spiritual sun is the sole substance from which
all things are (according to the spiritual ideas of the angels,
n. 300).

*In the substances and matters of which lands are formed there is
nothing of the Divine in itself, but still they are from the Divine
in itself*

305. From the origin of lands (treated of in the preceding
chapter), it can be seen, that in their substances and matters
there is nothing of the Divine in itself, but that they are devoid
of all that is Divine in itself. For they are, as was said, the
endings and closings of the atmospheres, whose heat has died
away into cold, whose light into darkness, and whose activity
into inertness. Nevertheless, by continuation from the substance of the spiritual sun, they have brought with them what
there was in that substance from the Divine, which (as said
above, n. 291–298), was the sphere encompassing God-man, or
the Lord. From that sphere, by continuation from the sun

through the atmospheres as mediums, have arisen the substances and matters of which the lands are formed.

306. The origin of lands from the spiritual sun through the atmospheres, as mediums, can no otherwise be described by expressions flowing out of natural ideas, but may by expressions flowing out of spiritual ideas, because these are apart from space, and for this reason, they do not fall into any expressions of natural language. That spiritual thoughts, speech, and writings differ so entirely from natural thoughts, speech, and writings, that they have nothing in common, and have communication only by correspondences, may be seen above (n. 295). It may suffice, therefore, if the origin of lands be perceived in some measure naturally.

All uses, which are ends of creation, are in forms, which forms they take from substances and matters such as are in lands

307. All things treated of hitherto, as the sun, atmospheres, and lands, are only means to ends. The ends of creation are those things that are produced by the Lord as a sun, through the atmospheres, out of lands; and these ends are called uses. In their whole extent these are all things of the vegetable kingdom, all things of the animal kingdom, and finally the human race, and the angelic heaven which is from it. These are called uses, because they are recipients of Divine love and Divine wisdom, also because they have regard to God the creator from whom they are, and thereby conjoin him to his great work; by which conjunction it comes that, as they spring forth from him, so do they have unceasing existence from him. They are said to have regard to God the creator from whom they are, and to conjoin him to his great work, but this is to speak according to appearance. It is meant that God the creator causes them to have regard and to conjoin themselves to him as it were of themselves; but how they have regard and thereby

conjoin will be declared in what follows. Something has been said before on these subjects in their place, as that Divine love and Divine wisdom must necessarily have being and form in other things created by themselves (n. 37–51); that all things in the created universe are recipients of Divine love and Divine wisdom (n. 55–60); that the uses of all created things ascend by degrees to man, and through man to God the creator from whom they are (n. 65–68).

308. Who does not see clearly that uses are the ends of creation, when he considers that from God the creator nothing can have form, and therefore nothing can be created, except use; and that to be use, it must be for the sake of others; and that use for the sake of self is also for the sake of others, since a use for the sake of self looks to one's being in a state to be of use to others? Who so considers this is also able to see, that use which is use cannot spring from man, but must be in man from that being from whom everything that comes forth is use, that is, from the Lord.

309. But as the forms of uses are here treated of, the subject shall be set forth in the following order:

(1) In lands there is a conatus to produce uses in forms, that is, forms of uses.

(2) In all forms of uses there is a kind of image of the creation of the universe.

(3) In all forms of uses there is a kind of image of man.

(4) In all forms of uses there is a kind of image of the Infinite and the Eternal.

310. (1) *In lands there is a conatus to produce uses in forms, that is, forms of uses.* That there is this conatus in lands, is evident from their source, since the substances and matters of which lands consist are endings and closings of atmospheres which proceed as uses from the spiritual sun (as may be seen

above, n. 305, 306). And because the substances and matters of
which lands consist are from that source, and their aggregations
are held in connection by the pressure of the surrounding
atmospheres, it follows that they have from that a perpetual
conatus to bring forth forms of uses. The very quality that
makes them capable of bringing forth they derive from their
source, as being the outmosts of atmospheres, with which they
are constantly in accord. Such a conatus and quality are said to
be in lands, but it is meant that they are present in the substances and matters of which lands consist, whether these are in
the lands or in the atmospheres as exhalations from the lands.

That atmospheres are full of such things is well known. That
there is such a conatus and such quality in the substances and
matters of lands is plain from the fact that seeds of all kinds,
opened by means of heat even to their inmost core, are
impregnated by the most subtle substances (which can have no
other than a spiritual origin), and through this they have power
to conjoin themselves to use, from which comes their prolific
principle. Then through conjunction with matters from a
natural origin they are able to produce forms of uses, and
thereafter to deliver them as from a womb, that they may come
forth into light, and thus sprout up and grow. This conatus is
afterwards continuous from the lands through the root even to
outmosts, and from outmosts to firsts, wherein use itself is in
its origin.

Thus uses pass into forms; and forms, in their progression
from firsts to outmosts and from outmosts to firsts, derive from
use (which is like a soul) that each and every thing of the form
is of some use. Use is said to be like a soul, since its form is
like a body. It also follows that there is a conatus more
interior, that is, the conatus to produce uses for the animal
kingdom through vegetable growths, since by these animals of
every kind are nourished. It further follows that in all these

there is an inmost conatus, the conatus to perform use to the human race. From all this these things follow: (1) that there are outmosts, and in outmosts are all prior things simultaneously in their order, according to what has been frequently explained above; (2) that as there are degrees of both kinds in the greatest and least of all things (as was shown above, n. 222–229), so there are likewise in this conatus; (3) that as all uses are brought forth by the Lord out of outmosts, so in outmosts there must be a conatus to uses.

311. Still none of these are living conatus, for they are the conatus of life's outmost forces; within which forces there exists, from the life out of which they spring, a striving to return at last to their origin through the means afforded. In outmosts, atmospheres become such forces; and by these forces, substances, and matters, such as are in the lands, are molded into forms and held together in forms both within and without. But the subject is too large to allow a more extended explanation here.

312. The first production from these earthy matters, while they were still new and in their simple state, was production of seed; the first conatus therein could not be any other.

313. (2) *In all forms of uses there is a kind of image of creation.* Forms of uses are of a threefold kind; forms of uses of the mineral kingdom, forms of uses of the vegetable kingdom, and forms of uses of the animal kingdom. The forms of uses of the mineral kingdom cannot be described, because they are not visible to the eye. The first forms are the substances and matters of which the lands consist, in their minutest divisions; the second forms are aggregates of these, and are of infinite variety; the third forms come from plants that have fallen to dust, and from animal remains, and from the continual evaporations and exhalations from these, which are added to lands and make their soil. These forms of the mineral kingdom in three

degrees represent creation in an image in this, that, made active
by the sun through the atmospheres and their heat and light,
they bring forth uses in forms, which uses were creative ends.
This image of creation lies deeply hidden within their conatus
(of which see above, n. 310).

314. In the forms of uses of the vegetable kingdom an image
of creation appears in this, that from their firsts they proceed
to their outmosts, and from outmosts to firsts. Their firsts are
seeds, their outmosts are stalks clothed with bark; and by
means of the bark which is the outmost of the stalk, they tend
to seeds which, as was said, are their firsts. The stalks clothed
with layers of bark represent the globe clothed with lands, out
of which come the creation and formation of all uses.

That vegetation is effected through the outer and inner barks
and coatings, by a climbing up, by means of the coverings of
the roots (which are continued around the stalks and branches),
into the beginnings of the fruit, and in like manner through the
fruits into the seeds, is known to many. An image of creation
is displayed in forms of uses in the progress of the formation of
uses from firsts to outmosts, and from outmosts to firsts; also
in this, that in the whole progression there lies the end of
producing fruit and seeds, which are uses. From what has been
said above it is plain, that the progression of the creation of the
universe was from its First (which is the Lord encircled by the
sun) to outmosts which are lands, and from these through uses
to its First, that is, the Lord; also that the ends of the whole
creation were uses.

315. It should be known that to this image of creation the
heat, light, and atmospheres of the natural world contribute
nothing whatever. It is only the heat, light, and atmospheres of
the sun of the spiritual world that do this, bringing that image
with them, and clothing it with the forms of uses of the vegetable kingdom. The heat, light, and atmospheres of the natural

world simply open the seeds, keep their products in a state of expansion, and clothe them with the matters that give them fixedness. And this is done not by any forces from their own sun (which viewed in themselves are null), but by forces from the spiritual sun, by which the natural forces are unceasingly impelled to these services. Natural forces contribute nothing whatever towards forming this image of creation, for the image of creation is spiritual. But that this image may be manifest and perform use in the natural world, and may stand fixed and be permanent, it must be materialized, that is, filled in with the matters of that world.

316. In the forms of uses of the animal kingdom there is a similar image of creation, in that the animal body, which is the outmost thereof, is formed by a seed deposited in a womb or an ovum, and this body, when mature, brings forth new seed. This progression is similar to the progression of the forms of uses of the vegetable kingdom: seeds are the beginnings; the womb or the ovum is like the ground; the state before birth is like the state of the seed in the ground while it takes root; the state after birth until the animal becomes prolific is like the growth of a tree until it reaches its state of fruit bearing. From this parallelism it is plain that there is a likeness of creation in the forms of animals as well as in the forms of plants, in that there is a progression from firsts to outmosts, and from outmosts to firsts.

A like image of creation exists in every single thing there is in man; for there is a like progression of love through wisdom into uses, consequently a like progression of the will through the understanding into acts, and of charity through faith into deeds. Will and understanding, also charity and faith, are the firsts as their source; acts and deeds are the outmosts; from these, by means of the enjoyments of uses, a return is made to their firsts, which, as was said, are the will and understanding, or charity and faith. That the return is effected by means of the enjoyments of uses is very evident from the enjoyments felt in those acts and deeds which are from any love, in that they flow back to the first of the love from which they spring and that thereby conjunction is effected. The enjoyments of acts and deeds are what are called the enjoyments of uses. A like progression from firsts to outmosts, and from outmosts to firsts, is exhibited in the forms most purely organic of affections and thoughts in man. In his brains there are those starlike forms called the cineritious substances; out of these go forth fibers through the medullary substance by the neck into the body; passing through to the outmosts of the body, and from outmosts returning to their firsts.

This return of fibers to their firsts is made through the blood vessels. There is a like progression of all affections and thoughts, which are changes and variations of state of those forms or substances, for the fibers issuing out of those forms or substances are comparatively like the atmospheres from the spiritual sun, which are containers of heat and light; while bodily acts are like the things produced from the lands by means of atmospheres, the enjoyments of their uses returning to the source from which they sprang. But that the progression of these is such, and that within this progression there is an image of creation, can hardly be comprehended fully by the understanding, both because thousands and myriads of forces operating in act appear as one, and because the enjoyments of uses do not appear as ideas in the thought, but only affect without distinct perception.

On this subject see what has been declared and explained above, as follows: The uses of all created things ascend by degrees of height to man, and through man to God the creator from whom they are (n. 65–68). The end of creation takes form in outmosts, which end is that all things may return to the creator and that there may be conjunction (n. 167–172). But these things will appear in still clearer light in the following chapter, where the correspondence of the will and understanding with the heart and lungs will be treated of.

317. (3) *In all forms of uses there is a kind of image of man.* This has been shown above (n. 61–64). That all uses, from firsts to outmosts and from outmosts to firsts, have relation to all parts of man and have correspondence with them, consequently that man is, in a kind of image, a universe, and conversely that the universe viewed as to uses is in image a man, will be seen in the following chapter.

318. (4) *In all forms of uses there is a kind of image of the infinite and the eternal.* The image of the infinite in these forms is plain from their conatus and power to fill the spaces of the whole world, and even of many worlds, to infinity. For a single seed produces a tree, shrub, or plant, which fills its own space; and each tree, shrub, or plant produces seeds, in some cases thousands of them, which, when sown and grown up, fill their own spaces; and if from each seed of these there should proceed as many more, reproduced again and again, in the course of years the whole world would be filled; and if the production were still continued, many worlds would be filled; and this to infinity. Estimate a thousand seeds from one, and multiply the thousand by a thousand ten times, twenty times, even to a hundred times, and you will see.

There is a like image of the Eternal in these forms; seeds are propagated from year to year, and the propagations never cease; they have not ceased from the creation of the world till now, and will not cease to eternity. These two are standing proofs and attesting signs that all things of the universe have been created by an infinite and eternal God. Beside these images of the infinite and eternal, there is another image of the infinite and eternal in varieties, in that there can never be a substance, state, or thing in the created universe the same as or identical with any other, neither in atmospheres, nor in lands, nor in the forms arising out of these. Thus not in any of the things which fill the universe can anything the same be produced to eternity. This is plainly to be seen in the variety of the faces of human beings; no one face can be found throughout the world which is the same as another, nor can there be to all eternity, consequently not one mind, for the face is the type of the mind.

All things of the created universe, viewed in reference to uses, represent man in an image, and this testifies that God is a man

319. By the ancients man was called a microcosm, from his representing the macrocosm, that is, the universe in its whole complex; but it is not known at the present day why man was so called by the ancients, for no more of the universe or macrocosm is manifest in him than that he derives nourishment and bodily life from its animal and vegetable kingdoms, and that he is kept in a living condition by its heat, sees by its light, and hears and breathes by its atmospheres. Yet these things do not make man a microcosm, as the universe with all things thereof is a macrocosm. The ancients called man a microcosm, or little universe, from truth which they derived from the knowledge of correspondences, in which the most ancient people were, and from their communication with angels of heaven; for angels of heaven know from the things which they see about them that all things of the universe, viewed as to uses, represent man as an image.

320. But the truth that man is a microcosm, or little universe, because the created universe, viewed as to uses is, in image, a man, cannot come into the thought and from that into the

knowledge of anyone on earth from the idea of the universe as
it is viewed in the spiritual world; and therefore it can be
corroborated only by an angel, who is in the spiritual world,
or by someone to whom it has been granted to be in that
world, and to see things which are there. As this has been
granted to me, I am able, from what I have seen there, to
disclose this arcanum.

321. It should be known that the spiritual world is, in
external appearance, wholly like the natural world. Lands,
mountains, hills, valleys, plains, fields, lakes, rivers, springs of
water are to be seen there, as in the natural world; thus all
things belonging to the mineral kingdom. Paradises, gardens,
groves, woods, and in them trees and shrubs of all kinds bearing fruit and seeds; also plants, flowers, herbs, and grasses are
to be seen there; thus all things pertaining to the vegetable
kingdom. There are also to be seen there beasts, birds, and fish
of every kind; thus all things pertaining to the animal kingdom.
Man there is an angel or spirit. This is premised that it may be
known that the universe of the spiritual world is wholly like
the universe of the natural world, with this difference only,
that things in the spiritual world are not fixed and settled like
those in the natural world, because in the spiritual world
nothing is natural but everything is spiritual.

322. That the universe of that world represents man in an
image can be clearly seen from this, that all things just mentioned (n. 321) appear to the life, and take form about the
angel, and about the angelic societies, as if they were produced
or created by them; they are about them permanently, and do
not pass away. That they are as if they were produced or
created by them is seen by their no longer appearing when the
angel goes away, or when the society passes to another place;
also when other angels come in place of these the appearance
of all things about them is changed—in the paradises the trees

and fruits are changed, in the flower gardens the flowers and
seeds, in the fields the herbs and grasses, also the kinds of
animals and birds are changed. Such things take form and are
changed in this manner, because all these things take form
according to the affections and consequent thoughts of the
angels, for they are correspondences. And because things that
correspond make one with that to which they correspond they
are an image representative of it. The image itself is not seen
when these things are viewed in their forms; it is seen only
when they are viewed in respect to uses. It has been granted me
to perceive that angels, when their eyes were opened by the
Lord, and they saw these things from the correspondence of
uses, recognized and saw themselves therein.

323. Inasmuch as these things which have existence about the
angels, corresponding to their affections and thoughts, represent
a universe, in that there are lands, plants, and animals, and
these constitute an image representative of the angel, it is evident why the ancients called man a microcosm.

324. That this is so has been abundantly confirmed in *Arcana
Coelestia*, also in the work *Heaven and Hell*, and occasionally in
the preceding pages where correspondence is treated of. It has
been there shown also that nothing is to be found in the
created universe which has not a correspondence with something in man, not only with his affections and their thoughts,
but also with his bodily organs and viscera; not with these
however as substances, but as uses. From this it is that in the
Word, where the church and the man of the church are treated
of, such frequent mention is made of trees, such as "olives,"
"vines," and "cedars"; of "gardens," "groves" and "woods"; and
of the "beasts of the earth," "birds of the air," and "fish of the
sea." They are there mentioned because they correspond, and
by correspondence make one, as was said above; consequently,
when such things are read in the Word by man, these objects

are not perceived by angels, but the church or the men of the church in respect to their states are perceived instead.

325. Since all things of the universe have relation in an image to man, the wisdom and intelligence of Adam are described by the "garden of Eden," wherein were all kinds of trees, also rivers, precious stones, and gold, and animals to which he gave names; by all of which are meant such things as were in Adam, and constitute that which is called man. Nearly the same things are said of Ashur, by whom the church in respect to intelligence is signified (Ezek. 31:3–9); and of Tyre, by which the church in respect to knowledges of good and truth is signified (Ezek. 28:12, 13).

326. From all this it can be seen that all things in the universe, viewed from uses, have relation in an image to man, and that this testifies that God is a man. For such things as have been mentioned above take form about the angelic man, not from the angels, but from the Lord through the angels. For they take their form from the influx of the Lord's Divine love and Divine wisdom into the angel, who is a recipient, and before whose eyes all this is brought forth like the creation of a universe. From this they know there that God is a man, and that the created universe, viewed in its uses, is an image of God.

All things created by the Lord are use; they are uses in the order, degree, and respect in which they have relation to man, and through man to the Lord, from whom [they are]

327. In respect to this it has been shown above: That from God the creator nothing can take form except uses (n. 308); that the uses of all created things ascend by degrees from outmost things to man, and through man to God the creator, from whom they are (n. 65–68); that the end of creation takes form in outmosts, which end is, that all things may return to God the creator, and that there may be conjunction (n. 167–172); that things are uses so far as they have regard to the creator (n. 307); that the Divine must necessarily have being and form in other things created by itself (n. 47–51); that all things of the universe are recipients according to uses, and this according to degrees (n. 58); that the universe, viewed from uses, is an image of God (n. 59); and many other things. From all which this truth is plain, that all things created by the Lord are uses, and that they are uses in that order, degree, and respect in which they have relation to man, and through man to the Lord from whom [they are]. It remains now that some things should be said in detail respecting uses.

328. By man, to whom uses have relation, is meant not alone an individual but an assembly of men, also a society smaller or larger, as a commonwealth, kingdom, or empire, or that largest society, the whole world, for each of these is a man. Likewise in the heavens, the whole angelic heaven is as one man before the Lord, and equally every society of heaven; from this it is that every angel is a man. That this is so may be seen in the work *Heaven and Hell* (n. 68–103). This makes clear what is meant by man in what follows.

329. The end of the creation of the universe clearly shows what use is. The end of the creation of the universe is the existence of an angelic heaven; and as the angelic heaven is the end, man also or the human race is the end, since heaven is from that. From which it follows that all created things are mediate ends, and that these are uses in that order, degree, and respect in which they have relation to man, and through man to the Lord.

330. Inasmuch as the end of creation is an angelic heaven out of the human race, and thus the human race itself, all other

created things are mediate ends, and these, as having relation to man, with a view to his conjunction with the Lord, refer themselves to these three things in him, his body, his rational, and his spiritual. For man cannot be conjoined to the Lord unless he be spiritual, nor can he be spiritual unless he be rational, nor can he be rational unless his body is in a sound state. These three are like a house; the body like the foundation, the rational like the superstructure, the spiritual like those things which are in the house, and conjunction with the Lord like dwelling in it. From this can be seen in what order, degree, and respect uses (which are the mediate ends of creation) have relation to man, namely (1) for sustaining his body, (2) for perfecting his rational, (3) for receiving what is spiritual from the Lord.

331. Uses for sustaining the body relate to its nourishment, its clothing, its habitation, its recreation and enjoyment, its protection and the preservation of its state. The uses created for the nourishment of the body are all things of the vegetable kingdom suitable for food and drink, as fruits, grapes, grain, pulse, and herbs; in the animal kingdom all things which are eaten, as oxen, cows, calves, deer, sheep, kids, goats, lambs, and the milk they yield; also fowls and fish of many kinds. The uses created for the clothing of the body are many other products of these two kingdoms; in like manner, the uses for habitation, also for recreation, enjoyment, protection, and preservation of state. These are not mentioned because they are well known, and their mere enumeration would fill pages. There are many things, to be sure, which are not used by man; but what is superfluous does not do away with the use, but ensures its continuance. Misuse of uses is also possible, but misuse does not do away with use, even as falsification of truth does not do away with truth except with those who falsify it.

332. Uses for perfecting the rational are all things that give instruction about the subjects above mentioned, and are called

sciences and branches of study, pertaining to natural, economical, civil, and moral affairs, which are learned either from parents and teachers, or from books, or from interaction with others, or by reflection on these subjects by oneself. These things perfect the rational so far as they are uses in a higher degree, and they are permanent as far as they are applied to life. Space forbids the enumeration of these uses, by reason both of their multitude and of their varied relation to the common good.

333. Uses for receiving the spiritual from the Lord, are all things that belong to religion and to worship therefrom; thus all things that teach the acknowledgment and knowledge of God and the knowledge and acknowledgment of good and truth and thus eternal life, which are acquired in the same way as other learning, from parents, teachers, discourses, and books, and especially by applying to life what is so learned; and in the Christian world, by doctrines and discourses from the Word, and through the Word from the Lord. These uses in their full extent may be described under the same heads as the uses of the body, as nourishment, clothing, habitation, recreation and enjoyment, and preservation of state, if only they are applied to the soul; as nutrition to goods of love, clothing to truths of wisdom, habitation to heaven, recreation and enjoyment to felicity of life and heavenly joy, protection to safety from infesting evils, and preservation of state to eternal life. All these things are given by the Lord according to the acknowledgment that all bodily things are also from the Lord, and that a man is only as a servant and house steward appointed over the goods of his Lord.

334. That such things have been given to man to use and enjoy, and that they are free gifts, is clearly evident from the state of angels in the heavens, who have, like men on earth, a body, a rational, and a spiritual. They are nourished freely, for food is given them daily; they are clothed freely, for garments are given them; their dwellings are free, for houses are given

them; nor have they any care about all these things; and so far as they are rational-spiritual do they have enjoyment, protection, and preservation of state. The difference is that angels see that these things, because created according to the state of their love and wisdom, are from the Lord (as was shown in the preceding chapter, n. 322); but men do not see this, because their harvest returns yearly, and is not in accord with the state of their love and wisdom, but in accord with the care bestowed by them.

335. These things are called uses, because through man they have relation to the Lord; nevertheless, they must not be said to be uses from man for the Lord's sake, but from the Lord for man's sake, inasmuch as in the Lord all uses are infinitely one, but in man there are no uses except from the Lord; for man cannot do good from himself, but only from the Lord, and good is what is called use.

The essence of spiritual love is doing good to others, not for the sake of self but for the sake of others; infinitely more is this the essence of Divine love. It is like the love of parents for their children, in that parents do good to their children from love, not for their own sake but for their children's sake. This is especially manifest in a mother's love for her offspring. Because the Lord is to be adored, worshiped and glorified, he is supposed to love adoration, worship, and glory for his own sake; but he loves these for man's sake, because by means of them man comes into a state in which the Divine can flow in and be perceived; since by means of them man puts away that which is his own, which hinders influx and reception, for what is man's own, which is self-love, hardens the heart and shuts it up.

This is removed by man's acknowledging that from himself comes nothing but evil and from the Lord nothing but good; from this acknowledgment there is a softening of the heart and humiliation, out of which flow forth adoration and worship. From all this it follows, that the use which the Lord performs for himself through man is that man may be able to do good from love, and since this is the Lord's love, its reception is the enjoyment of his love. Therefore, let no one believe that the Lord is with those who merely worship him; he is with those who do his commandments, thus who perform uses; with such he has his abode, but not with the former. (See what was said above on this subject, n. 47–49.)

Evil uses were not created by the Lord, but originated together with hell

336. All good things that take form in act are called uses; and all evil things that take form in act are also called uses, but evil uses, while the former are called good uses. Now, since all good things are from the Lord and all evil things from hell, it follows that none but good uses were created by the Lord, and that evil uses arose out of hell. By the uses specially treated of in this chapter are meant all those things which are to be seen upon the earth, as animals of every kind and plants of every kind.

Such things of both kingdoms as are useful to man are from the Lord, but those which are harmful to man are from hell. By uses from the Lord are likewise meant all things that perfect the rational of man, and cause him to receive the spiritual from the Lord; but by evil uses are meant all things that destroy the rational, and make man unable to become spiritual. Those things that are harmful to man are called uses because they are of use to the evil in doing evil, and also are serviceable in absorbing malignities and thus also as remedies. "Use" is employed in both senses, as love is when we speak of good love and evil love; moreover, everything that love does it calls use.

337. That good uses are from the Lord, and evil uses from hell, will be shown in the following order.

(1) What is meant by evil uses on the earth.

(2) All things that are evil uses are in hell, and all things that are good uses are in heaven.

(3) There is unceasing influx from the spiritual world into the natural world.

(4) Those things that are evil uses are effected by the operation of influx from hell, wherever there are such things as correspond thereto.

(5) This is done by the lowest spiritual separated from what is above it.

(6) There are two forms into which the operation by influx takes place, the vegetable and the animal.

(7) Both these forms receive the ability to propagate their kind and the means of propagation.

338. (1) *What is meant by evil uses on the earth.* By evil uses on earth are meant all noxious things in both the animal and vegetable kingdom, also in the mineral kingdom. It is needless to enumerate all the noxious things in these kingdoms, for to do so would merely heap up names, and doing this without indicating the noxious effect that each kind produces would not contribute to the object which this work has in view. For the sake of information a few examples will suffice: In the animal kingdom there are poisonous serpents, scorpions, crocodiles, great snakes, horned owls, screech owls, mice, locusts, frogs, spiders; also flies, drones, moths, lice, mites; in a word, creatures that destroy grasses, leaves, fruits, seed, food, and drink, and are harmful to beast and man. In the vegetable kingdom there are all hurtful, virulent, and poisonous herbs, with leguminous plants and shrubs of like character; and in the mineral kingdom all poisonous earths. From these few examples it can be seen what is meant by evil uses on earth; for evil uses are all things that are opposite to good uses (of which, in the preceding paragraph, n. 336).

339. (2) *All things that are evil uses are in hell, and all things that are good uses are in heaven.* Before it can be seen that all evil uses that take form on earth are not from the Lord but from hell, something must be premised concerning heaven and hell, without a knowledge of which evil uses as well as good may be attributed to the Lord, and it may be believed that they are together from creation; or they may be attributed to nature, and their origin to the sun of nature.

From these two errors man cannot be delivered, unless he knows that nothing whatever takes form in the natural world that does not derive its cause and therefore its origin from the spiritual world, and that good is from the Lord, and evil from the devil, that is, from hell. By the spiritual world is meant both heaven and hell. In heaven are to be seen all those things that are good uses (of which in a preceding article, n. 336). In hell are to be seen all those that are evil uses (see just above, n. 338, where they are enumerated).

These are wild creatures of every kind, as serpents, scorpions, great snakes, crocodiles, tigers, wolves, foxes, swine, owls of different kinds, bats, rats, and mice, frogs, locusts, spiders, and noxious insects of many kinds; also hemlocks and aconites, and all kinds of poisons, both of herbs and of earths; in a word, everything hurtful and deadly to man. Such things appear in the hells to the life precisely like those on and in the earth.

They are said to appear there; yet they are not there as on earth, for they are mere correspondences of lusts that swarm out of their evil loves, and present themselves in such forms before others. Because there are such things in the hells, these abound in foul smells, cadaverous, fecal, urinous, and putrid, wherein the diabolical spirits there take delight, as animals do in rank stenches. From this it can be seen that like things in the natural world did not derive their origin from the Lord, and were not created from the beginning, neither did they spring from nature through her sun, but are from hell. That they are not from nature through her sun is plain, for the spiritual inflows into the natural, and not the reverse. And that they are not from the Lord is plain, because hell is not from him, therefore nothing in hell corresponding to the evils of its inhabitants is from him.

340. (3) *There is unceasing influx out of the spiritual world into the natural world.* he who does not know that there is a spiritual world, or that it is distinct from the natural world, as what is prior is distinct from what is subsequent, or as cause from the thing caused, can have no knowledge of this influx. This is the reason why those who have written on the origin of plants and animals could not do otherwise than ascribe that origin to nature; or if to God, then in the sense that God had implanted in nature from the beginning a power to produce such things, not knowing that no power has been implanted in nature, since nature, in herself, is dead, and contributes no more to the production of these things than a tool does, for instance, to the work of a mechanic, the tool acting only as it is continually moved.

It is the spiritual, deriving its origin from the sun where the Lord is, and proceeding to the outmosts of nature, that produces the forms of plants and animals, exhibiting the marvels that exist in both, and filling the forms with matters from the earth, that they may become fixed and enduring. But because it is now known that there is a spiritual world, and that the spiritual is from the spiritual sun, in which the Lord is and which is from the Lord, and that the spiritual is what impels nature to act, as what is living impels what is dead, also that like things exist in the spiritual world as in the natural world, it can now be seen that plants and animals have had their existence only from the Lord through that world, and through that world they have perpetual existence.

Thus there is unceasing influx from the spiritual world into the natural. That this is so will be abundantly corroborated in the next chapter. Noxious things are produced on earth through influx from hell, by the same law of permission whereby evils themselves from hell flow into men. This law will be set forth in *Angelic Wisdom Concerning Divine Providence*.

341. (4) *Those things that are evil uses are effected by the operation of influx from hell, wherever there are such things as correspond thereto.* The things that correspond to evil uses, that is, to hurtful plants and noxious animals, are cadaverous, putrid, excrementitious, fecal, rancid, and urinous matters; consequently, in places where these are, such herbs and such animalcules spring forth as are mentioned above; and in the torrid zone, like things of larger size, as serpents, basilisks, crocodiles, scorpions, rats, and so forth.

Everyone knows that swamps, stagnant ponds, dung, fetid bogs, are full of such things; also that noxious insects fill the atmosphere in clouds, and noxious vermin walk the earth in armies, and consume its herbs to the very roots. I once observed in my garden, that in the space of a half yard, nearly all the dust was turned into minute insects, for when it was stirred with a stick, they rose in clouds. That cadaverous and putrid matters are in accord with these noxious and useless little things, and that the two are homogeneous, is evident from mere observation; and it is still more clearly seen from the cause, which is, that like stenches and fumes exist in the hells, where such little things are likewise to be seen.

Those hells are therefore named accordingly; some are called cadaverous, some fecal, some urinous, and so on. But all these hells are covered over, that those vapors may not escape from them. For when they are opened a very little, which happens when novitiate devils enter, they excite vomiting and cause headache, and such as are also poisonous induce fainting. The very dust there is also of the same nature, wherefore it is there called damned dust. From this it is evident that there are such noxious insects wherever there are such stenches, because the two correspond.

342. It now becomes a matter of inquiry whether such things spring from eggs conveyed to the spot by means of air, or rain, or water oozing through the soil, or whether they spring from the damp and stenches themselves. That these noxious animalcules and insects mentioned above are hatched from eggs which have been carried to the spot, or which have lain hidden everywhere in the ground since creation, is opposed to all observation. For worms spring forth in minute seeds, in the kernels of nuts, in wood, in stones, and even from leaves, and upon plants and in plants there are lice and grubs which are accordant with them.

Of flying insects, too, there are such as appear in houses, fields, and woods, which arise in like manner in summer, with no oviform matters sufficient to account for them; also such as devour meadows and lawns, and in some hot localities fill and infest the air; besides those that swim and fly unseen in filthy waters, wines becoming sour, and pestilential air. These facts of observation support those who say that the odors, effluvia, and exhalations emitted from plants, earths, and ponds, are what give the initiative to such things. That when they have come forth, they are afterwards propagated either by eggs or offshoots, does not disprove their immediate generation; since every living creature, along with its minute viscera, receives organs of generation and means of propagation (see below, n. 347). In agreement with these phenomena is the fact heretofore unknown that there are like things also in the hells.

343. That the hells mentioned above have not only communication but conjunction with such things in the earths may be concluded from this, that the hells are not distant from men, but are about them, yea, are within those who are evil; thus they are contiguous to the earth; for man, in regard to his affections and lusts, and consequent thoughts, and in regard to his actions springing from these, which are good or evil uses, is in the midst either of angels of heaven or of spirits of hell; and as such things as are on the earth are also in the heavens and hells, it follows that influx therefrom directly produces such things when the conditions are favorable.

All things, in fact, that appear in the spiritual world, whether in heaven or in hell, are correspondences of affections or lusts, for they take form there in accordance with these; consequently when affections or lusts, which in themselves are spiritual, meet with homogeneous or corresponding things in the earths, there are present both the spiritual that furnishes a soul, and the material that furnishes a body. Moreover, within everything spiritual there is a conatus to clothe itself with a body. The hells are about men, and therefore contiguous to the earth, because the spiritual world is not in space, but is where there is a corresponding affection.

344. I heard two presidents of the English Royal Society, Sir Hans Sloane and Martin Folkes, conversing together in the spiritual world about the existence of seeds and eggs, and about productions from them in the earths. The former ascribed them to nature, and contended that nature was endowed from creation with a power and force to produce such effects by means of the sun's heat. The other maintained that this force is in nature unceasingly from God the creator. To settle the discussion, a beautiful bird appeared to Sir Hans Sloane, and he was asked to examine it to see whether it differed in the smallest particle from a similar bird on earth. He held it in his hand, examined it, and declared that there was no difference. He knew indeed that it was nothing but an affection of some angel represented outside of the angel as a bird, and that it would vanish or cease with its affection. And this came to pass.

By this experience Sir Hans Sloane was convinced that nature contributes nothing whatever to the production of plants and animals, that they are produced solely by what flows into the natural world out of the spiritual world. If that bird, he said, were to be infilled, in its minutest parts, with corresponding matters from the earth, and thus fixed, it would be a lasting bird, like the birds on the earth; and that it is the same with such things as are from hell. To this he added that had he known what he now knew of the spiritual world, he would have ascribed to nature no more than this, that it serves the spiritual, which is from God, in fixing the things which flow in unceasingly into nature.

345. (5) *This is effected by the lowest spiritual separated from what is above it.* It was shown in chapter 3 that the spiritual flows down from its sun even to the outmosts of nature through three degrees, which are called the celestial, the spiritual, and the natural; that these three degrees are in man from creation; consequently from birth; that they are opened according to man's life; that if the celestial degree which is the highest and inmost is opened, man becomes celestial; if the spiritual degree which is the middle is opened, he becomes spiritual; but if only the natural degree which is the lowest and outermost is opened, he becomes natural; that if man becomes natural only, he loves only corporeal and worldly things; and that so far as he loves these, so far he does not love celestial and spiritual things, and does not look to God, and so far he becomes evil. From all this it is evident that the lowest spiritual, which is called the spiritual-natural, can be separated from its higher degrees, and is separated in such men as hell consists of.

This lowest spiritual can separate itself from its higher parts, and look to hell, in men only; it cannot be so separated in beasts, or in soils. From which it follows that these evil uses mentioned above are effected on the earth by this lowest spiritual separated from what is above it, such as it is in those who are in hell. That the noxious things on the earth have their origin in man, thus from hell, may be shown by the state of the land of Canaan, as described in the Word; in that when the children of Israel lived according to the commandments, the earth yielded its increase, likewise the flocks and herds; but when they lived contrary to the commandments the ground was barren, and as it is said, accursed; instead of harvests it yielded thorns and briars, the flocks and herds miscarried, and wild beasts broke in. The same may be inferred from the locusts, frogs, and lice in Egypt.

346. (6) *There are two forms into which the operation by influx takes place, the vegetable and the animal form.* That there are only two universal forms produced out of the earth is known from the two kingdoms of nature, called the animal and the vegetable kingdoms, also that all the subjects of either kingdom possess many things in common. Thus the subjects of the animal kingdom have organs of sense and organs of motion and members and viscera that are actuated by brains, hearts, and lungs. So the subjects of the vegetable kingdom send down a root into the ground, and bring forth stem, branches, leaves, flowers, fruits, and seeds. Both the animal and the vegetable kingdoms, as regards the production of their forms, derive their origin from spiritual influx and operation out of the sun of heaven where the Lord is, and not from the influx and operation of nature out of her sun; from this they derive nothing except their fixation, as was said above.

All animals, great and small, derive their origin from the spiritual in the outmost degree, which is called the natural; man alone from all three degrees, called the celestial, spiritual, and natural. As each degree of height or discrete degree decreases from its perfection to its imperfection, as light to shade, by continuity, so do animals; there are therefore perfect, less perfect, and imperfect animals. The perfect animals are elephants, camels, horses, mules, oxen, sheep, goats, and others which are of the herd or the flock; the less perfect are birds; and the imperfect are fish and shellfish; these, as being the lowest of that degree, are as it were in shade, while the former are in light. Yet animals, since they live only from the lowest spiritual degree, which is called the natural, can look nowhere else than towards the earth and to food there, and to their own kind for the sake of propagation; the soul of all these is natural affection and appetite.

The subjects of the vegetable kingdom comprise, in like manner, the perfect, less perfect, and imperfect; the perfect are fruit trees, the less perfect are vines and shrubs, and the imperfect are grasses. But plants derive from the spiritual out of which they spring that they are uses, while animals derive from the spiritual out of which they spring that they are affections and appetites, as was shown above.

347. (7) *Each of these forms receives with its existence the means of propagation.* In all products of the earth, which pertain, as was said above, either to the vegetable or to the animal kingdom, there is a kind of image of creation, and a kind of image of man, and also a kind of image of the infinite and the eternal; this was shown above (n. 313–318); also that the image of the infinite and the eternal is clearly manifest in the capacity of all these for infinite and eternal propagation. They all, therefore, receive means of propagation; the subjects of the animal kingdom through seed, in the egg or in the womb or by spawning; and the subjects of the vegetable kingdom through seeds in the ground. From which it can be seen that although

the more imperfect and the noxious animals and plants originate through immediate influx out of hell, yet afterwards they
are propagated mediately by seeds, eggs, or grafts; consequently,
the one position does not annul the other.

348. That all uses, both good and evil, are from a spiritual
origin, thus from the sun where the Lord is, may be illustrated
by this experience. I have heard that goods and truths have
been sent down through the heavens by the Lord to the hells,
and that these same, received by degrees to the lowest deep,
were there turned into evils and falsities, which are the opposite
of the goods and truths sent down. This took place because
recipient subjects turn all things that inflow into such things as
are in agreement with their own forms, just as the white light
of the sun is turned into ugly colors or into black in those
objects whose substances are interiorly of such a form as to
suffocate and extinguish the light, and as stagnant ponds, dung
hills, and dead bodies turn the heat of the sun into stenches.
From all this it can be seen that even evil uses are from the
spiritual sun, but that good uses are changed in hell into evil
uses. It is evident, therefore, that the Lord has not created and
does not create any except good uses, but that hell produces
evil uses.

The visible things in the created universe bear witness that nature
has produced and does produce nothing, but that the Divine out of
itself, and through the spiritual world, has produced and does
produce all things

349. Speaking from appearances, most men say that the sun
by heat and light produces whatever is to be seen in plains,
fields, gardens, and forests; also that the sun by its heat hatches
worms from eggs, and makes prolific the beasts of the earth and
the fowls of the air; and that it even gives life to man. Those
who speak from appearances only may speak in this way

without ascribing these things to nature, because they are not thinking about the matter; as there are those who speak of the sun as rising and setting, and causing days and years, and being now at this or that altitude; such persons speak from appearances, and in doing so, do not ascribe such effects to the sun, because they are not thinking of the sun's fixity or the earth's revolution. But those who confirm themselves in the idea that the sun produces the things that appear upon the earth by means of its heat and light, end by ascribing all things to nature, even the creation of the universe, and become naturalists and, at last, atheists. These may continue to say that God created nature and endowed her with the power of producing such things, but this they say from fear of losing their good name; and by God the creator they still mean nature, and some mean the innermost of nature, and then the Divine things taught by the church they regard as of no account.

350. There are some who are excusable for ascribing certain visible things to nature, for two reasons. First, because they have had no knowledge of the sun of heaven, where the Lord is, or of influx therefrom, or of the spiritual world and its state, or even of its presence with man, and therefore had no other idea than that the spiritual is a purer natural; consequently, that angels are in the ether or in the stars; and that the devil is either man's evil or if an actual existence, that he is in the air or the abyss; also that the souls of men, after death, are either in the interior of the earth, or in an undetermined somewhere till the day of judgment; and other like things deduced by fancy out of ignorance of the spiritual world and its sun.

Secondly, they are excusable, because they are unable to see how the Divine could produce everything that appears on the earth, where there are not only good things but also evil things; and they are afraid to confirm themselves in such an idea, lest they ascribe the evil things also to God, and form a material conception of God, and make God and nature one, and thus confound the two.

For these two reasons those are excusable who have believed that nature produces the visible world by a power implanted in her by creation. But those who have made themselves atheists by confirmations in favor of nature are not excusable, because they might have confirmed themselves in favor of the Divine. Ignorance indeed excuses, but does not remove, falsity which has been confirmed, for such falsity coheres with evil, thus with hell. Consequently, those same persons who have confirmed themselves in favor of nature to such an extent as to separate the Divine from nature, regard nothing as sin, because all sin is against the Divine, and this they have separated, and thus have rejected it; and those who in spirit regard nothing as sin, after death when they become spirits, since they are in bonds to hell, rush into wickednesses which are in accord with the lusts to which they have given rein.

351. Those who believe in a Divine operation in all the details of nature, are able by very many things they see in nature to confirm themselves in favor of the Divine, as fully as others confirm themselves in favor of nature, yea, more fully. For those who confirm themselves in favor of the Divine give attention to the wonders which are displayed in the production both of plants and animals. In the production of plants, how out of a little seed cast into the ground there goes forth a root, and by means of the root a stem, and branches, leaves, flowers, and fruits in succession, even to new seeds; just as if the seed knew the order of succession, or the process by which it is to renew itself.

Can any reasonable person think that the sun, which is mere fire, has this knowledge, or that it is able to empower its heat and light to effect these results, or is able to fashion these wonderful things in plants, and to contemplate use? Any man of elevated reason who sees and weighs these things cannot think otherwise than that they come from him who has infinite reason, that is, from God. Those who acknowledge the Divine also see and think this, but those who do not acknowledge the Divine do not see or think this because they do not wish to; thus they sink their rational into the sensual, which draws all its ideas from the lumen which is proper to the bodily senses and which confirms their illusions, saying, Do you not see the sun effecting these things by its heat and light? What is a thing that you do not see? Is it anything?

Those who confirm themselves in favor of the Divine give attention to the wonders which are displayed in the production of animals; to mention here only, in reference to eggs, how the chick in its seed or beginning lies hidden therein, with everything requisite till it is hatched, also with everything pertaining to its subsequent development, until it becomes a bird or winged thing of the same form as its parent. And if one observes the living form, it is such as to fill anyone with astonishment who thinks deeply, seeing that in the minutest as in the largest living creatures, even in the invisible, as in the visible, there are the organs of sense, namely, sight, hearing, smell, taste, and touch; and organs of motion which are muscles, for they fly and walk; also viscera surrounding the heart and lungs, which are set in action by brains.

That even the commonest insects enjoy such organs is shown in their anatomy as described by some writers, and especially by Swammerdam, in his *Biblia Naturae*. Those who ascribe everything to nature, see all these things, but they merely perceive that they exist, and say that nature produces them. They say this because they have turned their minds away from thinking about the Divine; and those who have done this are unable, when they see the wonderful things in nature, to think rationally, still less spiritually; but they think sensually and materially; and then they think in nature from nature, and not above nature, just as

those do who are in hell. They differ from beasts only in having
the power to think rationally, that is, in being able to understand, and therefore to think otherwise, if they choose.

352. Those who have averted themselves from thinking about
the Divine when observing the wonderful things in nature, and
who thereby become sensual, do not reflect that the sight of
the eye is so gross as to see many little insects as an obscure
speck, when yet each one of these is organized to feel and to
move, and is accordingly furnished with fibers and vessels, also
with a minute heart, pulmonary tubes, viscera, and brains; also
that these organs are woven out of the purest substances in
nature, their tissues corresponding to that somewhat of life by
which their minutest parts are separately moved. When the
sight of the eye is so gross that many such creatures, with
innumerable particulars in each, appear to it as an obscure
speck, and yet those who are sensual think and judge by that
sight, it is clear how dulled their minds are, and therefore what
thick darkness they are in concerning spiritual things.

353. Anyone who chooses may confirm himself in favor of
the Divine from things seen in nature, and whoever thinks
about God in reference to life does so confirm himself; as when
he observes the birds of the air, how each species knows its
food and where to find it, recognizes its kind by sound and
sight, and which among other kinds are its friends and which
its enemies; how also they mate, have knowledge of the sexual
relation, skillfully build nests, lay eggs therein, sit upon these,
know the period of incubation, and this having elapsed, bring
forth their young, love them most tenderly, cherish them under
their wings, bring them food and feed them, until they can do
for themselves, perform the same offices, and bring forth a
family to perpetuate their kind.

Anyone who is willing to reflect on the Divine influx
through the spiritual world into the natural can see such influx

in these things, and if he will, can say from his heart, Such knowledges cannot flow into these creatures out of the sun through its rays of light, for the sun, from which nature derives its origin and essence, is mere fire, consequently its rays of light are wholly dead; and thus he may conclude that such things are from the influx of Divine wisdom into the outmosts of nature.

354. Anyone may confirm himself in favor of the Divine from things visible in nature, when he sees larvae, from the delight of some impulse, desiring and longing to change their terrestrial state to a certain likeness of the heavenly state, and for this purpose creeping into corners, and putting themselves as it were into a womb in order to be born again, and there becoming chrysalises, aurelias, caterpillars, nymphs, and at length butterflies; and having undergone this metamorphosis, and each after its kind been decked with beautiful wings, they ascend into the air as into their heaven, and there disport themselves joyfully, form marriage unions, lay eggs, and provide for themselves a posterity, nourished meanwhile with pleasant and sweet food from flowers. Who that confirms himself in favor of the Divine from the visible things in nature can help seeing a kind of image of man's earthly state in these as larvae, and in them as butterflies an image of the heavenly state? Those who confirm themselves in favor of nature see the same things, but because in heart they have rejected the heavenly state of man they call them merely natural instincts.

355. Anyone may confirm himself in favor of the Divine from things seen in nature by giving attention to what is known about bees: that they know how to collect wax and suck honey from herbs and flowers, and to build cells like little houses, and set them in the form of a city, with streets through which to come in and go out; that they scent at long distances the flowers and herbs from which they collect wax for their houses and honey for food, and laden with these fly back in a direct line to their

hive; thus providing themselves with food and habitation for the coming winter, as if they had foresight and knowledge of it.

They also set over them a mistress as queen, out of whom a posterity may be propagated; and for her they build a sort of a palace over themselves with guards around it; and when her time of bringing forth is at hand, she goes attended by her guards from cell to cell, and lays her eggs, which the crowd of followers smear over to protect them from the air, from which a new progeny springs forth for them. When this progeny becomes mature enough to do the same, it is driven from the hive. The expelled swarm first collects, and then in a close body, to preserve its integrity, flies away in quest of a home for itself. Moreover, in the autumn the useless drones are led out and are deprived of their wings to prevent their returning and consuming the food for which they have not labored; not to mention other particulars. From all this it can be seen that bees, because of their use to the human race, have from influx from the spiritual world, a form of government similar to that among men on earth, and even like that of angels in heaven. Can any man of unimpaired reason fail to see that these doings of the bees are not from the natural world? What has that sun, from which nature springs, in common with a government that vies with and resembles the government of heaven? From these things and others very similar to them in the brute creation, the confessor and worshiper of nature confirms himself in favor of nature, while the confessor and worshiper of God confirms himself from the same things in favor of the Divine; for the spiritual man sees in them spiritual things and the natural man natural things, thus each according to his character.

As for myself, such things have been proofs to me of an influx of the spiritual into the natural, that is, of the spiritual world into the natural world, thus of an influx from the Lord's Divine wisdom. Consider, moreover, whether you can think analytically concerning any form of government, or any civil law, or moral virtue, or spiritual truth, unless the Divine out of his wisdom flows in through the spiritual world? For myself, I could not and cannot. For having now observed that influx perceptibly and sensibly for about nineteen years continually, I speak as an eyewitness.

356. Can anything natural regard use as an end and dispose uses into series and forms? No one can do this unless he be wise; and no one but God, whose wisdom is infinite, can so give order and form to the universe. Who else or what else is able to foresee and provide all things needful for the food and clothing of man, food from the fruits of earth and from animals, and clothing from the same? How marvelous that so insignificant a creature as the silkworm should clothe in silk and splendidly adorn both women and men, from queens and kings to maidservants and menservants, and that insignificant insects like the bees should supply wax for the candles by which temples and palaces are made brilliant. These and many other things are manifest proofs that the Lord from himself by means of the spiritual world, brings about everything that comes into existence in nature.

357. To this must be added that those who have confirmed themselves in favor of nature, from the visible things of the world, until they have become atheists, have been seen by me in the spiritual world; and in the spiritual light their understanding appeared open below, but closed above, because in thought they had looked downward toward the earth, and not upward toward heaven. Above their sensual, which is the bottom of the understanding, appeared something like a veil; which in some flashed with hellish fire, in some was black like soot, and in some livid like a corpse. Therefore let everyone beware of confirmations in favor of nature; let him confirm himself in favor of the Divine; there is no lack of material.

Chapter 5
[The Goal of Creation]

Two receptacles and abodes for himself, called will and understanding, have been created and formed by the Lord in man; the will for his Divine love, and the understanding for his Divine wisdom

358. The Divine love and Divine wisdom of God the Creator, who is the Lord from eternity, and also the creation of the universe, have been treated of; something shall now be said of the creation of man. We read (in Gen. 1:26) that man was created "in the image of God, after his likeness." By "image of God" is there meant the Divine wisdom, and by "likeness" of God the Divine love; since wisdom is nothing but an image of love, for in wisdom love presents itself to be seen and recognized, and because it is seen and recognized in wisdom, wisdom is an image of it. Moreover love is the *esse* of life, and wisdom is the *existere* of life therefrom. In angels the likeness and image of God clearly appear, since love from within shines forth in their faces, and wisdom in their beauty, and their beauty is a form of their love. I have seen and know.

359. Man cannot be an image of God, after his likeness, unless God is in him and is his life from the inmost. That God is in man and, from the inmost, is his life, follows from what has been shown above (n. 4–6), that God alone is life, and that men and angels are recipients of life from him. Moreover, that God is in man and that he makes his abode with him, is known from the Word; for which reason it is customary for preachers to declare that men ought to prepare themselves to receive God, that he may enter into them, and be in their hearts, that they may be his dwelling place. The devout man says the same in his prayers, and some speak more openly respecting the Holy Spirit, which they believe to be in them when they are in holy zeal, and from that zeal they think, speak, and preach. That the Holy Spirit is the Lord, and not a God who is a person by himself, has been shown in the *Doctrine of the New Jerusalem Concerning the Lord* (n. 51–53). For the Lord declares:

> In that day ye shall know that ye are in Me, and I in you (John 14:20; 15:4, 5; 17:23).

360. Now because the Lord is Divine love and Divine wisdom, and these two essentially are himself, it is necessary, in order that he may abide in man and give life to man, that he should create and form in man receptacles and abodes for himself; the one for love and the other for wisdom. These receptacles and abodes in man are called will and understanding; the receptacle and abode of love is called the will, and the receptacle and abode of wisdom is called the understanding. That these two are the Lord's in man, and that from these two man has all his life, will be seen in what follows.

361. That every man has these two, will and understanding, and that they are distinct from each other, as love and wisdom are distinct, is known and is not known in the world. It is known from common perception, but it is not known from thought and still less from thought when written out; for who does not know from common perception that the will and the understanding are two distinct things in man? For everyone perceives this when he hears it stated, and may himself say to another, This man means well, but does not understand clearly; while that one's understanding is good, but his will is not; I like the man whose understanding and will are both good; but I do not like him whose understanding is good and his will bad. Yet when he thinks about the will and the understanding he does not make them two and distinguish them, but confounds them, since his thought then acts in common with the bodily sight. When writing he apprehends still less that will and understanding are two distinct things, because his thought then acts in common with the sensual, that is, with what is the man's own. From this it is that some can think and speak well, but cannot write well. This is common with women. It is the same with many other things. Is it not known by everyone from common perception that a man whose life is good is saved, but that a man whose life is bad is condemned? Also that one whose life is good will enter the society of angels, and will there see, hear, and speak like a man? Also that one who from justice does what is just and from what is right does right, has a conscience?

But if one lapses from common perception, and submits these things to thought, he does not know what conscience is; or that the soul can see, hear, and speak like a man; or that the good of life is anything except giving to the poor. And if from thought you write about these things, you confirm them by appearances and fallacies, and by words of sound but of no substance. For this reason many of the learned who have thought much, and especially who have written much, have weakened and obscured, yea, have destroyed their common perception; while the simple see more clearly what is good and true than those who think themselves their superiors in wisdom.

This common perception comes by influx from heaven, and descends into thought even to sight; but thought separated from common perception falls into imagination from the sight and from what is man's own. You may observe that this is so. Tell some truth to anyone that is in common perception, and he will see it; tell him that from God and in God we are and live and are moved, and he will see it; tell him that God dwells with man in love and in wisdom, and he will see it; tell him further that the will is the receptacle of love, and the understanding of wisdom, and explain it a little, and he will see it; tell him that God is love itself and wisdom itself, and he will see it; ask him what conscience is, and he will tell you. But say the same things to one of the learned, who has not thought from common perception, but from principles or from ideas obtained from the world through sight, and he will not see. Then consider which is the wiser.

Will and understanding, which are the receptacles of love and wisdom, are in the brains, in the whole and in every part of them, and therefrom in the body, in the whole and in every part of it

362. This shall be shown in the following order:

(1) Love and wisdom, and will and understanding therefrom, make the very life of man.

(2) The life of man in its first principles is in the brains, and in its derivatives in the body.

(3) Such as life is in its first principles, such it is in the whole and in every part.

(4) By means of first principles life is in the whole from every part, and in every part from the whole.

(5) Such as the love is, such is the wisdom, consequently such is the man.

363. (1) *Love and wisdom, and will and understanding therefrom, make the very life of man.* Scarcely anyone knows what life is. When one thinks about life, it seems as if it were a fleeting something, of which no distinct idea is possible. It so seems because it is not known that God alone is life, and that his life is Divine love and Divine wisdom. From this it is evident that in man life is nothing else than love and wisdom, and that there is life in man in the degree in which he receives these. It is known that heat and light go forth from the sun, and that all things in the universe are recipients and grow warm and bright in the degree in which they receive. So do heat and light go forth from the sun where the Lord is; the heat going forth therefrom is love, and the light wisdom (as shown in chapter 2). Life, therefore, is from these two which go forth from the Lord as a sun. That love and wisdom from the Lord is life can be seen also from this, that man grows torpid as love recedes from him, and stupid as wisdom recedes from him, and that were they to recede altogether he would become extinct.

There are many things pertaining to love which have received other names because they are derivatives, such as affections, desires, appetites, and their pleasures and enjoyments; and there are many things pertaining to wisdom, such as perception, reflection, recollection, thought, intention to an end; and there are many pertaining to both love and wisdom, such as consent, conclusion, and determination to action; besides others. All of these, in fact, pertain to both, but they are designated from the more prominent and nearer of the two. From these two are derived ultimately sensations, those of sight, hearing, smell, taste, and touch, with their enjoyments and pleasures. It is according to appearance that the eye sees; but it is the understanding that sees through the eye; consequently seeing is predicated also of the understanding.

The appearance is that the ear hears, but it is the understanding that hears through the ear; consequently hearing is predicated also of attention and giving heed, which pertain to the understanding. The appearance is that the nose smells and the tongue tastes, but it is the understanding that smells and also tastes by virtue of its perception; therefore smelling and tasting are predicated also of perception. So in other cases. The sources of all these are love and wisdom; from which it can be seen that these two make the life of man.

364. Everyone sees that the understanding is the receptacle of wisdom, but few see that the will is the receptacle of love. This is because the will does not act at all by itself, but only through the understanding; also because the love of the will, in passing over into the wisdom of the understanding, is first changed into affection, and thus passes over; and affection is not perceived except by something pleasant in thinking, speaking, and acting, which is not noticed. Still it is evident that love is from the will, for the reason that everyone wills what he loves, and does not will what he does not love.

365. (2) *The life of man in its first principles is in the brains, and in its derivatives in the body.* In first principles means in its firsts, and in derivatives means in what is brought forth and formed from its firsts. By life in first principles is meant will and understanding. These two are what are in their first principles in the brains, and in their derivatives in the body. It is evident that the first principles or firsts of life are in the brains:

(a) From the feeling itself; since man perceives, when he exerts his mind and thinks, that he thinks in the brain. He draws in as it were the sight of the eye, contracts the forehead, and perceives the mental process to be within, especially inside the forehead and somewhat above it.

(b) From man's formation in the womb; in that the brain or head is first developed, and continues for some time larger than the body.

(c) In that the head is above and the body below; and it is according to order for the higher to act upon the lower, and not the reverse.

(d) In that, when the brain is injured in the womb or by a wound or by disease, or by excessive application, thought is weakened and sometimes the mind becomes deranged.

(e) In that all the external senses of the body, sight, hearing, smell, and taste, with touch (the universal sense) as also speech, are in the front part of the head, which is called the face, and communicate immediately through fibers with the brains, and derive therefrom their sensitive and active life.

(f) It is from this that affections, which are of love, appear imaged forth in the face, and that thoughts, which are of wisdom, are revealed in a kind of sparkle of the eyes.

(g) Anatomy teaches that all fibers descend from the brains through the neck into the body, and that none ascend from the body through the neck into the brains. And where the fibers are in their first principles or firsts, there life is in its first principles or firsts. Will anyone venture to deny that life has its origin where the fibers have their origin?

(h) Ask anyone of common perception where his thought resides or where he thinks, and he will say, In the head. Then appeal to someone who has assigned the seat of the soul to some gland or to the heart or somewhere else, and ask him where affection and thought therefrom are in their firsts, whether they are not in the brain? And he will answer, No, or that he does not know. The cause of this ignorance may be seen above (n. 361).

366. (3) *Such as life is in its first principles, such it is in the whole and in every part.* That this may be perceived, it shall now be told where in the brains these first principles are, and how they become derivative. Anatomy shows where in the brains these first principles are; it teaches that there are two brains; that these are continued from the head into the spinal column; that they consist of two substances, called cortical substance and medullary substance; that cortical substance consists of innumerable gland-like forms, and medullary substance of innumerable fiber-like forms. Now as these little glands are heads of fibrils, they are also their first principles. For from these, fibers begin and thereupon go forth, gradually bundling themselves into nerves. These bundles or nerves, when formed, descend to the organs of sense in the face, and to the organs of motion in the body, and form them. Consult anyone skilled in the science of anatomy, and you will be convinced.

This cortical or glandular substance constitutes the surface of the cerebrum, and also the surface of the corpora striata, from which proceeds the medulla oblongata; it also constitutes the middle of the cerebellum, and the middle of the spinal marrow. But medullary or fibrillary substance everywhere begins in and proceeds from the cortical; out of it nerves arise, and from them all things of the body. That this is true is proved by dissection. They who know these things, either from the study of anatomical science or from the testimony of those who are skilled in the science, can see that the first principles of life are in the same place as the beginnings of the fibers, and that fibers cannot go forth from themselves, but must go forth from first principles.

These first principles, that is, beginnings, which appear as little glands, are almost countless; their multitude may be compared to the multitude of stars in the universe; and the multitude of fibrils coming out of them may be compared to the multitude of rays going forth from the stars and bearing their heat and light to the earth.

The multitude of these little glands may also be compared to the multitude of angelic societies in the heavens, which also are countless, and, I have been told, are in like order as the glands. Also the multitude of fibrils going out from these little glands may be compared to the spiritual truths and goods which in like manner flow down from the angelic societies like rays. From this it is that man is like a universe, and like a heaven in least form (as has been frequently said and shown above).

From all which it can now be seen that such as life is in first principles, such it is in derivatives; or such as it is in its firsts in the brains, such it is in the things arising therefrom in the body.

367. (4) *By means of first principles life is in the whole from every part, and in every part from the whole.* This is because the whole, which is the brain and the body together, is originally made up of nothing but fibers proceeding from their first principles in the brains. It has no other origin, as is evident from what has been shown just above (n. 366); consequently, the whole is from every part; and by means of these first principles life is in every part from the whole, because the whole dispenses to each part its task and needs, thereby making it to be a part in the whole. In a word, the whole has existence from the parts, and the parts have permanent existence from the whole. That there is such reciprocal communion, and conjunction thereby, is clear from many things in the body. For the same order prevails there as in a state, commonwealth, or kingdom; the community has its existence from the individuals which are its parts, and the parts or individuals have permanent existence from the community. It is the same with everything that has form, most of all in man.

368. (5) *Such as the love is, such is the wisdom, consequently such is the man.* For such as the love and wisdom are, such are the will and understanding, since the will is the receptacle of love, and the understanding of wisdom, as has been shown above; and these two make the man and his character. Love is manifold, so manifold that its varieties are limitless; as can be seen from the human race on the earths and in the heavens.

There is no man or angel so like another that there is no difference. Love is what distinguishes; for every man is his own love. It is supposed that wisdom distinguishes; but wisdom is from love; it is the form of love; love is the *esse* of life, and wisdom is the *existere* of life from that *esse*. In the world it is believed that the understanding makes the man; but this is believed because the understanding can be elevated, as was shown above, into the light of heaven, giving man the appearance of being wise; yet so much of the understanding as transcends, that is to say, so much as is not of the love, although it appears to be man's and therefore to determine man's character, is only an appearance.

For so much of the understanding as transcends is, indeed, from the love of knowing and being wise, but not at the same time from the love of applying to life what man knows and is wise in. Consequently, in the world it either in time passes away or lingers outside of the things of memory in its mere borders as something ready to drop off; and therefore after death it is separated, no more of it remaining than is in accord with the spirit's own love. Inasmuch as love makes the life of man, and thus the man himself, all societies of heaven, and all angels in societies, are arranged according to affections belonging to love, and no society nor any angel in a society according to anything of the understanding separate from love. So likewise in the hells and their societies, but in accordance with loves opposite to the heavenly loves. From all this it can be seen that such as the love is such is the wisdom, and consequently such is the man.

369. It is acknowledged, indeed, that man is such as his reigning love is, but only in respect to his mind and disposition, not in respect to his body, thus not wholly. But it has been made known to me by much experience in the spiritual world, that man from head to foot, that is, from things primary in the head to the outmosts in the body, is such as his love is. For all in the spiritual world are forms of their own love: the angels forms of heavenly love, the devils of hellish love; the devils deformed in face and body, but the angels beautiful in face and body. Moreover, when their love is assailed their faces are changed, and if much assailed they wholly disappear. This is peculiar to that world, and so happens because their bodies make one with their minds. The reason is evident from what has been said above, that all things of the body are derivatives, that is, are things woven together by means of fibers out of first principles, which are receptacles of love and wisdom.

Whatever these first principles may be, their derivatives cannot be different; therefore wherever first principles go their derivatives follow, and cannot be separated. For this reason he who raises his mind to the Lord is wholly raised up to him, and he who casts his mind down to hell is wholly cast down thither; consequently the whole man, in conformity to his life's love, comes either into heaven or into hell. That man's mind is a man because God is a man, and that the body is the mind's external, which feels and acts, and that they are thus one and not two, is a matter of angelic wisdom.

370. It is to be observed that the very forms of man's members, organs, and viscera, as regards the structure itself, are from fibers that arise out of their first principles in the brains; but these become fixed by means of such substances and matters as are in earths, and from earths in air and in ether. This is effected by means of the blood. Consequently, in order that all parts of the body may be maintained in their formation and rendered permanent in their functions, man requires to be nourished by material food, and to be continually renewed.

There is a correspondence of the will with the heart, and of the understanding with the lungs

371. This shall be shown in the following series:

(1) All things of the mind have relation to the will and understanding, and all things of the body to the heart and lungs.

(2) There is a correspondence of the will and understanding with the heart and lungs, consequently a correspondence of all things of the mind with all things of the body.

(3) The will corresponds to the heart.

(4) The understanding corresponds to the lungs.

(5) By means of this correspondence many arcana relating to the will and understanding, thus also to love and wisdom, may be disclosed.

(6) Man's mind is his spirit, and the spirit is the man, while the body is the external by means of which the mind or spirit feels and acts in its world.

(7) The conjunction of man's spirit with his body is by means of the correspondence of his will and understanding with his heart and lungs, and their separation is from noncorrespondence.

372. (1) *All things of the mind have relation to the will and understanding, and all things of the body to the heart and lungs.* By the mind nothing else is meant than the will and understanding, which in their complex are all things that affect man and all that he thinks, thus all things of man's affection and thought. The things that affect man are of his will, and the things that he thinks are of his understanding. That all things of man's thought are of his understanding is known, since he thinks from the understanding; but it is not so well known that all things of man's affection are of his will; this is not so well known because when man is thinking he pays no attention to the affection, but only to what he is thinking; just as when he hears a person speaking, he pays no attention to the tone of the voice but only to the language.

Yet affection is related to thought as the tone of the voice is to the language; consequently the affection of the one speaking is known by the tone, and his thought by the language.

Affection is of the will, because all affection is of love, and the will is the receptacle of love, as was shown above. He that is not aware that affection is of the will confounds affection with understanding, for he declares it to be one with thought, yet they are not one but act as one. That they are confounded is evident from the common expression, "I think I will do this," meaning, I will to do it. But that they are two is also evident from a common expression, "I wish to think about this matter"; and when one thinks about it, the affection of the will is present in the thought of the understanding, like the tone in speech, as was said before. That all parts of the body have relation to the heart and lungs is known, but that there is a correspondence of the heart and lungs with the will and understanding is not known. This subject will therefore be treated in what follows.

373. Because the will and understanding are the receptacles of love and wisdom, these two are organic forms, or forms organized out of the purest substances; for such they must be to be receptacles. It is no objection that their organization is imperceptible to the eye; it lies beyond the reach of vision, even when this is increased by the microscope. The smallest insects are also too small to be seen, yet they have organs of sense and motion, for they feel, walk, and fly. That they have brains, hearts, pulmonary pipes, and viscera, acute observers have discovered from their anatomy by means of the microscope. Since minute insects themselves are not visible, and still less so their component viscera, and since it is not denied that they are organized even to each single particle in them, how can it be said that the two receptacles of love and wisdom, called will and understanding, are not organic forms? How can love and wisdom, which are life from the Lord, act upon what is not a subject, or upon what has no substantial existence?

Without organic forms, how can thought inhere; and from thought inherent in nothing can one speak? Is not the brain, where thought comes forth, complete and organized in every part? The organic forms themselves are there visible even to the naked eye; and the receptacles of the will and understanding, in their first principles, are plainly to be seen in the cortical substance, where they are perceptible as minute glands (on which see above, n. 366). Do not, I pray, think of these things from an idea of vacuum. Vacuum is nothing, and in nothing nothing takes place, and from nothing nothing comes forth. (On the idea of vacuum, see above, n. 82.)

374. (2) *There is a correspondence of the will and understanding with the heart and lungs, consequently a correspondence of all things of the mind with all things of the body.* This is new: it has hitherto been unknown because it has not been known what the spiritual is, and how it differs from the natural; therefore it has not been known what correspondence is; for there is a correspondence between things spiritual and things natural, and by means of correspondence they are conjoined.

It is said that heretofore there has been no knowledge of what the spiritual is, or of what its correspondence with the natural is and therefore what correspondence is; yet these might have been known. Who does not know that affection and thought are spiritual, therefore that all things of affection and thought are spiritual? Who does not know that action and speech are natural, therefore that all things of action and speech are natural? Who does not know that affection and thought, which are spiritual, cause man to act and to speak? From this who cannot see what correspondence is between things spiritual and things natural?

Does not thought make the tongue speak, and affection together with thought make the body act? There are two distinct things: I can think without speaking, and I can will without acting; and the body, it is known, neither thinks nor wills, but thought falls into speech, and will descends into action.

Does not affection also beam forth from the face, and there exhibit a type of itself? This everyone knows. Is not affection, regarded in itself, spiritual, and the change of countenance, called the expression, natural? From this who might not conclude that there is correspondence; and further, a correspondence of all things of the mind with all things of the body; and since all things of the mind have relation to affection and thought, or what is the same, to the will and understanding, and all things of the body to the heart and lungs, that there is a correspondence of the will with the heart and of the understanding with the lungs? Such things have remained unknown, though they might have been known, because man has become so external as to be unwilling to acknowledge anything except the natural. This has become the joy of his love, and from that the joy of his understanding; consequently it has become distasteful to him to raise his thought above the natural to anything spiritual separate from the natural; therefore, from his natural love and its delights, he can think of the spiritual only as a purer natural, and of correspondence only as a something flowing in by continuity; yea, the merely natural man cannot think of anything separate from the natural; any such thing to him is nothing.

Again, these things have not heretofore been seen and known, because everything of religion, that is, everything called spiritual, has been banished from the sight of man by the dogma of the whole Christian world, that matters theological, that is, spiritual, which councils and certain leaders have decreed, are to be believed blindly because (as they say) they transcend the understanding. Some, therefore, have imagined the spiritual to be like a bird flying above the air in an ether to which the sight of the eye does not reach; when yet it is like a bird of paradise, which flies near the eye, even touching the pupil with its beautiful wings and longing to be seen. By "the sight of the eye" intellectual vision is meant.

375. The correspondence of the will and understanding with the heart and lungs cannot be abstractly proved, that is, by mere reasonings, but it may be proved by effects. It is much the same as it is with the causes of things which can be seen rationally, yet not clearly except by means of effects; for causes are in effects, and by means of effects make themselves visible; and until causes are thus made visible, the mind is not assured respecting them. In what follows, the effects of this correspondence will be described. But lest anyone should fall into ideas of this correspondence imbibed from hypotheses about the soul, let him first read over carefully the propositions in the preceding chapter, as follows: Love and wisdom, and the will and understanding therefrom, make the very life of man (n. 363, 364). The life of man is in first principles in the brains, and in derivatives in the body (n. 365). Such as life is in first principles, such it is in the whole and in every part (n. 366). By means of these first principles life is in the whole from every part, and in every part from the whole (n. 367). Such as the love is, such is the wisdom, consequently such is the man (n. 368).

376. It is permitted to introduce here, in the way of evidence, a representation of the correspondence of the will and understanding with the heart and lungs which was seen in heaven among the angels. By a wonderful flowing into spiral movements, such as no words can express, the angels formed the likeness of a heart and the likeness of lungs, with all the interior structures therein; and in this they were falling in with the flow of heaven, for heaven from the inflowing of love and wisdom from the Lord strives to come into such forms. They thus represented the conjunction of the heart and lungs, and at the same time the correspondence of these with the love of the will and with the wisdom of the understanding. This correspondence and union they called the heavenly marriage; saying that in the whole body, and in its several members, organs, and viscera, it is the same as in the things belonging to the heart and lungs; also that where the heart and lungs do not act, each in its turn, there can be no motion of life from any voluntary principle, and no sensation of life from any intellectual principle.

377. Inasmuch as the correspondence of the heart and lungs with the will and understanding is treated of in what now follows, and upon this correspondence is based that of all parts of the body, namely, the members, the organs of the senses, and the viscera throughout the body, and inasmuch as the correspondence of natural things with spiritual has been heretofore unknown, and yet is amply shown in two works, one of which treats of heaven and hell and the other, *Arcana Coelestia,* treats of the spiritual sense of the Word in Genesis and Exodus, I will here point out what has been written and shown in those two works respecting correspondence. In the work *Heaven and Hell:* the correspondence of all things of heaven with all things of man (n. 87–102), the correspondence of all things of heaven with all things on earth (n. 103–115).

In *Arcana Coelestia,* the work on the spiritual sense of the Word in Genesis and Exodus: the correspondence of the face and its expressions with the affections of the mind (n. 1568, 2988, 2989, 3631, 4796, 4797, 4800, 5165, 5168, 5695, 9306), the correspondence of the body, its gestures and actions, with things intellectual and things voluntary (n. 2988, 3632, 4215), the correspondence of the senses in general (n. 4318–4330), the correspondence of the eyes and of sight (n. 4403–4420), the correspondence of the nostrils and of smell (n. 4624–4634), the correspondence of the ear and of hearing (n. 4652–4660), the correspondence of the tongue and of taste (n. 4791–4805), the correspondence of the hands, arms, shoulders, and feet (n. 4931–4953), the correspondence of the loins and organs of generation (n. 5050–5062), the correspondence of the internal viscera of the body, especially of the stomach, thymus gland, the receptacle and ducts of the chyle and lacteals, and of the mesentery (n. 5171–5181, 5189), the correspondence of the spleen (n. 9698), the correspondence of the peritoneum, kidneys, and bladder (n. 5377–5385), the correspondence of the liver, and of the hepatic, cystic, and pancreatic ducts (n. 5183–5185), the correspondence of the intestines (n. 5392–5395, 5379), the correspondence of the bones (n. 5560–5564), the correspondence of the skin (n. 5552–5559), the correspondence of heaven with man (n. 911, 1900, 1982, 2996–2998, 3624–3649, 3741–3745, 3884, 4051, 4279, 4403, 4423, 4524, 4525, 6013, 6057, 9279, 9632).

All things that exist in the natural world and in its three kingdoms correspond to all things which appear in the spiritual world (n. 1632, 1831, 1881, 2758, 2990–2993, 2997–3003, 3213–3227, 3483, 3624–3649, 4044, 4053, 4116, 4366, 4939, 5116, 5377, 5428, 5477, 8211, 9280). All things that appear in the heavens are correspondences (n. 1521, 1532, 1619–1625, 1807, 1808, 1971, 1974, 1977, 1980, 1981, 2299, 2601, 3213–3226, 3349, 3350, 3475–3485, 3748, 9481, 9570, 9576, 9577), the correspondence of the sense of the letter of the Word and of its spiritual sense is treated of in the *Arcana Coelestia* throughout; and on this subject see also the *Doctrine of the New Jerusalem Concerning the Sacred Scripture* (n. 5–65).

378. (3) *The will corresponds to the heart.* This cannot be seen so clearly taken by itself as when the will is considered in its effects (as was said above). Taken by itself it can be seen by this, that all affections, which are of love, induce changes in the heart's pulsations, as is evident from the pulse of the arteries, which act synchronously with the heart. The heart's changes and pulsations in accordance with the love's affections are innumerable. Those felt by the finger are only that the beats are slow or quick, high or low, weak or strong, regular or irregular, and so on; thus that there is a difference in joy and in sorrow, in tranquillity of mind and in wrath, in fearlessness and in fear, in hot diseases and in cold, and so on.

Because the two motions of the heart, systolic and diastolic, change and vary in this manner according to the affections of each one's love, many of the ancient and after them some modern writers have assigned the affections to the heart, and have made the heart their dwelling place. From this have come into common language such expressions as a stout heart, a timid heart, a joyful heart, a sad heart, a soft heart, a hard heart, a great heart, a weak heart, a whole heart, a broken heart, a heart of flesh, a heart of stone; likewise being gross, or soft, or tender in heart; giving the heart to a thing, giving a single heart, giving a new heart, laying up in the heart, receiving in the heart, not reaching the heart, hardening one's heart, a friend at heart; also the terms concord, discord, folly *[vecordia]*, and other similar terms expressive of love and its affections. There are like expressions in the Word, because the Word was written by correspondences. Whether you say love or will it is the same, because the will is the receptacle of love, as was explained above.

379. It is known that there is vital heat in man and in every living creature; but its origin is not known. Everyone speaks of it from conjecture, consequently such as have known nothing of the correspondence of natural things with spiritual have ascribed its origin, some to the sun's heat, some to the activity of the parts, some to life itself; but as they have not known what life is, they have been content with the mere phrase. But anyone who knows that there is a correspondence of love and its affections with the heart and its derivations may know that the origin of vital heat is love.

For love goes forth as heat from the spiritual sun where the Lord is, and moreover is felt as heat by the angels. This spiritual heat which in its essence is love, is what inflows by correspondence into the heart and its blood, and imparts heat to it, and at the same time vivifies it. That a man grows hot, and, as it were, is fired, according to his love and the degree of it, and grows torpid and cold according to its decrease, is known, for it is felt and seen; it is felt by the heat throughout the body, and seen by the flushing of the face; and on the other hand, extinction of love is felt by coldness in the body, and is seen by paleness in the face.

Because love is the life of man, the heart is the first and the last of his life; and because love is the life of man, and the soul maintains its life in the body by means of the blood, in the Word blood is called the soul (Gen. 9:4; Lev. 17:14). The various meanings of soul will be explained in what follows.

380. The redness, also, of the blood is from the correspondence of the heart and the blood with love and its affection; for in the spiritual world there are all kinds of colors, of which red and white are the fundamental, the rest deriving their varieties from these and from their opposites, which are a dusky fire color and black. Red there corresponds to love, and white to wisdom. Red corresponds to love because it originates in the fire of the spiritual sun, and white corresponds to wisdom because it originates in the light of that sun. And because there is a correspondence of love with the heart, the blood must needs be red, and reveal its origin. For this reason in the heavens where love to the Lord reigns the light is flame colored, and the angels there are clothed in purple garments; and in the heavens where wisdom reigns the light is white, and the angels there are clothed in white linen garments.

381. The heavens are divided into two kingdoms, one called celestial, the other spiritual; in the celestial kingdom love to the Lord reigns, and in the spiritual kingdom wisdom from that love. The kingdom where love reigns is called heaven's cardiac kingdom, the one where wisdom reigns is called its pulmonic kingdom. Be it known, that the whole angelic heaven in its aggregate represents a single man, and before the Lord appears as a single man; consequently its heart makes one kingdom and its lungs another. For there is a general cardiac and pulmonic movement throughout heaven, and a particular movement therefrom in each angel.

The general cardiac and pulmonic movement is from the Lord alone, because love and wisdom are from him alone. For these two movements are in the sun where the Lord is and which is from the Lord, and from that in the angelic heavens and in the universe. Banish spaces and think of omnipresence, and you will be convinced that it is so. That the heavens are divided into two kingdoms, celestial and spiritual, see the work *Heaven and Hell* (n. 20–28); and that the whole angelic heaven in the aggregate represents a single man (n. 59–67).

382. (4) *The understanding corresponds to the lungs.* This follows from what has been said of the correspondence of the will with the heart; for there are two things, will and understanding, which reign in the spiritual man, that is, in the mind, and there are two things, heart and lungs, which reign in the natural man, that is, in the body; and there is correspondence (as was said above) of all things of the mind with all things of the body; from which it follows that as the will corresponds to the heart, so the understanding corresponds to the lungs. Moreover, that the understanding corresponds to the lungs anyone may observe in himself, both from his thought and from his speech. (a) From thought: No one is able to think except with the concurrence and concordance of the pulmonary respiration; consequently, when he thinks tacitly he breathes tacitly, if he thinks deeply he breathes deeply; he draws in the breath and lets it out, contracts and expands the lungs, slowly or quickly, eagerly, gently, or intently, all in conformity to his thought, thus to the influx of affection from love; yea, if he hold the breath entirely he is unable to think, except in his spirit by its respiration, which is not manifestly perceived.

(b) From speech: Since not the least vocal sound flows forth from the mouth without the concurrent aid of the lungs—for the sound, which is articulated into words, comes forth from the lungs through the trachea and epiglottis—therefore, according to the inflation of these bellows and the opening of the passage the voice is raised even to a shout, and according to their contraction it is lowered; and if the passage is entirely closed speech ceases and thought with it.

383. Since the understanding corresponds to the lungs and thought therefrom to the respiration of the lungs, in the Word, "soul" and "spirit" signify the understanding; for example:

> Thou shalt love the Lord thy God with all thy heart and with all thy soul (Matt. 22:37).

> God will give a new heart and a new spirit (Ezek. 36:26; Ps. 51:10).

That "heart" signifies the love of the will was shown above; therefore "soul" and "spirit" signify the wisdom of the understanding. That the spirit of God, also called the Holy Spirit, means Divine wisdom, and therefore Divine truth which is the light of men, may be seen in the *Doctrine of the New Jerusalem Concerning the Lord* (n. 50, 51), therefore,

> The Lord breathed on his disciples, and said, Receive ye the Holy Spirit (John 20:22);

for the same reason it is said that:

> Jehovah God breathed into the nostrils of Adam the breath of lives, and he was made into a living soul (Gen. 2:7;)

also he said to the prophet:

> Prophesy upon the breath, and say unto the wind, Come from the four winds, O breath, and breathe upon these slain, that they may live (Ezek. 37:9);

likewise in other places; therefore the Lord is called "the breath of the nostrils," and "the breath of life." Because respiration passes through the nostrils, perception is signified by them; and an intelligent man is said to be keen-scented, and an unintelligent man to be dull-scented. For the same reason, "spirit" and "wind" in the Hebrew, and in some other languages, are the same word; for the word "spirit" is derived from a word that means breathing; and therefore when a man dies he is said to give up the ghost *[anima]*. It is for the same reason that men believe the spirit to be wind, or an airy something like breath breathed out from the lungs, and the soul to be of like nature. From all this it can be seen that to "love God with all the heart and all the soul" means to love him with all the love and with all the understanding, and to "give a new heart and a new spirit" means to give a new will and a new understanding. Because "spirit" signifies understanding, it is said of Bezaleel:

> That he was filled with the spirit of wisdom, of intelligence, and of knowledge (Exod. 31:3);

and of Joshua:

> That he was filled with the spirit of wisdom (Deut. 34:9);

and Nebuchadnezzar says of Daniel:

> That an excellent spirit of knowledge, of intelligence, and of wisdom, was in him (Dan. 5:11, 12, 14);

and it is said in Isaiah:

> They that err in spirit shall learn intelligence (29:24);

likewise in many other places.

384. Since all things of the mind have relation to the will and understanding, and all things of the body to the heart and lungs, there are in the head two brains, distinct from each other as will and understanding are distinct. The cerebellum is especially the organ of the will, and the cerebrum of the understanding. Likewise the heart and lungs in the body are distinct from the remaining parts there.

They are separated by the diaphragm, and are enveloped by their own covering, called the pleura, and form that part of the body called the chest. In the other parts of the body, called members, organs, and viscera, there is a joining together of the two, and thus there are pairs; for instance, the arms, hands, loins, feet, eyes, and nostrils; and within the body the kidneys, ureters, and testicles; and the viscera which are not in pairs are divided into right and left. Moreover, the brain itself is divided into two hemispheres, the heart into two ventricles, and the lungs into two lobes; the right of all these having relation to the good of truth, and the left to the truth of good, or, what is the same, the right having relation to the good of love from which is the truth of wisdom, and the left having relation to the truth of wisdom which is from the good of love. And because the conjunction of good and truth is reciprocal, and by means of that conjunction the two become as it were one, therefore the pairs in man act together and conjointly in functions, motions, and senses.

385. (5) *By means of this correspondence many arcana relating to the will and understanding, thus also to love and wisdom, may be disclosed.* In the world it is scarcely known what the will is or what love is, for the reason that man is not able, by himself, to love, and from love to will, although he is able as it were by himself to exercise intelligence and thought; just as he is not able of himself to cause the heart to beat, although he is able of himself to cause the lungs to respire. Now because it is scarcely known in the world what the will is or what love is, but it is known what the heart and the lungs are—for these are objects of sight and can be examined, and have been examined and described by anatomists, while the will and the understanding are not objects of sight, and cannot be so examined—therefore when it is known that these correspond, and by correspondence act as one, many arcana relating to the will and understanding may be disclosed that could not otherwise be disclosed; those for instance relating to the conjunction of the will with the understanding, and the reciprocal conjunction of the understanding with the will; those relating to the conjunction of love with wisdom, and the reciprocal conjunction of wisdom with love; also those relating to the derivation of love into affections, and to the consociation of affections, to their influx into perceptions and thoughts, and finally their influx according to correspondence into the bodily acts and senses. These and many other arcana may be both disclosed and illustrated by the conjunction of the heart and lungs, and by the influx of the blood from the heart into the lungs, and reciprocally from the lungs into the heart, and therefrom through the arteries into all the members, organs, and viscera of the body.

386. (6) *Man's mind is his spirit, and the spirit is the man, while the body is an external by means of which the mind or spirit feels and acts in its world.* That man's mind is his spirit, and that the spirit is the man, can hardly enter the faith of those who have supposed the spirit to be wind, and the soul to be an airy something like breath breathed out from the lungs. For they say, How can the spirit, when it is spirit, be the man, and how can the soul, when it is soul, be the man? They think in the same way of God because he is called a Spirit.

This idea of the spirit and the soul has come from the fact that spirit and wind in some languages are the same word; also, that when a man dies, he is said to give up the ghost or spirit; also, that life returns, after suffocation or swooning, when the spirit or breath of the lungs comes back. Because in these cases nothing but the breath or air is perceived, it is concluded from the eye and bodily sense that the spirit and soul of man after death is not the man. From this corporeal conclusion about the spirit and soul, various hypotheses have arisen, and these have given birth to a belief that man after death does not become a man until the day of the last judgment, and that meanwhile his spirit remains somewhere or other awaiting reunion with the body, according to what has been shown in the *Continuation Concerning the Last Judgment* (n. 32–38). Because man's mind is his spirit, the angels, who also are spirits, are called minds.

387. Man's mind is his spirit, and the spirit is the man, because by the mind all things of man's will and understanding are meant, which things are in first principles in the brains and in derivatives in the body; therefore in respect to their forms they are all things of man. This being so, the mind (that is, the will and understanding) impels the body and all its belongings at will. Does not the body do whatever the mind thinks and wills? Does not the mind incite the ear to hear, and direct the eye to see, move the tongue and the lips to speak, impel the hands and fingers to do whatever it pleases, and the feet to walk whither it will? Is the body, then, anything but obedience to its mind; and can the body be such unless the mind is in its derivatives in the body? Is it consistent with reason to think that the body acts from obedience simply because the mind so wills? In which case they should be two, the one above and the other below, one commanding, the other obeying.

As this is in no way consistent with reason, it follows that man's life is in its first principles in the brains, and in its derivatives in the body (according to what has been said above, n. 365); also that such as life is in first principles, such it is in the whole and in every part (n. 366); and by means of these first principles life is in the whole from every part, and in every part from the whole (n. 367). That all things of the mind have relation to the will and understanding, and that the will and understanding are the receptacles of love and wisdom from the Lord, and that these two make the life of man, has been shown in the preceding pages.

388. From what has now been said it can also be seen that man's mind is the man himself. For the primary texture of the human form, that is, the human form itself with each and every thing thereof, is from first principles continued from the brain through the nerves, in the manner described above. It is this form into which man comes after death, who is then called a spirit or an angel, and who is in all completeness a man, but a spiritual man. The material form that is added and superinduced in the world, is not a human form by itself, but only by virtue of the spiritual form, to which it is added and superinduced that man may be enabled to perform uses in the natural world, and also to draw to himself out of the purer substances of the world a fixed container of spiritual things, and thus continue and perpetuate life. It is a truth of angelic wisdom that man's mind, not alone in general, but in every particular, is in a perpetual conatus toward the human form, for the reason that God is a man.

389. That man may be man there must be no part lacking, either in head or in body, that has existence in the complete man; since there is nothing therein that does not enter into the human form and constitute it; for it is the form of love and wisdom, and this, in itself considered, is Divine. In it are all terminations of love and wisdom, which in God-man are infinite, but in his image, that is, in man, angel, or spirit, are finite. If any part that has existence in man were lacking, there would be lacking something of termination from the love and wisdom corresponding to it, whereby the Lord might be from firsts in outmosts with man, and might from his Divine love through his Divine wisdom provide uses in the created world.

390. (7) *The conjunction of man's spirit with his body is by means of the correspondence of his will and understanding with his heart and lungs, and their separation is from non-correspondence.* As it has heretofore been unknown that man's mind, by which is meant the will and understanding, is his spirit, and that the spirit is a man; and as it has been unknown that man's spirit, as well as his body, has a pulse and respiration, it could not be known that the pulse and respiration of the spirit in man flow into the pulse and respiration of his body and produce them. Since, then, man's spirit, as well as his body, enjoys a pulse and respiration, it follows that there is a like correspondence of the pulse and respiration of man's spirit with the pulse and respiration of his body, for, as was said, his mind is his spirit; consequently, when the two pairs of motions cease to correspond, separation takes place, which is death. Separation or death ensues when from any kind of disease or accident the body comes into such a state as to be unable to act in unison with its spirit, for thus correspondence perishes, and with it conjunction; not, however, when respiration alone ceases, but when the heart's pulsation ceases. For so long as the heart is moved, love with its vital heat remains and preserves life, as is evident in cases of swoon and suffocation, and in the condition of fetal life in the womb. In a word, man's bodily life depends on the correspondence of its pulse and respiration with the pulse and respiration of his spirit; and when that correspondence ceases, the bodily life ceases, and his spirit departs and continues its life in the spiritual world, which is so similar to his life in the natural world that he does not know that he has died. Men generally enter the spiritual world two days after the death of the body. For I have spoken with some after two days.

391. That a spirit, as well as a man on earth in the body, enjoys a pulse and a respiration, can only be proved by spirits and angels themselves, when privilege is granted to speak with them. This privilege has been granted to me. When questioned about the matter they declared that they are just as much men as those in the world are, and possess a body as well as they, but a spiritual body, and feel the beat of the heart in the chest, and the beat of the arteries in the wrist, just as men do in the natural world. I have questioned many about the matter, and they all gave like answer.

That man's spirit respires within his body has been granted me to learn by personal experience. On one occasion angels were allowed to control my respiration, and to diminish it at pleasure, and at length to withdraw it, until only the respiration of my spirit remained, which I then perceived by sense.

A like experience was granted me when permitted to learn the state of the dying (as may be seen in the work *Heaven and Hell*, n. 449). I have sometimes been brought into the respiration of my spirit only, which I have then sensibly perceived to be in accord with the common respiration of heaven. Also many times I have been in a state like that of angels, and also raised up into heaven to them, and being then out of the body in spirit, I talked with angels with a respiration in like manner as in the world. From this and other personal evidence it has been made clear to me that man's spirit respires, not only in the body but also after it has left the body; that the respiration of the spirit is so silent as not to be perceptible to man; and that it inflows into the manifest respiration of the body almost as cause flows into effect, or thought into the lungs and through the lungs into speech. From all this it is also evident that conjunction of spirit and body in man is by means of the correspondence of the cardiac and pulmonic movement in both.

392. These two movements, the cardiac and the pulmonic, derive their origin and persistence from this, that the whole angelic heaven, in general and in particular, is in these two movements of life; and the whole angelic heaven is in these movements because the Lord pours them in from the sun, where he is, and which is from him; for these two movements are maintained by that sun from the Lord. It is evident that such is their origin, since all things of heaven and all things of the world depend on the Lord through that sun in a connection, by virtue of form, like a chain-work from the first to outmosts, also since the life of love and wisdom is from the Lord, and all the forces of the universe are from life. That the variation of these movements is according to the reception of love and wisdom, also follows.

393. More will be said in what follows of the correspondence of these movements, as what the nature of that correspondence is in those who respire with heaven, and what it is in those who respire with hell; also what it is in those who speak with heaven, but think with hell, thus what it is with hypocrites, flatterers, deceivers, and others.

From the correspondence of the heart with the will and of the lungs with the understanding, everything may be known that can be known about the will and understanding, or about love and wisdom, therefore about the soul of man

394. Many in the learned world have wearied themselves with inquiries respecting the soul; but as they knew nothing of the spiritual world, or of man's state after death, they could only frame theories, not about the nature of the soul, but about its operation on the body. Of the nature of the soul they could have no idea except as something most pure in the ether, and of its containing form they could have no idea except as being ethereal. But knowing that the soul is spiritual, they dared not say much about the matter openly, for fear of ascribing to the soul something natural.

With this conception of the soul, and yet knowing that the soul operates on the body, and produces all things in it that relate to its sensation and motion, they have wearied themselves, as was said, with inquiries respecting the operation of the soul on the body. This has been held by some to be effected by influx, and by some to be effected by harmony. But as this investigation has disclosed nothing in which the mind anxious to see the real truth can acquiesce, it has been granted me to speak with angels, and to be enlightened on the subject by their wisdom; the fruits of which are as follows: man's soul, which lives after death, is his spirit, and is in complete form a man; the soul of this form is the will and understanding, and the soul of these is love and wisdom from the Lord; these two are what constitute man's life, which is from the Lord alone; yet for the sake of man's reception of him, he causes life to appear as if it were man's; but that man may not claim life for himself as his, and thus withdraw himself from this reception of the Lord, the Lord has also taught that everything of love, which is called good, and everything of wisdom, which is called truth, is from him, and nothing of these from man; and as these two are life, that everything of life which is life is from him.

395. Since the soul in its very *esse* is love and wisdom, and these two in man are from the Lord, there are created in man two receptacles, which are also the abodes of the Lord in man; one for love, the other for wisdom, the one for love called the will, the other for wisdom called the understanding. Now since Love and Wisdom in the Lord are one distinctly (as may be seen above, n. 17–22), and Divine love is of his Divine wisdom, and Divine wisdom is of his Divine love (n. 34–39), and since these so go forth from God-man, that is, from the Lord, therefore these two receptacles and abodes of the Lord in man,

the will and understanding, are so created by the Lord as to be distinctly two, and yet make one in every operation and every sensation; for in these the will and understanding cannot be separated. Nevertheless, to enable man to become a receptacle and an abode of the Lord, it is provided, as necessary to this end, that man's understanding can be raised above his proper love into some light of wisdom in the love of which the man is not, and that he can thereby see and be taught how he must live if he would come also into that higher love, and thus enjoy eternal happiness. But by the misuse of this power to elevate the understanding above his proper love, man has subverted in himself that which might have been the receptacle and abode of the Lord (that is, of love and wisdom from the Lord), by making the will an abode for the love of self and the world, and the understanding an abode for whatever confirms those loves. From this it has come that these two abodes, the will and understanding, have become abodes of infernal love, and by confirmations in favor of these loves, abodes of infernal thought, which in hell is esteemed as wisdom.

396. The reason why the love of self and love of the world are infernal loves, and yet man has been able to come into them and thus subvert the will and understanding within him, is as follows: the love of self and the love of the world by creation are heavenly loves; for they are loves of the natural man serviceable to spiritual loves, as a foundation is to a house. For man, from the love of self and the world, seeks the welfare of his body, desires food, clothing, and habitation, is solicitous for the welfare of his family, and to secure employment for the sake of use, and even, in the interest of obedience, to be honored according to the dignity of the affairs which he administers, and to find delight and refreshment in worldly enjoyment; yet all this for the sake of the end, which must be use. For through these things man is in a state to serve the

Lord and to serve the neighbor. When, however, there is no love of serving the Lord and serving the neighbor, but only a love of serving himself by means of the world, then from being heavenly that love becomes hellish, for it causes a man to sink his mind and disposition in what is his own, and that in itself is wholly evil.

397. Now that man may not by the understanding be in heaven while by the will he is in hell, as is possible, and may thereby have a divided mind, after death everything of the understanding which transcends its own love is removed; whereby it comes that in everyone the will and understanding finally make one. With those in heaven the will loves good and the understanding thinks truth; but with those in hell the will loves evil and the understanding thinks falsity. The same is true of man in this world when he is thinking from his spirit, as he does when alone; yet many, so long as they are in the body, when they are not alone think otherwise. They then think otherwise because they raise their understanding above the proper love of their will, that is, of their spirit. These things have been said, to make known that the will and understanding are two distinct things, although created to act as one, and that they are made to act as one after death, if not before.

398. Now since love and wisdom, and therefore will and understanding, are what are called the soul, and how the soul acts upon the body, and effects all its operations, is to be shown in what follows, and since this may be known from the correspondence of the heart with the will, and of the lungs with the understanding, by means of that correspondence what follows has been disclosed:

(1) Love or the will is man's very life.

(2) Love or the will strives unceasingly towards the human form and all things of that form.

(3) Love or the will is unable to effect anything by its human form without a marriage with wisdom or the understanding.

(4) Love or the will prepares a house or bridal chamber for its future wife, which is wisdom or the understanding.

(5) Love or the will also prepares all things in its human form, that it may act conjointly with wisdom or the understanding.

(6) After the nuptials, the first conjunction is through affection for knowing, from which springs affection for truth.

(7) The second conjunction is through affection for understanding, from which springs perception of truth.

(8) The third conjunction is through affection for seeing truth, from which springs thought.

(9) Through these three conjunctions love or the will is in its sensitive life and in its active life.

(10) Love or the will introduces wisdom or the understanding into all things of its house.

(11) Love or the will does nothing except in conjunction with wisdom or the understanding.

(12) Love or the will conjoins itself to wisdom or the understanding, and causes wisdom or the understanding to be reciprocally conjoined to it.

(13) Wisdom or the understanding, from the potency given to it by love or the will, can be elevated, and can receive such things as are of light out of heaven, and perceive them.

(14) Love or the will can in like manner be elevated and can perceive such things as are of heat out of heaven, provided it loves its consort in that degree.

(15) Otherwise love or the will draws down wisdom or the understanding from its elevation, that it may act as one with itself.

(16) Love or the will is purified by wisdom in the understanding, if they are elevated together.

(17) Love or the will is defiled in the understanding and by it, if they are not elevated together.

(18) Love, when purified by wisdom in the understanding, becomes spiritual and celestial.

(19) Love, when defiled in the understanding and by it, becomes natural and sensual.

(20) The capacity to understand called rationality and the capacity to act called freedom still remain.

(21) Spiritual and celestial love is love towards the neighbor and love to the Lord; and natural and sensual love is love of the world and love of self.

(22) It is the same with charity and faith and their conjunction as with the will and understanding and their conjunction.

399. (1) *Love or the will is man's very life.* This follows from the correspondence of the heart with the will (considered above, n. 378–381). For as the heart acts in the body, so does the will act in the mind; and as all things of the body depend for existence and motion upon the heart, so do all things of the mind depend for existence and life upon the will. It is said, upon the will, but this means upon the love, because the will is the receptacle of love, and love is life itself (see above, n. 1–3), and love, which is life itself, is from the Lord alone. By the heart and its extension into the body through the arteries and veins it can be seen that love or the will is the life of man, for the reason that things that correspond to each other act in a like manner, except that one is natural and the other spiritual.

How the heart acts in the body is evident from anatomy, which shows that wherever the heart acts by means of the vessels put forth from it, everything is alive or subservient to life; but where the heart by means of its vessels does not act, everything is lifeless. Moreover, the heart is the first and last thing to act in the body. That it is the first is evident from the fetus, and that it is the last is evident from the dying, and that it may act without the cooperation of the lungs is evident from cases of suffocation and swooning; from which it can be seen that the life of the mind depends solely upon the will, in the same way as the substitute life of the body depends on the heart alone; and that the will lives when thought ceases, in the same way as the heart lives when breathing ceases. This also is evident from the fetus, from the dying, and from cases of suffocation and swooning. From which it follows that love or the will is man's very life.

400. (2) *Love or the will strives unceasingly towards the human form and all things of that form.* This is evident from the correspondence of heart and will. For it is known that all things of the body are formed in the womb, and that they are formed by means of fibers from the brains and blood vessels from the heart, and that out of these two the tissues of all organs and viscera are made; from which it is evident that all things of man have their existence from the life of the will, which is love, from their first principles, out of the brains, through the fibers; and all things of his body out of the heart through the arteries and veins. From this it is clearly evident that life (which is love and the will therefrom), strives unceasingly towards the human form. And as the human form is made up of all the things there are in man, it follows that love or the will is in a continual conatus and effort to form all these.

There is such a conatus and effort towards the human form, because God is a man, and Divine love and Divine wisdom is his life, and from his life is everything of life. Anyone can see that unless Life which is very man acted into that which in itself is not life, the formation of anything such as exists in man would be impossible, in whom are thousands of thousands of things that make a one, and that unanimously aspire to an image of the life from which they spring, that man may become a receptacle and abode of that life. From all this it can be seen that love, and out of the love the will, and out of the will the heart, strive unceasingly towards the human form.

401. (3) *Love or the will is unable to effect anything by its human form without a marriage with wisdom or the understanding.* This also is evident from the correspondence of the heart with the will. The embryo man lives by the heart, not by the lungs. For in the fetus the blood does not flow from the heart into the lungs, giving it the ability to respire; but it flows through the oval opening into the left ventricle of the heart; consequently the fetus is unable to move any part of its body, but lies enswathed, neither has it sensation, for its organs of sense are closed. So is it with love or the will, from which the fetus lives indeed, though obscurely, that is, without sensation or action. But as soon as the lungs are opened, which is the case after birth, he begins to feel and act, and likewise to will and think. From all this it can be seen, that love or the will is unable to effect anything by means of its human form without a marriage with wisdom or the understanding.

402. (4) *Love or the will prepares a house or bridal chamber for its future wife, which is wisdom or the understanding.* In the created universe and in each of its particulars there is a marriage of good and truth; and this is so because good is of love and truth is of wisdom, and these two are in the Lord, and out of him all things are created. How this marriage has existence in man can be seen mirrored in the conjunction of the heart with the lungs; since the heart corresponds to love or good, and the lungs to wisdom or truth (see above, n. 378–384). From that conjunction it can be seen how love or the will betroths to itself wisdom or the understanding, and afterwards weds it, that is, enters into a kind of marriage with it. Love betroths to itself wisdom by preparing for it a house or bridal chamber, and marries it by conjoining it to itself by affections, and afterwards lives wisely with it in that house. How this is cannot be fully described except in spiritual language, because love and wisdom, consequently will and understanding, are spiritual; and spiritual things can, indeed, be expressed in natural language, but can be perceived only obscurely, from a lack of knowledge of what love is, what wisdom is, what affections for good are, and what affections for wisdom, that is, affections for truth, are.

Yet the nature of the betrothal and of the marriage of love with wisdom, or of will with understanding, can be seen by the parallel that is furnished by their correspondence with the heart and lungs. What is true of these is true of love and wisdom, so entirely that there is no difference whatever except that one is natural and the other spiritual. Thus it is evident from the heart and lungs, that the heart first forms the lungs, and afterwards joins itself to them; it forms the lungs in the fetus, and joins itself to them after birth. This the heart does in its abode which is called the breast, where the two are encamped together, separated from the other parts of the body by a partition called the diaphragm and by a covering called the pleura. So it is with love and wisdom or with will and understanding.

403. (5) *Love or the will prepares all things in its own human form, that it may act conjointly with wisdom or the understanding.* We say, will and understanding, but it is to be carefully borne in mind that the will is the entire man; for it is the will that, with the understanding, is in first principles in the brains, and in derivatives in the body, consequently in the whole and in every part (see above, n. 365–367). From this it can be seen that the will is the entire man as regards his very form, both the general form and the particular form of all parts; and that the understanding is its partner, as the lungs are the partner of

the heart. Beware of cherishing an idea of the will as something separate from the human form, for it is that same form. From this it can be seen not only how the will prepares a bridal chamber for the understanding, but also how it prepares all things in its house (which is the whole body) that it may act conjointly with the understanding. This it prepares in such a way that as each and every thing of the body is conjoined to the will, so is it conjoined to the understanding; in other words, that as each and every thing of the body is submissive to the will, so is it submissive to the understanding.

How each and every thing of the body is prepared for conjunction with the understanding as well as with the will, can be seen in the body only as in a mirror or image, by the aid of anatomical knowledge, which shows how all things in the body are so connected, that when the lungs respire each and every thing in the entire body is moved by the respiration of the lungs, and at the same time from the beating of the heart. Anatomy shows that the heart is joined to the lungs through the auricles, which are continued into the interiors of the lungs; also that all the viscera of the entire body are joined through ligaments to the chamber of the breast; and so joined that when the lungs respire, each and all things, in general and in particular, partake of the respiratory motion.

Thus when the lungs are inflated, the ribs expand the thorax, the pleura is dilated, and the diaphragm is stretched wide, and with these all the lower parts of the body, which are connected with them by ligaments therefrom, receive some action through the pulmonic action; not to mention further facts, lest those who have no knowledge of anatomy, on account of their ignorance of its terms should be confused in regard to the subject. Consult any skillful and discerning anatomist whether all things in the entire body, from the breast down be not so bound together, that when the lungs expand by respiration, each and all of them are moved to action synchronous with the pulmonic action. From all this the nature of the conjunction prepared by the will between the understanding and each and every thing of the human form is now evident. Only explore the connections well and scan them with an anatomical eye; then, following the connections, consider their cooperation with the breathing lungs and with the heart; and finally, in thought, substitute for the lungs the understanding, and for the heart the will, and you will see.

404. (6) *After the nuptials, the first conjunction is through affection for knowing, from which springs affection for truth.* By the nuptials is meant man's state after birth, from a state of ignorance to a state of intelligence, and from this to a state of wisdom. The first state which is one of pure ignorance, is not meant here by nuptials, because there is then no thought from the understanding, and only an obscure affection from the love or will. This state is initiatory to the nuptials. In the second state, which belongs to man in childhood, there is, as we know, an affection for knowing, by means of which the infant child learns to speak and to read, and afterwards gradually learns such things as belong to the understanding. That it is love, belonging to the will, that effects this, cannot be doubted; for unless it were effected by love or the will it would not be done.

That every man has, after birth, an affection for knowing, and through that acquires the knowledge by which his understanding is gradually formed, enlarged, and perfected, is acknowledged by everyone who thoughtfully takes counsel of experience. It is also evident that from this comes affection for truth; for when man, from affection for knowing, has become intelligent, he is led not so much by affection for knowing as by affection for reasoning and forming conclusions on subjects which he loves, whether economical or civil or moral. When this affection is raised to spiritual things, it becomes affection for spiritual truth. That its first initiatory state was affection for knowing, may be seen from the fact that affection for truth is an exalted affection for knowing; for to be affected by truths is the same as to wish from affection to know them, and when found, to drink them in from the joy of affection.

(7) *The second conjunction is through affection for understanding, from which springs perception of truth.* This is evident to anyone who is willing by rational insight to examine the matter. From rational insight it is clear that affection for truth and perception of truth are two powers of the understanding, which in some persons harmonize as one, and in others do not.

They harmonize as one in those who wish to perceive truths with the understanding, but do not in those who only wish to know truths. It is also clear that everyone is in perception of truth so far as he is in an affection for understanding; for if you take away affection for understanding truth, there will be no perception of truth; but give the affection for understanding truth, and there will be perception of truth according to the degree of affection for it. No man of sound reason ever lacks perception of truth, so long as he has affection for understanding truth. That every man has a capacity to understand truth, which is called rationality, has been shown above.

(8) *The third conjunction is through affection for seeing truth, from which springs thought.* That affection for knowing is one thing, affection for understanding another, and affection for seeing truth another, or that affection for truth is one thing, perception of truth another, and thought another, is seen but obscurely by those who cannot perceive the operations of the mind as distinct, but is seen clearly by those who can. This is obscurely seen by those who do not perceive the operations of the mind as distinct, because with those who are in affection for truth and in perception of truth, these operations are simultaneous in the thought, and when simultaneous they

cannot be distinguished. Man is in manifest thought when his spirit thinks in the body, which is especially the case when he is in company with others; but when he is in affection for understanding, and through that comes into perception of truth, he is then in the thought of his spirit, which is meditation. This passes, indeed, into the thought of the body, but into silent thought; for it is above bodily thought, and looks upon what belongs to thought from the memory as below itself, drawing therefrom either conclusions or confirmations. But real affection for truth is perceived only as a pressure of will from something pleasurable which is interiorly in meditation as its life, and is little noticed.

From all this it can now be seen that these three, affection for truth, perception of truth, and thought, follow in order from love, and that they have existence only in the understanding. For when love enters into the understanding, which it does when their conjunction is accomplished, it first brings forth affection for truth, then affection for understanding that which it knows, and lastly, affection for seeing in the bodily thought that which it understands; for thought is nothing but internal sight. It is true that thought is the first to be manifest, because it is of the natural mind; but thought from perception of truth which is from affection for truth is the last to be manifest; this thought is the thought of wisdom, but the other is thought from the memory through the sight of the natural mind. All operations of love or the will not within the understanding have relation not to affections for truth, but to affections for good.

405. That these three from the will's love follow in order in the understanding can, indeed, be comprehended by the rational man, but yet cannot be clearly seen and thus so proved as to command belief. But as love that is of the will acts as one with the heart by correspondence, and wisdom that is of the understanding acts as one with the lungs (as has been shown above) therefore what has been said (in n. 404) about affection for truth, perception of truth, and thought, can nowhere be more clearly seen and proved than in the lungs and the mechanism thereof. These, therefore, shall be briefly described.

After birth, the heart discharges the blood from its right ventricle into the lungs; and after passing through these it is emptied into the left ventricle: thus the heart opens the lungs. This it does through the pulmonary arteries and veins. The lungs have bronchial tubes which ramify, and at length end in air cells, into which the lungs admit the air, and thus respire. Around the bronchial tubes and their ramifications there are also arteries and veins called the bronchial, arising from the azygous veins or vena cava, and from the aorta. These arteries and veins are distinct from the pulmonary arteries and veins. From this it is evident that the blood flows into the lungs by two ways, and flows out from them by two ways. This enables the lungs to respire nonsynchronously with the heart. That the alternate movements of the heart and the alternate movements of the lungs do not act as one is well known.

Now, inasmuch as there is a correspondence of the heart and lungs with the will and understanding (as shown above), and inasmuch as conjunction by correspondence is of such a nature that as one acts so does the other, it can be seen by the flow of the blood out of the heart into the lungs how the will flows into the understanding, and produces the results mentioned just above (n. 404) respecting affection for and perception of truth, and respecting thought. By correspondence this and many other things relating to the subject, which cannot be explained in a few words, have been disclosed to me. Whereas love or the will corresponds to the heart, and wisdom or the understanding to the lungs, it follows that the blood vessels of the heart in the lungs correspond to affections for truth, and the ramifications of the bronchia of the lungs to perceptions and thoughts from those affections. Whoever will trace out all the tissues of the lungs from these origins, and disclose the analogy with the love of the will and the wisdom of the understanding, will be able to see in a kind of image the things mentioned above (n. 404), and thereby attain to a confirmed belief. But since a few only are familiar with the anatomical details respecting the heart and lungs, and since confirming a thing by what is unfamiliar induces obscurity, I omit further demonstration of the analogy.

406. (9) *Through these three conjunctions love or the will is in its sensitive life and in its active life.* Love without the understanding, or affection which is of love without thought, which is of the understanding, can neither feel nor act in the body; since love without the understanding is as it were blind, and affection without thought is as it were in thick darkness, for the understanding is the light by which love sees. The wisdom of the understanding, moreover, is from the light that proceeds from the Lord as a sun.

Since, then, the will's love, without the light of the understanding, sees nothing and is blind, it follows that without the light of the understanding even the bodily senses would be blind and blunted, not only sight and hearing, but the other senses also, the other senses, because all perception of truth is a property of love in the understanding (as was shown above), and all the bodily senses derive their perception from their mind's perception. The same is true of every bodily act; for action from love without understanding is like man's action in the dark, when he does not know what he is doing; consequently in such action there would be nothing of intelligence and wisdom. Such action cannot be called living action, for action derives its *esse* from love and its quality from intelligence. Moreover, the whole power of good is by means of truth; consequently good acts in truth, and thus by means of truth; and good is of love, and truth is of the understanding. From all this it can be seen that love or the will through these three conjunctions (see above, n. 404) is in its sensitive life and in its active life.

407. That this is so can be proved to the life by the conjunction of the heart with the lungs, because the correspondence between the will and the heart, and between the understanding and the lungs, is such that just as the love acts with the understanding spiritually, so does the heart act with the lungs naturally: from this, what has been said above can be seen as in an image presented to the eye. That man has neither any sensitive life nor any active life, so long as the heart and the lungs do not act together, is evident from the state of the fetus or the infant in the womb, and from its state after birth. So long as man is a fetus, that is, in the womb, the lungs are closed, wherefore he has no feeling nor any action; the organs of sense are closed up, the hands are bound, likewise the feet; but after birth the lungs are opened, and as they are opened man feels and acts; the lungs are opened by means of the blood sent into them from the heart.

That man has neither sensitive life nor active life without the cooperation of the heart and the lungs, is evident also in swoons, when the heart alone acts, and not the lungs, for respiration then ceases; in this case there is no sensation and no action, as is well known. It is the same with persons suffocated, either by water or by anything obstructing the larynx and closing the respiratory passage; it is well known that the man then appears to be dead, he feels nothing and does nothing; and yet he is alive in the heart; for he returns to both his sensitive and his active life as soon as the obstructions to the lungs are removed. The blood, it is true, circulates in the meantime through the lungs, but through the pulmonary arteries and veins, not through the bronchial arteries and veins, and these last are what give man the power of breathing. It is the same with the influx of love into the understanding.

408. (10) *Love or the will introduces wisdom or the understanding into all things of its house.* By the house of love or the will is meant the whole man as to all things of his mind; and as these correspond to all things of the body (as shown above), by the house is meant also the whole man as to all things of his body, called members, organs, and viscera. That the lungs are introduced into all these things just as the understanding is introduced into all things of the mind, can be seen from what has been shown above, namely, that love or the will prepares a house or bridal chamber for its future wife, which is wisdom or the understanding (n. 402); and that love or the will prepares all things in its own human form, that is, in its house, that it may act conjointly with wisdom or the understanding (n. 403). From what is there said, it is evident that each and all things in the whole body are so connected by ligaments issuing from the ribs, vertebrae, sternum, and diaphragm, and from the peritoneum which depends on these, that when the lungs respire all are likewise drawn and borne along in alternate movements. Anatomy shows that the alternate waves of respiration even enter into the very viscera to their inmost recesses; for the ligaments above mentioned cleave to the sheaths of the viscera, and these sheaths, by their extensions, penetrate to their innermost parts, as do the arteries and veins also by their ramifications.

From this it is evident that the respiration of the lungs is in entire conjunction with the heart in each and every thing of the body; and in order that the conjunction may be complete in every respect, even the heart itself is in pulmonic motion, for it lies in the bosom of the lungs and is connected with them by the auricles, and reclines upon the diaphragm, whereby its arteries also participate in the pulmonic motion. The stomach, too, is in similar conjunction with the lungs, by the coherence of its esophagus with the trachea. These anatomical facts are adduced to show what kind of a conjunction there is of love or the will with wisdom or the understanding, and how the two in consort are conjoined with all things of the mind; for the spiritual and the bodily conjunction are similar.

409. (11) *Love or the will does nothing except in conjunction with wisdom or the understanding.* For as love has no sensitive nor any active life apart from the understanding, and as love introduces the understanding into all things of the mind (as was shown above, n. 407, 408), it follows that love or the will does nothing except in conjunction with the understanding. For what is it to act from love without the understanding? Such action can only be called irrational; for the understanding teaches what ought to be done and how it ought to be done. Apart from the understanding love does not know this; consequently such is the marriage between love and the understanding, that although they are two, they act as one.

There is a like marriage between good and truth, for good is of love and truth is of the understanding. In every particular thing of the universe as created by the Lord there is such a marriage, their use having relation to good, and the form of their use to truth. From this marriage it is that in each and every thing of the body there is a right and a left, the right having relation to the good from which truth proceeds, and the left to truth from good, thus to their conjunction.

From this it is that there are pairs in man; there are two brains, two hemispheres of the brain, two ventricles of the heart, two lobes of the lungs, two eyes, ears, nostrils, arms, hands, loins, feet, kidneys, testicles, etc.; and where there are not pairs, there is a right and a left side, all this for the reason that good looks to truth that it may take form, and truth looks to good that it may have being. It is the same in the angelic heavens and in their several societies. On this subject more may be seen above (n. 401), where it is shown that love or the will is unable to effect anything by its human form without a marriage with wisdom or the understanding. Conjunction of evil and falsity, which is opposite to the conjunction of good and truth, will be spoken of elsewhere.

410. (12) *Love or the will conjoins itself to wisdom or the understanding, and causes wisdom or the understanding to be reciprocally conjoined to it.* That love or the will conjoins itself to wisdom or the understanding is plain from their correspondence with the heart and lungs. Anatomical observation shows that the heart is in its life's motion when the lungs are not yet in motion; this it shows by cases of swooning and of suffocation, also by the fetus in the womb and the chick in the egg.

Anatomical observation shows also that the heart, while acting alone, forms the lungs and so adjusts them that it may carry on respiration in them; also that it so forms the other viscera and organs that it may carry on various uses in them, the organs of the face that it may have sensation, the organs of motion that it may act, and the remaining parts of the body that it may exhibit uses corresponding to the affections of love. From all this it can now for the first time be shown that as the heart produces such things for the sake of the various functions which it is afterwards to discharge in the body, so love, in its receptacle called the will, produces like things for the sake of the various affections that constitute its form, which is the human form (as was shown above). Now as the first and nearest of love's affections are affection for knowing, affection for understanding, and affection for seeing what it knows and understands, it follows, that for these affections love forms the understanding and actually enters into them when it begins to feel and to act and to think. To this the understanding contributes nothing, as is evident from the analogy of the heart and lungs (of which above). From all this it can be seen, that love or the will conjoins itself to wisdom or the understanding, and not wisdom or the understanding to love or the will; also from this it is evident that knowledge, which love acquires to itself by the affection for knowing, and perception of truth, which it acquires by the affection for understanding, and thought which it acquires by the affection for seeing what it knows and understands, are not of the understanding but of love.

Thoughts, perceptions, and knowledges therefrom, flow in, it is true, out of the spiritual world, yet they are received not by the understanding but by love, according to its affections in the understanding. It appears as if the understanding received them, and not love or the will, but this is an illusion. It appears also as if the understanding conjoined itself to love or the will, but this too, is an illusion; love or the will conjoins itself to the understanding, and causes the understanding to be reciprocally conjoined to it. This reciprocal conjunction is from love's marriage with wisdom, wherefrom a conjunction seemingly reciprocal, from the life and consequent power of love, is effected.

It is the same with the marriage of good and truth; for good is of love and truth is of the understanding. Good does everything and it receives truth into its house and conjoins itself with it so far as the truth is accordant. Good can also admit truths which are not accordant; but this it does from an affection for knowing, for understanding, and for thinking its own things, whilst it has not as yet determined itself to uses, which are its ends and are called its goods. Of reciprocal conjunction, that is, the conjunction of truth with good, there is none whatever. That truth is reciprocally conjoined is from the life belonging to good. From this it is that every man and every spirit and angel is regarded by the Lord according to his love or good, and no one according to his intellect, or his truth separate from love or good. For man's life is his love (as was shown above), and his life is qualified according as he has exalted his affections by means of truth, that is, according as he has perfected his affections by wisdom. For the affections of love are exalted and perfected by means of truths, thus by means of wisdom. Then love acts conjointly with its wisdom, as though from it; but it acts from itself through wisdom, as through its own form, and this derives nothing whatever from the understanding, but everything from a kind of determination of love called affection.

411. All things that favor it love calls its goods, and all things that as means lead to goods it calls its truths; and because these are means they are loved and come to be of its affection and thus become affections in form; therefore truth is nothing else than a form of the affection that is of love. The human form is nothing else than the form of all the affections of love; beauty is its intelligence, which it procures for itself through truths received either by sight or by hearing, external and internal. These are what love disposes into the form of its affections; and these forms exist in great variety; but all derive a likeness from their general form, which is the human. To the love all such forms are beautiful and lovely, but others are unbeautiful and unlovely. From this, again, it is evident that love conjoins itself to the understanding, and not the reverse, and that the reciprocal conjunction is also from love. This is what is meant by love or the will causing wisdom or the understanding to be reciprocally conjoined to it.

412. What has been said may be seen in a kind of image and thus corroborated by the correspondence of the heart with love and of the lungs with the understanding (of which above). For if the heart corresponds to love, its determinations, which are arteries and veins, correspond to affections, and in the lungs to affections for truth; and as there are also other vessels in the

lungs called air vessels, whereby respiration is carried on, these vessels correspond to perceptions. It must be distinctly understood that the arteries and veins in the lungs are not affections, and that respirations are not perceptions and thoughts, but that they are correspondences, that is, they act correspondently or synchronously; likewise that the heart and the lungs are not the love and understanding, but correspondences; and inasmuch as they are correspondences the one can be seen in the other.

Whoever from anatomy has come to understand the whole structure of the lungs can see clearly, when he compares it with the understanding, that the understanding does not act at all by itself, does not perceive nor think by itself, but acts wholly by affections which are of love. These, in the understanding, are called affection for knowing, for understanding, and for seeing truth (which have been treated of above). For all states of the lungs depend on the blood from the heart and from the vena cava and aorta; and respirations, which take place in the bronchial branches, proceed in accordance with the state of those vessels; for when the flow of the blood stops, respiration stops.

Much more may be disclosed by comparing the structure of the lungs with the understanding, to which the lungs correspond; but as few are familiar with anatomical science, and to try to demonstrate or prove anything by what is unknown renders it obscure, it is not well to say more on this subject. By what I know of the structure of the lungs I am fully convinced that love through its affections conjoins itself to the understanding, and that the understanding does not conjoin itself to any affection of love, but that it is reciprocally conjoined by love, to the end that love may have sensitive life and active life. But it must not be forgotten that man has a twofold respiration, one of the spirit and another of the body; and that the respiration of the spirit depends on the fibers from the brains, and the respiration of the body on the blood vessels from the heart, and from the vena cava and aorta. It is evident, moreover, that thought produces respiration; it is evident, also, that affection, which is of love, produces thought, for thought without affection is precisely like respiration without a heart, a thing impossible. From this it is clear that affection, which is of love, conjoins itself to thought, which is of the understanding (as was said above), in like manner as the heart does in the lungs.

413. (13) *Wisdom or the understanding, from the potency given to it by love, can be elevated and can receive such things as are of light out of heaven, and perceive them.* That man has the ability to perceive arcana of wisdom when he hears them, has been shown above in many places. This capacity of man is called rationality. It belongs to every man by creation. It is the capacity to understand things interiorly, and to decide what is just and right, and what is good and true; and by it man is distinguished from beasts. This, then, is what is meant when it is said, that the understanding can be elevated and receive things that are of light out of heaven, and perceive them. That this is so can also be seen in a kind of image in the lungs, for the reason that the lungs correspond to the understanding. In the lungs it can be seen from their cellular substance, which consists of bronchial tubes continued down to the minutest air cells, which are receptacles of air in respirations; these are what the thoughts make one with by correspondence.

This cell-like substance is such that it can be expanded and contracted in a twofold mode, in one mode with the heart, in the other almost separate from the heart. In the former, it is expanded and contracted through the pulmonary arteries and veins, which are from the heart alone; in the latter, through the bronchial arteries and veins, which are from the vena cava and aorta, and these vessels are outside of the heart. This takes place in the lungs for the reason that the understanding is capable of being raised above its proper love, which corresponds to the heart, and to receive light from heaven. Still, when the understanding is raised above its proper love, it does not withdraw from it, but derives from it what is called the affection for knowing and understanding, with a view to somewhat of honor, glory, or gain in the world; this clings to every love as a surface, and by it the love shines on the surface, but with the wise, the love shines through. These things respecting the lungs are brought forward to prove that the understanding can be elevated and can receive and perceive things that are of the light of heaven; for the correspondence is plenary. To see from correspondence is to see the lungs from the understanding, and the understanding from the lungs, and thus from both together to perceive proof.

414. (14) *Love or the will can in like manner be elevated and can receive such things as are of heat out of heaven provided it loves wisdom, its consort, in that degree.* That the understanding can be elevated into the light of heaven, and from that light draw forth wisdom, has been shown in the preceding chapter and in many places above; also that love or the will can be elevated as well, provided it loves those things that are of the light of heaven or that are of wisdom, has also been shown in many places.

Yet love or the will cannot be thus elevated through anything of honor, glory, or gain as an end, but only through a love of use, thus not for the sake of self, but for the sake of the neighbor; and because this love is given only by the Lord out of heaven, and is given by the Lord when man flees from evils as sins, therefore it is that love or the will can be elevated by these means, and cannot without these means. But love or the will is elevated into heaven's heat, while the understanding is elevated into its light. When both are elevated, a marriage of the two takes place there, which is called celestial marriage, because it is a marriage of celestial love and wisdom; consequently it is said that love also is elevated if it loves wisdom, its consort, in that degree. The love of wisdom, that is, the genuine love of the human understanding, is love toward the neighbor from the Lord. It is the same with light and heat in the world. Light exists without heat and with heat; light is without heat in winter and with heat in summer; and when heat is with light all things flourish. The light with man that corresponds to the light of winter is wisdom without its love; and the light with man that corresponds to the light of summer is wisdom with its love.

415. This conjunction and disjunction of wisdom and love can be seen effigied, as it were, in the conjunction of the lungs with the heart. For the heart can be conjoined to the clustering vesicles of the bronchia by blood sent out from itself, and also by blood sent out not from itself but from the vena cava and the aorta. Thereby the respiration of the body can be separated from the respiration of the spirit; but when blood from the heart alone acts the respirations cannot be separated.

Now since thoughts act as one with respirations by correspondence it is plain, from the twofold state of the lungs in respirations, that man is able to think and from thoughts to speak and act in one way when in company with others, and to think and from thought to speak and act in another way when not in company, that is, when he has no fear of loss of reputation; for he can then think and speak against God, the neighbor, the spiritual things of the church, and against moral and civil laws; and he can also act contrary to them, by stealing, by being revengeful, by blaspheming, by committing adultery. But in company with others, where he is afraid of losing reputation, he can talk, preach, and act precisely like a spiritual, moral, and civil man. From all this it can be seen that

love or the will as well as the understanding can be elevated
and can receive such things as are of the heat or love of heaven,
provided it loves wisdom in that degree, and if it does not love
wisdom, that it can as it were be separated.

416. (15) *Otherwise love or the will draws down wisdom, or the
understanding, from its elevation, that it may act as one with
itself.* There is natural love and there is spiritual love. A man
who is in natural and in spiritual love both at once, is a
rational man; but one who is in natural love alone, although
able to think rationally, precisely like a spiritual man, is not a
rational man; for although he elevates his understanding even
to heavenly light, thus to wisdom, yet the things of wisdom,
that is, of heavenly light, do not belong to his love. His love,
it is true, effects the elevation, but from desire for honor, glory,
and gain. But when he perceives that he gains nothing of the
kind from that elevation (as is the case when he thinks with
himself from his own natural love), then he does not love the
things of heavenly light or wisdom; consequently he then draws
down the understanding from its height, that it may act as one
with himself.

For example: when the understanding by its elevation is in
wisdom, then the love sees what justice is, what sincerity is,
what chastity is, even what genuine love is. This the natural
love can see by its capacity to understand and contemplate
things in heavenly light; it can even talk and preach about these
and explain them as at once moral and spiritual virtues. But
when the understanding is not elevated, the love, if it is merely
natural, does not see these virtues, but instead of justice it sees
injustice, instead of sincerity deceit, instead of chastity lewd-
ness, and so on. If it then thinks of the things it spoke of when
its understanding was in elevation, it can laugh at them and
speak of them merely as serviceable to it in captivating the
souls of men. From all this it can be seen how it is to be

understood that love, unless it loves wisdom, its consort, in that degree, draws wisdom down from its elevation, that it may act as one with itself. That love is capable of elevation if it loves wisdom in that degree, can be seen above (n. 414).

417. Now as love corresponds to the heart, and the understanding to the lungs, the foregoing statements may be corroborated by their correspondence; as, for instance, how the understanding can be elevated above its own love even into wisdom; and how, if that love is merely natural, the understanding is drawn down by it from that elevation. Man has a twofold respiration; one of the body, the other of the spirit. These two respirations may be separated and they may be conjoined; with men merely natural, especially with hypocrites, they are separated, but rarely with men who are spiritual and sincere. Consequently a merely natural man and hypocrite, whose understanding has been elevated, and in whose memory therefore various things of wisdom remain, can talk wisely in company by thought from the memory; but when not in company, he does not think from the memory, but from his spirit, thus from his love. He also respires in like manner, inasmuch as thought and respiration act correspondently. That the structure of the lungs is such that they can respire both by blood from the heart and by blood from outside of the heart has been shown above.

418. It is the common opinion that wisdom makes the man; therefore when anyone is heard to talk and teach wisely he is believed to be wise; yea, he himself believes it at the time, because when he talks or teaches in company he thinks from the memory, and if he is a merely natural man, from the surface of his love, which is a desire for honor, glory, and gain; but when the same man is alone he thinks from the more inward love of his spirit, and then not wisely, but sometimes insanely. From all this it can be seen that no one is to be judged of by wise speaking, but by his life; that is, not by wise speaking separate from life, but by wise speaking conjoined to life. By life is meant love. That love is the life has been shown above.

419. (16) *Love or the will is purified in the understanding, if they are elevated together.* From birth man loves nothing but self and the world, for nothing else appears before his eyes, consequently nothing else occupies his mind. This love is corporeal-natural, and may be called material love. Moreover, this love has become impure by reason of the separation of heavenly love from it in parents. This love could not be separated from its impurity unless man had a power to raise his understanding into the light of heaven, and to see how he ought to live in order that his love, as well as his understanding, may be elevated into wisdom. By means of the understanding, love, that is, the man, sees what the evils are that defile and corrupt the love; he also sees that if he flees from those evils as sins and turns away from them, he loves the things that are opposite to those evils; all of which are heavenly. Then also he perceives the means by which he is enabled to flee from and turn away from those evils as sins. This the love, that is, the man, sees, by the exercise of his power to elevate his understanding into the light of heaven, which is the source of wisdom. Then so far as love gives heaven the first place and the world the second, and at the same time gives the Lord the first place and self the second, so far love is purged of its uncleanness and is purified; in other words, is raised into the heat of heaven, and conjoined with the light of heaven in which the understanding is; and the marriage takes place that is called the marriage of good and truth, that is, of love and wisdom.

Anyone can comprehend intellectually and see rationally, that so far as he flees from and turns away from theft and cheating, so far he loves sincerity, rectitude and justice; so far as he flees and turns away from revenge and hatred, so far he loves the neighbor; and so far as he flees and turns away from adulteries, so far he loves chastity; and so on. And yet scarcely anyone knows what there is of heaven and the Lord in sincerity, rectitude, justice, love towards the neighbor, chastity, and other affections of heavenly love, until he has removed their opposites. When he has removed the opposites, then he is in those affections, and therefrom recognizes and sees them. Previously there is a kind of veil interposed, that does, indeed, transmit to love the light of heaven; yet inasmuch as the love does not in that degree love its consort, wisdom, it does not receive it, yea, may even contradict and rebuke it when it returns from its elevation.

Still man flatters himself that the wisdom of his understanding may be made serviceable as a means to honor, glory, or gain. Then man gives self and the world the first place, and the Lord and heaven the second, and what has the second place is loved only so far as it is serviceable, and if it is not serviceable it is disowned and rejected; if not before death, then after it. From all this the truth is now evident, that love or the will is purified in the understanding if they are elevated together.

420. The same thing is imaged in the lungs, whose arteries and veins correspond to the affections of love, and whose respirations correspond to the perceptions and thoughts of the understanding, as has been said above. That the heart's blood is purified of undigested matters in the lungs, and nourishes itself with suitable food from the inhaled air, is evident from much observation. (a) That the blood is purified of undigested matter in the lungs, is evident not only from the influent blood, which is venous, and therefore filled with the chyle collected from food and drink, but also from the moisture of the outgoing breath and from its odor as perceived by others, as well as from the diminished quantity of the blood flowing

back into the left ventricle of the heart. (b) That the blood
nourishes itself with suitable food from the inhaled air is
evident from the immense volumes of odors and exhalations
continually flowing forth from fields, gardens, and woods; from
the immense supply of salts of various kinds in the water that
rises from the ground and from rivers and ponds, and from the
immense quantity of exhalations and effluvia from human
beings and animals with which the air is impregnated.

That these things flow into the lungs with the inhaled air is
undeniable; it is therefore undeniable also that from them the
blood draws such things as are useful to it; and such things are
useful as correspond to the affections of its love. For this reason
there are, in the vesicles or innermost recesses of the lungs,
little veins in great abundance with tiny mouths that absorb
these suitable matters; consequently, the blood that flows back
into the left ventricle of the heart is changed into arterial blood
of brilliant hue.

These facts prove that the blood purifies itself of heterogeneous things and nourishes itself with homogeneous things.
That the blood in the lungs purifies and nourishes itself
correspondently to the affections of the mind is as yet unknown; but in the spiritual world it is very well known, for
angels in the heavens find delight only in the odors that
correspond to the love of their wisdom, while the spirits in hell
find delight only in the odors that correspond to a love
opposed to wisdom; these are foul odors, but the former are
fragrant. It follows that men in the world impregnate their
blood with similar things according to correspondence with the
affections of their love; for what the spirit of a man loves, his
blood according to correspondence craves and by respiration
attracts. From this correspondence it results that man as regards
his love is purified if he loves wisdom, and is defiled if he does
not love it. Moreover, all purification of man is effected by

means of the truths of wisdom, and all pollution of man is effected by means of falsities that are opposite to the truths of wisdom.

421. (17) *Love or the will is defiled in the understanding and by it, if they are not elevated together.* This is because love, if not elevated, remains impure (as stated above, n. 419, 420); and while it remains impure it loves what is impure, such as revenges, hatreds, deceits, blasphemies, adulteries, for these are then its affections that are called lusts, and it rejects what belongs to charity, justice, sincerity, truth, and chastity. Love is said to be defiled in the understanding, and by it; in the understanding, when love is affected by these impure things; by the understanding, when love makes the things of wisdom to become its servants, and still more when it perverts, falsifies, and adulterates them.

Of the corresponding state of the heart, or of its blood in the lungs, there is no need to say more than has been said above (n. 420), except that instead of the purification of the blood its defilement takes place; and instead of the nutrition of the blood by fragrant odors its nutrition is effected by stenches, precisely as it is respectively in heaven and in hell.

422. (18) *Love, when purified by wisdom in the understanding, becomes spiritual and celestial.* Man is born natural, but in the measure in which his understanding is raised into the light of heaven, and his love conjointly is raised into the heat of heaven, he becomes spiritual and celestial; he then becomes like a garden of Eden, which is at once in vernal light and vernal heat. It is not the understanding that becomes spiritual and celestial, but the love; and when the love has so become, it makes its consort, the understanding, spiritual and celestial. Love becomes spiritual and celestial by a life according to the truths of wisdom which the understanding teaches and requires. Love imbibes these truths by means of its understanding, and not from itself; for love cannot elevate itself unless it knows truths, and these it can learn only by means of an elevated and enlightened understanding; and then so far as it loves truths in the practice of them so far it is elevated; for to understand is one thing and to will is another; or to say is one thing and to do is another. There are those who understand and talk about the truths of wisdom, yet neither will nor practice them.

When, therefore, love puts in practice the truths of light which it understands and speaks, it is elevated. This one can see from reason alone; for what kind of a man is he who understands the truths of wisdom and talks about them while he lives contrary to them, that is, while his will and conduct are opposed to them? Love purified by wisdom becomes spiritual and celestial, for the reason that man has three degrees of life, called natural, spiritual, and celestial (of which in chapter 3 of this work), and he is capable of elevation from one degree into another. Yet he is not elevated by wisdom alone, but by a life according to wisdom, for a man's life is his love. Consequently, so far as his life is according to wisdom, so far he loves wisdom; and his life is so far according to wisdom as he purifies himself from uncleannesses, which are sins; and so far as he does this does he love wisdom.

423. That love purified by the wisdom in the understanding becomes spiritual and celestial cannot be seen so clearly by their correspondence with the heart and lungs, because no one can see the quality of the blood by which the lungs are kept in their state of respiration. The blood may abound in impurities, and yet not be distinguishable from pure blood. Moreover, the respiration of a merely natural man appears the same as the respiration of a spiritual man. But the difference is clearly discerned in heaven, for there everyone respires according to the marriage of love and wisdom; therefore as angels are recognized according to that marriage, so are they recognized according to their respiration. For this reason it is that when one who is not in that marriage enters heaven, he is seized with anguish in the breast, and struggles for breath like a man in the agonies of death; such persons therefore throw themselves headlong from the place, nor do they find rest until they are among those who are in a respiration similar to their own; for then by correspondence they are in similar affection, and therefore in similar thought. From all this it can be seen that with the spiritual man it is the purer blood, called by some the animal spirit, which is purified; and that it is purified so far as the man is in the marriage of love and wisdom. It is this purer blood which corresponds most nearly to that marriage; and because this blood inflows into the blood of the body, it follows that the latter blood is also purified by means of it.

The reverse is true of those in whom love is defiled in the understanding. But, as was said, no one can test this by any experiment on the blood; but he can by observing the affections of love, since these correspond to the blood.

424. (19) *Love, when defiled in the understanding and by it, becomes natural, sensual, and corporeal.* Natural love separated from spiritual love is the opposite of spiritual love; because natural love is love of self and of the world, and spiritual love is love to the Lord and love to the neighbor; and love of self and the world looks downward and outward, and love to the Lord looks upward and inward. Consequently when natural love is separated from spiritual love it cannot be elevated above what is man's own, but remains immersed in it, and so far as it loves it, is glued to it. Then if the understanding ascends, and sees by the light of heaven such things as are of wisdom, this natural love draws down such wisdom, and joins her to itself in what is its own; and there either rejects the things of wisdom or falsifies them or encircles itself with them, that it may talk about them for reputation's sake. As natural love can ascend by degrees and become spiritual and celestial, in the same way it can descend by degrees and become sensual and corporeal, and it does descend so far as it loves dominion from no love of use, but solely from love of self. It is this love which is called the devil. Those who are in this love are able to speak and act in the same manner as those who are in spiritual love; but they do this either from memory or from the understanding elevated by itself into the light of heaven.

Nevertheless, what they say and do is comparatively like fruit that appears beautiful on the surface but is wholly rotten within; or like almonds which from the shell appear sound but are wholly worm-eaten within. These things in the spiritual world are called fantasies, and by means of them harlots, there called sirens, make themselves appear handsome, and adorn themselves with beautiful garments; but when the fantasy is dissipated the sirens appear like ghosts, and are like devils who make themselves angels of light. For when that corporeal love draws its understanding down from its elevation, as it does when man is alone and thinks from his own love, then he thinks against God in favor of nature, against heaven in favor of the world, and against the truths and goods of the church in favor of the falsities and evils of hell; thus against wisdom.

From this the character of those who are called corporeal men can be seen: for they are not corporeal in understanding, but corporeal in love; that is, they are not corporeal in understanding when they converse in company, but are so when they hold converse with themselves in spirit; and being such in spirit, therefore after death they become, both in love and in understanding, spirits that are called corporeal. Those who in the world had been in a supreme love of ruling from the love of self, and had also surpassed others in elevation of understanding, then appear in body like Egyptian mummies, and in mind gross and silly. Who in the world at the present day is aware that this love in itself is of such a nature? Yet a love of ruling from love of use is possible, but only from love of use for the sake of the common good, not for the sake of self. It is difficult, however, for man to distinguish the one love from the other, although the difference between them is like that between heaven and hell. The differences between these two loves of ruling may be seen in the work *Heaven and Hell* (n. 551–565).

425. (20) *The capacity to understand called rationality and the capacity to act called freedom still remain.* These two capacities belonging to man have been treated of above (n. 264–267). Man has these two capacities that he may from being natural become spiritual, that is, may be regenerated. For, as was said above, it is man's love that becomes spiritual, and is regenerated; and it cannot become spiritual or be regenerated unless it knows, by means of its understanding, what evil is and what good is, and therefore what truth is and what falsity is.

When it knows this it can choose either one or the other; and if it chooses good it can, by means of its understanding, be instructed about the means by which to attain to good. All the means by which man is enabled to attain good are provided. It is by rationality that man is able to know and understand these means, and by freedom that he is able to will and to do them. There is also a freedom to will to know, to understand, and to think these means. Those who hold from church doctrine that things spiritual or theological transcend the understanding, and are therefore to be believed apart from the understanding, know nothing of these capacities called rationality and freedom. These cannot do otherwise than deny that there is a capacity called rationality. Those, too, who hold from church doctrine that no one is able to do good from himself, and consequently that good is not to be done from any will to be saved, cannot do otherwise than deny, from a principle of religion, the existence of both these capacities which belong to man.

Therefore, those who have confirmed themselves in these things, after death, in agreement with their faith, are deprived of both these capacities; and in place of heavenly freedom, in which they might have been, are in infernal freedom, and in place of angelic wisdom from rationality, in which they might have been, are in infernal insanity; and what is wonderful, they claim that both these capacities have place in doing what is evil and thinking what is false, not knowing that the exercise of freedom in doing what is evil is slavery, and that the exercise of the reason to think what is false is irrational. But it is to be carefully noted that these capacities, freedom and rationality, are neither of them man's, but are of the Lord in man, and that they cannot be appropriated to man as his; nor indeed, can they be given to man as his, but are continually of the Lord in man, and yet are never taken away from man; and this because without them man cannot be saved, for without them he cannot be regenerated (as has been said above).

For this reason man is instructed by the church that from himself he can neither think what is true nor do what is good. But inasmuch as man perceives no otherwise than that he thinks from himself what is true and does from himself what is good, it is very evident that he ought to believe that he thinks as if from himself what is true, and does as if from himself what is good. For if he does not believe this, either he does not think what is true nor do what is good, and therefore has no religion, or he thinks what is true and does what is good from himself, and thus ascribes to himself that which is Divine. That man ought to think what is true and do good as if from himself, may be seen in the *Doctrine of Life for the New Jerusalem*, from beginning to end.

426. (21) *Spiritual and celestial love is love toward the neighbor and love to the Lord; and natural and sensual love is love of the world and love of self.* By love toward the neighbor is meant the love of uses, and by love to the Lord is meant the love of doing uses (as has been shown before). These loves are spiritual and celestial, because loving uses and doing them from a love of them, is distinct from the love of what is man's own; for whoever loves uses spiritually looks not to self, but to others outside of self for whose good he is moved. Opposed to these loves are the loves of self and of the world, for these look to uses not for the sake of others but for the sake of self; and those who do this invert Divine order, and put self in the Lord's place, and the world in the place of heaven; as a consequence they look backward, away from the Lord and away from heaven, and looking backward away from these is looking to hell. (More about these loves may be seen above, n. 424.) Yet man does not feel and perceive the love of performing uses for the sake of uses as he feels and perceives the love of performing uses for the sake of self; consequently when he is performing uses he does not know whether he is doing them for the sake of uses or for the sake of self. But let him know that he is performing uses for the sake of uses in the measure in which he flees from evils; for so far as he flees from evils, he performs uses not for himself, but from the Lord. For evil and good are opposites; so far as one is not in evil he is in good.

No one can be in evil and in good at the same time, because no one can serve two masters at the same time. All this has been said to show that although man does not sensibly perceive whether the uses which he performs are for the sake of use or for the sake of self, that is, whether the uses are spiritual or merely natural, still he can know it by this, whether or not he considers evils to be sins. If he regards them as sins, and for that reason abstains from doing them, the uses which he does are spiritual. And when one who does this flees from sins from

a feeling of aversion, he then begins to have a sensible perception of the love of uses for the sake of uses, and this from
spiritual enjoyment in them.

427. (22) *It is the same with charity and faith and their
conjunction as with the will and understanding and their
conjunction.* There are two loves, according to which the
heavens are distinct, celestial love and spiritual love. Celestial
love is love to the Lord, and spiritual love is love towards the
neighbor. These loves are distinguished by this, that celestial
love is the love of good, and spiritual love the love of truth;
for those who are in celestial love perform uses from love of
good, and those in spiritual love from love of truth. The
marriage of celestial love is with wisdom, and the marriage of
spiritual love with intelligence; for it is of wisdom to do good
from good, and it is of intelligence to do good from truth,
consequently celestial love does what is good, and spiritual
love does what is true.

The difference between these two loves can be defined only
in this way, that those who are in celestial love have wisdom
inscribed on their life, and not on the memory, for which
reason they do not talk about Divine truths, but do them;
while those who are in spiritual love have wisdom inscribed
on their memory, therefore they talk about Divine truths,
and do them from principles in the memory. Because those
who are in celestial love have wisdom inscribed on their life,
they perceive instantly whether whatever they hear is true or
not; and when asked whether it is true, they answer only, It
is, or It is not. These are they who are meant by the words
of the Lord:

> Let your speech be Yea, yea, Nay, nay (Matt. 5:37).

And because they are such, they are unwilling to hear
anything about faith, saying, What is faith? Is it not wisdom?
And what is charity? Is it not doing? And when told that

faith is believing what is not understood, they turn away, saying, The man is crazy. These are they who are in the third heaven, and who are the wisest of all. Such have they become who in the world have applied the Divine truths which they have heard immediately to the life by turning away from evils as infernal, and worshiping the Lord alone. These, since they are in innocence, appear to others as infants; and since they never talk about the truths of wisdom and there is nothing of pride in their discourse, they also appear simple. Nevertheless, when they hear anyone speaking, they perceive from the tone all things of his love, and from the speech all things of his intelligence. These are they who are in the marriage of love and wisdom from the Lord; and who represent the heart region of heaven, mentioned above.

428. Those, however, who are in spiritual love, which is love towards the neighbor, do not have wisdom inscribed on their life, but intelligence; for it is of wisdom to do good from affection for good, while it is of intelligence to do good from affection for truth (as has been said above). Neither do these know what faith is. When faith is mentioned they understand truth, and when charity is mentioned they understand doing the truth; and when told that they must believe, they call it empty talk, and ask, Who does not believe what is true? This they say because they see truth in the light of their own heaven; therefore, to believe what they do not see they call either simplicity or foolishness. These are they who constitute the lung region of heaven, also mentioned above.

429. But those who are in spiritual-natural love have neither wisdom nor intelligence inscribed on their life, but only something of faith out of the Word, so far as this has been conjoined with charity. Inasmuch as these do not know what charity is, or whether faith be truth, they cannot be among those in the heavens who are in wisdom and intelligence, but among those who are in knowledge only. Yet such of them as have fled from evil as sins are in the outmost heaven, and are in a light there like the light of the moon by night; while those who have not confirmed themselves in a faith in what is unknown, but have cherished a kind of affection for truth are instructed by angels, and according to their reception of truths and a life in agreement therewith, are raised into the societies of those who are in spiritual love and therefore in intelligence. Those become spiritual, the rest becoming spiritual-natural. But those who have lived in faith separate from charity are removed, and sent away into deserts, because they are not in any good, thus not in any marriage of good and truth, in which all are who are in the heavens.

430. All that has been said of love and wisdom in this chapter may be said of charity and faith, if by charity spiritual love is understood, and by faith the truth whereby there is intelligence. It is the same whether the terms will and understanding, or love and intelligence be used, since the will is the receptacle of love, and the understanding of intelligence.

431. To this I will add the following notable experience: in heaven all who perform uses from affection for use, because of the communion in which they live, are wiser and happier than others; and with them performing uses is acting sincerely, uprightly, justly, and faithfully in the work proper to the calling of each. This they call charity; and observances pertaining to worship they call signs of charity, and other things they call obligations and favors; saying that when one performs the duties of his calling sincerely, uprightly, justly, and faithfully, the good of the community is maintained and perpetuated, and that this is to "be in the Lord," because all that flows in from the Lord is use, and it flows in from the parts into the community, and flows out from the community to the parts. The parts there are angels, and the community is a society of them.

What man's beginning is from conception

432. What man's beginning or primitive form is in the womb after conception no one can know, because it cannot be seen; moreover, it is made up of spiritual substance, which is not visible by natural light. Now because there are some in the world who are eager to investigate even the primitive form of man, which is seed from the father, from which conception is effected, and because many of these have fallen into the error of thinking that man is in his fullness from his first, which is the rudiment, and is afterwards perfected by growth, it has been disclosed to me what that rudiment or first is in its form. It has been disclosed to me by angels, to whom it was revealed by the Lord; and because they had made it a part of their wisdom, and it is the joy of their wisdom to communicate to others what they know, permission having been granted, they presented before my eyes in the light of heaven a type of man's initial form, which was as follows: There appeared as it were a tiny image of a brain with a delicate delineation of something like a face in front, with no appendage.

This primitive form in the upper convex part was a structure of contiguous globules or spherules, and each spherule was a joining together of those more minute, and each of these in like manner of those most minute. It was thus of three degrees. In front, in the flat part, a kind of delineation appeared for a face. The convex part was covered round about with a very delicate skin or membrane which was transparent. The convex part, which was a type of the brain in least forms, was also divided into two beds, as it were, just as the brain in its larger form is divided into hemispheres.

It was told me that the right bed was the receptacle of love, and the left the receptacle of wisdom; and that by wonderful interweavings these were like consorts and partners. It was further shown in the light of heaven, which fell brightly on it, that the structure of this little brain within, as to position and movement, was in the order and form of heaven, and that its outer structure was in direct opposition to that order and form. After these things were seen and pointed out, the angels said that the two interior degrees, which were in the order and form of heaven, were the receptacles of love and wisdom from the Lord; and that the exterior degree, which was in direct opposition to the order and form of heaven, was the receptacle of hellish love and insanity; for the reason that man, by hereditary corruption, is born into evils of every kind, and these evils reside there in the outermosts; and that this corruption is not removed unless the higher degrees are opened, which, as was said, are the receptacles of love and wisdom from the Lord. And as love and wisdom are very man, for love and wisdom in their essence are the Lord, and this primitive form of man is a receptacle, it follows that in that primitive form there is a continual effort towards the human form, which also it gradually assumes.

Index of Scripture Passages

Index

Abstract. *Abstract* things, being universals, are often better comprehended than things applied (n. 228).

Abuse. *Abuse* of rationality and freedom (n. 607).

Aconites. Origin of *aconites* (n. 339).

Acts. *Acts* of the body contain in them all the prior things from which they exist (n. 277, 278).

Action and Reaction. *Action* derives its *esse* from love, its quality from intelligence (n. 406). In life alone there is *action; reaction* is caused by the *action* of life (n. 68). In things greatest and least of the universe, both living and dead, there is *action and reaction* (n. 263). Without *reaction, action* would cease (n. 260). The equilibrium of all things is from *action and reaction* (n. 68, 263).

Adam. (See n. 287, 325). Errors respecting *Adam* (n. 117, 269).

Adoration and worship flow from softening of the heart and humiliation (n. 335).

Affection. *Affection* a determination of love (n. 410). Is of the will, because it is of love (n. 372). Arises from Divine love (n. 33).

Affection and thought are possible only by means of atmospheres purer than air (n. 176). From *affection* for knowing springs *affection* for truth; from *affection* for understanding springs perception of truth; and from *affection* for seeing truth springs thought (n. 404). *Affection* is related to thought as the tone is to speech (n. 372). *Affection* is not perceived except by something pleasant in thinking, speaking, and acting, which is not noticed (n. 364). *Affection,* thought, and action, are in a series of discrete degrees (n. 214). *Affections,* which are of love, appear imaged forth in the face; and thoughts, which are of wisdom, are revealed in a kind of sparkle of the eyes (n. 365). Thoughts, perceptions and *affections* are substances and forms, not entities abstracted from real and actual substance or form (n. 42); are not possible outside of their subjects, but are states of subjects (n. 209, 224, 291). All operations of love or the will outside of the understanding have relation not to *affections* for truth, but to

appearances remain *appearances* they are apparent truths; but when they are accepted as real truths they become falsities and fallacies (n. 108). Effect of speaking from *appearances* (n. 349) (See also n. 7, 10, 73, 109, 110, 113, 125, 363.)

Appetites. *Appetites* are derivations from love or the will (n. 363).

Arcana. *Arcana* concerning the Lord (n. 221, 223); the Word (n. 221); the natural mind in man (n. 257); the sun of the spiritual world (n. 294).

Arms. In the Word, *arms* signify power (n. 220). The right *arm* has reference to the good of truth, the left to the truth of good (n. 384, 409).

Arteries. Pulsation of the *arteries* with spirits and angels (n. 391). Bronchial and pulmonary *arteries* (n. 405, 407, 412, 413, 420). *Arteries* correspond to affections, and in the lungs to affections for truth (n. 412, 420).

Ascension. Threefold *ascension* of degrees of height (n. 235). There are six degrees of *ascent,* namely, three in the natural, and three in the spiritual world (n. 66, 67).

Ashur, Assyria. In the Word, *Ashur* or *Assyria* signifies the church in respect to intelligence (n. 325).

Atheists. Those who become *atheists* (n. 349). Their condition in the spiritual world (n. 357).

Atmospheres. *Atmospheres* are receptacles and containers of heat and light (n. 183, 191, 296, 299). There are *atmospheres* in the spiritual world, just as in the natural world only the former are spiritual, while the latter are natural (n. 173, 178). Both are divided substances or least forms (n. 174). Difference between spiritual and natural *atmospheres* (n. 175). The *atmospheres* in both worlds, in their outmosts, close into substances and matters such as are in the earth (n. 302–304). Respiration, speech, and hearing are effected by means of a lowest *atmosphere* which is called air; sight is possible only by means of an *atmosphere* purer than air; thought and affection are not possible except by means of still purer *atmosphere* (n. 176). All things belonging to the bodies of spirits and angels are held together in connection, form, and order by means of *atmospheres* (n. 152, 176). *Atmospheres* are active forces (n. 178). There are degrees of both kinds in the *atmospheres* of both worlds (n. 184, 225). (See also n. 147, 158, 300, 310.)

Auricles. (See n. 403, 408.)

Autumn. In the Word, *autumn* signifies the decline of the church (n. 73).

Azygos Vena. (See n. 405.)

Bark. How vegetation is brought about through the outer and inner *bark* (n. 314).

432). Injury to the *brain* (n. 365). The life of man in its first principles is in the *brains,* and in its derivatives in the body (n. 365). In the *brain* are substances and forms innumerable, in which every interior sense which pertains to the understanding and will has its seat (n. 42). The cerebellum is especially the organ of the will, and the cerebrum of the understanding (n. 384). (See also n. 367, 370, 409.)

Breadth. In the Word, *breadth* signifies the truth of a thing (n. 71).

Breast. The dwelling place of the heart and lungs (n. 402, 403).

Breath. Why men believe the soul or spirit to be an airy something like *breath* breathed out from the lungs (n. 383). The Lord called "the *breath* of life" (n. 383).

Bronchia. Ramifications of the *bronchia* in the lungs, correspondence of (n. 405, 412–415).

Butterflies. Metamorphosis of caterpillars into butterflies (n. 354).

Canaan. The state of that land corresponds to the state of its inhabitants (n. 345).

Capacities. Man has two *capacities* for life, from one of which he has will, from the other understanding (n. 30). Rationality and freedom are the two *capacities* from the Lord in man which distinguish him from the

beasts (n. 240, 264). Use and abuse of these (n. 267). Are never taken away; devils have them as well as angels (n. 162).

Cardiac. *Cardiac* kingdom of the heavens: that where love reigns (n. 381); represented by those who are in the marriage of love and wisdom from the Lord (n. 427). *Cardiac* and pulmonic movements in the body (n. 391, 392).

Cartilages. How formed (n. 304).

Caterpillars. Their change into butterflies (n. 354).

Cause. A *cause* alone not possible without an end from which and an effect in which it is (n. 167). The principal *cause* not perceived in the instrumental cause otherwise than as one with it (n. 4). Nothing of the real truth about *cause* can become known without a knowledge of degrees of both kinds (n. 188). All *causes* are in the spiritual world (n. 119). In *causes* there is nothing essential except the end (n. 197). *Causes* produce effects, not continuously but discretely (n. 185). *Causes* reveal effects (n. 119). To know effects from *causes* is to be wise; but to search for *causes* from effects is not to be wise (n. 119). *Causes* can be seen rationally yet not clearly except by means of effects (n. 375). See End and Effect.

Cellular. *Cellular* substance in the lungs, of what it consists (n. 413);

its twofold action (n. 413).

Changes. *Changes* of state impossible without a substantial form as a subject, just as sight is impossible without an eye (n. 273).

Charity. *Charity* is all the work of his calling which a man does from the Lord (n. 253); is of affection (n. 214). *Charity* and faith are essentials of the church (n. 253); are substance and form, and not abstractions; are not possible outside of subjects which are substances, but are states of subjects (n. 209). *Charity*, faith, and good works are in a series of discrete degrees (n. 214). Acting sincerely, uprightly, justly, and faithfully in the work proper to the calling of each is what the angels call *charity* (n. 431).

Church. Difference between *churches* before and after the Lord's advent (n. 233). By a man of the *church* is meant one in whom the *church* is (n. 118). A man of the *church* is an angel in respect to his interiors (n. 118). In the Word, times of the day and seasons of the year signify states of the *church* (n. 73).

Cineritious. *Cineritious* substances in the brain, what they are (n. 316).

Civil matters. *Civil matters* are not abstract but are substantial; do not exist outside of subjects which are substances, but are states of subjects (n. 209).

Clouds. By *clouds* in the Word, are meant spiritual *clouds*, which are thoughts (n. 147). In the spiritual world, thoughts from truths appear as shining white *clouds*, but thoughts from falsities as black *clouds* (ibid.).

Colors. There are all kinds of *colors* in the spiritual world, of which red and white are the fundamental, the rest deriving their varieties from these and from their opposites, which are a dusky fire color and black (n. 380). (See also n. 348.)

Communication. *Communication* among the three heavens is made only through correspondences (n. 202). Likewise between the natural and spiritual man or mind (n. 90, 252). *Communication* by correspondences is not sensibly felt (n. 238); is perceived in the understanding only by the fact that truths are seen in light; and is perceived in the will only by the fact that uses are performed from affection (n. 252).

Composites. All *composites* consist of degrees of height or discrete degrees (n. 184, 190).

Conatus. *Conatus* does nothing of itself, but acts through forces corresponding to it, thereby producing motion; it is the all in forces, and through forces is the all in motion (n. 218). In earths there is a *conatus* to produce uses

by means of a general *covering* which communicates with interiors and inmosts (n. 194). Cutaneous *covering* of the spiritual body, what composes it (n. 257, 388). How vegetation is effected through its coverings (n. 314).

Creation. Everything has been *created* for man as its end (n. 170). In everything *created* there are these three, end, cause, and effect (n. 154). To be *"created* into the image and likeness of God"* is to be *created* into the form of love and wisdom (n. 287, 358). *Creation* of the universe (n. 52–60, 151–156, 163–172); was not wrought from space to space, nor from time to time (n. 156); is brought within conception if space and time are removed from the thought (n. 155). The end of *creation* is that all things may return to the Creator, and that there may be conjunction (n. 167–172). The end of the *creation* of the universe is the existence of the angelic heaven from the human race (n. 329). In all forms of uses there is an image of *creation* (n. 313–316).

Crocodiles. Whence they originated (n. 339, 341).

Days. In the Word *days* signify states (n. 73).

Dead. Everything which derives its origin from the sun of the natural world is *dead* (n. 157).

What is *dead* does not act at all from itself, but is acted upon (n. 157). He is said to be *dead* whose mind is a hell (n. 276).

Death. When *death* of the body takes place (n. 390). What man becomes when he *dies* (n. 90).

Decrease. *Decrease* of spiritual heat and light is effected by degrees (n. 94, 186). In heaven, and in each society of heaven, light *decreases* from the middle to the outskirts (n. 253).

Degrees. *Degrees* are of a twofold kind, *degrees* of height or discrete *degrees,* and *degrees* of breadth or continuous *degrees* (n. 184–188). Lessenings or decreasings from grosser to finer, or rather growths and increasings from finer to grosser, are called continuous *degrees.* Discrete *degrees* are entirely different; they are like end, cause, and effect (n. 184). (See also n. 65–68.)

Delusions. *Delusions* in the spiritual world (n. 424).

Denial. The *denial* of God, and in the Christian world, the *denial* of the divinity of the Lord, constitute hell (n. 13).

Derivatives. All things of the body are *derivatives,* that is, are things woven together by means of fibers out of first principles, which are receptacles of love and wisdom (n. 369). The will and understanding are in their *derivatives* in the body (n. 365, 387). Wherever first principles

Divine essence. *Divine essence,* which is the Creator *[creatrix],* is Divine love and Divine wisdom (n. 33). It is one (n. 35).

Divine from which, in the trinity is called "the Father" (n. 146).

Divine life is Divine essence, and is one (n. 35).

Divine love and Divine wisdom. (See Contents, chapters 1 and 2.)

Divine Soul. The *Divine Soul* of God-man is meant by Divine *Esse* (n. 14).

Divine Truth. The Lord made Himself *Divine Truth* in ultimates by fulfilling all things of the Word concerning Himself in Moses and the Prophets (n. 221).

Dust. Damned *dust,* what it is (n. 341).

Dwelling Places. *Dwelling places* of the Lord in man (n. 170, 395). Of angels and spirits are according to their reception of love and wisdom (n. 121). An angel, unlike man in the world, knows his own house and his own *dwelling place* wherever he may go (n. 134).

Ear. The appearance is that the *ear* hears, but the understanding hears through the *ear* (n. 363). From sensation man knows nothing of the numberless things in the *ears* (n. 22). The more interiorly the *ear* is looked into the more do wonders present themselves, and they are interiorly more perfect according to discrete degrees (n. 201).

Earths. *Earths* are the passive forces from which all effects have existence (n. 178). In *earths* there is a conatus to produce uses in forms, that is, forms of uses (n. 310–312). The first production from these *earths,* while they were still new, was the production of seeds (n. 312). Origin of *earths* (n. 302–306). In the spiritual world there are *earths,* but they are spiritual (n. 173–178).

East. The *east* in the spiritual world is where the Lord appears as a sun, and from that the other quarters are determined (n. 119–123). At every turn of their bodies the angels have the *east* before their faces (n. 105). In the Word, the *east,* in the highest sense, signifies the Lord, and in a relative sense love to Him (n. 121, 122). In the spiritual world those who are in a higher degree of love dwell in the *east* (n. 121).

Eden. The Garden of *Eden* describes man in regard to wisdom and intelligence (n. 325, 422).

Effect. An *Effect* alone, that is, an *effect* without a cause and its end, is impossible (n. 167). The *effect* is the complex, container, and base of causes and ends (n. 212). Every *effect* is the fullness of causes (n. 217). From *effects* nothing but *effects* can be learned, and when they alone are considered no cause is brought to light (n. 119). *Effects* can only appear as it were in the darkness of night, unless the causes of the *effects* are seen at the same time (n. 107). To know *effects* from causes is to be wise, but to search out causes from *effects* is not to be wise (n. 119). To see from *effects* only is to see from fallacies (n. 187). All *effects* which are called last ends, become anew first ends in an uninterrupted succession from the First (n. 172). (See also n. 168, 256, 257.)

Effluvia. A wave of *effluvia* is constantly flowing forth out of every object in nature (n. 293). Effects which these *effluvia* have on the blood (n. 420).

Eggs. Propagation by seeds in the *egg* (n. 342, 347, 351).

Elevation. *Elevation* of man into the heat and light of heaven (n. 138, 256, 258, 422).

End. An *end* alone without a cause and an effect is impossible (n. 16, 17). The *end* begets the cause, and through the cause the effect (n. 189, 241). The *end* is the all of the cause, and also the all of the effect (n. 168, 197). There is a first *end,* middle *end,* and last *end,* or *end,* cause, and effect (n. 167, 197). Last *ends* become anew first *ends* in uninterrupted succession (n. 172). The *end* of creation is, that all things may return to the Creator and that

there may be conjunction (n. 167–172, 329, 330). The *ends* of the whole creation were uses (n. 314). The *end* qualifies the means (n. 261). See Cause and Effect.

Enjoyments. *Enjoyments* of man's life are from the affections of his love; and pleasantnesses are from the thoughts therefrom (n. 33). *Enjoyments* felt in the acts and deeds which are from anyone's love are *enjoyments* of uses (n. 316). *Enjoyments* are derivatives from love (n. 363).

Enlightenment. All *Enlightenment* is from the Lord alone (n. 150). Why *enlightenment* is said to be effected by the Spirit of Jehovah (n. 100). The *enlightenment* of the natural mind does not ascend by discrete degrees, but increases in a continuous degree (n. 256). Before the coming of the Lord, the *enlightenment* of men was mediate, but after His coming it was made immediate (n. 233).

Entity. Imaginary *Entities* (n. 43, 210).

Epiglottis. (n. 382).

Equilibrium. The *Equilibrium* of all things is from action and simultaneous reaction (n. 68, 263). Everything must be in *equilibrium* (n. 68). *Equilibrium* is destroyed when action overcomes reaction, or the reverse (n. 263).

Esse and Existere. Love and wisdom, taken together, are Divine *Esse;* but taken

fibers is, there is the origin of life (n. 365, 366). Action of *fibers* (n. 366; see also n. 207, 254, 367, 369, 370, 400). Motor *fibers* (n. 190, 192, 207, 215, 254, 277). Nervous *fibers* (n. 190, 192).

Fibrils. Their multitude compared to the multitude of rays going forth from the stars (n. 366).

Fibrillary. *Fibrillary* substance of the brain (n. 366).

Finite. The *finite* can exist only from the Infinite (n. 44).

Fire. *Fire* is dead and the solar fire is death itself (n. 89). The difference between spiritual *fire*, which is Divine love, and natural *fire*, is like the difference between what is alive and what is dead (n. 93). How the *fire* of the spiritual sun is adapted to angels in heaven by spiritual atmospheres, and in like manner the *fire* of the natural sun is adapted to men (n. 174). *"Fire"* in the Word, signifies love (n. 87); also the Lord as to Divine love (n. 98).

Figments. Mere *figments* of reason (n. 43, 210).

Firsts. The *first* principles or *firsts* of life are in the brains (n. 365). By life in *first* principles is meant will and understanding (n. 365). *First* things are each and all things of the animal kingdom (n. 65).

Flies. Their origin (n. 338, 339).

Flow in. Everything that *flows* in through the spiritual mind is from heaven, while everything that flows into the natural mind is from the world (n. 261). All *inflowing* is perceived and felt according to recipient forms and their states (n. 275).

Flowers. They are more perfect interiorly according to discrete degrees (n. 201). A wave of effluvia constantly flows forth out of *flowers* (n. 293).

Foolish. In the Word, he that doeth not is called *foolish* (n. 220).

Folkes. President of the Royal Society (n. 344).

Force. *Force* is conatus made active; it is produced by conatus, and produces motion (n. 218). Living forces in man are the interior constituents of his body (n. 219). It is contrary to order for dead *force* to act on living *force* (n. 166). Perfection of *forces* (n. 200). Active, mediate, and passive *forces* (n. 178). (See n. 311, 340, 344, 392.)

Forehead. Contracted when man exerts the mind and thinks (n. 365).

Form. *Form* in itself is Divine wisdom (n. 44–46). The substantial *form* of the natural mind (n. 273). The human *form* is nothing else than the *form* of all the affections of love (n. 411). The beginning or primitive *form* of man (n. 432). Material *form* of man (n. 388). *Form* of the will (n. 410). *Forms* of vegetables and animals, what produces them (n.

340). Origin of the *forms* of man's members, etc. (n. 370). Every spiritual *form* is like itself in what is greatest and what is least (n. 273, 275). What causes *forms* in the natural world to be fixed and enduring (n. 340). *Forms* are the containers of uses (n. 46). *Forms* of uses (n. 307–318). The *form* varies according to the excellence of the use (n. 80). There is no substance without *form* (n. 209, 223, 229). Substance and *form* (n. 41).

Formation. *Formation* of the body in the womb (n. 400).

Fountains. The *fountains* of all things of man's life are the Divine love and Divine wisdom (n. 33).

Foxes. Their origin (n. 339).

Freedom. *Freedom* is the ability to do what is good and true. It is a capacity of the will (n. 240, 264, 425). By virtue of *freedom* and rationality man is man, and is distinguished from beasts (n. 240, 264). These capacities are not man's, but are the Lord's in man (n. 116, 425). They are never taken away; they are with every man, good and evil alike (n. 162, 240, 247, 266, 425). The use and abuse of these capacities (n. 267). *Freedom* in doing what is evil is slavery (n. 425).

Frogs. Their origin (n. 339, 345).

Fruits are more perfect interiorly according to discrete degrees (n. 201). A wave of effluvia emanates unceasingly from *fruits* (n. 293).

Fullness. What it is to be in *fullness* (n. 217, 221).

Gifts. In the heavens all the necessaries of life are free *gifts* (n. 334).

Glandular substances. *Glandular substance* of the brain, in what it consists (n. 366).

Globe. The terraqueous *globe* is as a kind of base and support (n. 106, 165).

Glorification. *Glorification* of the Lord (n. 234). Described (n. 221).

Glory. A *glory* surrounds each love like the brightness of fire (n. 266). The Lord is to be adored, worshiped and glorified, not for His own *glory* but for man's sake (n. 335).

God. *God* is love itself because He is life itself (n. 4–6). He is not in space (n. 7–10, 21). He is very Man (n. 11–13, 16, 97). Existing not from Himself, but in Himself (n. 16). All things of the created universe, viewed in reference to uses, represent man in an image, and this proves that *God* is Man (n. 319–326). *God* by virtue of His own essence is called "Jehovah" (n. 100). *God* alone is Substance in itself, and therefore *Esse* itself (n. 283). In *God* we live, move, and have our being (n. 301). (See Jehovah and Lord. See also Contents, chapter 1.)

God-man. The *God-man* has a body and everything pertaining

to body (n. 18). From these come all like things in man (n. 22). All things from the one *God-man* (n. 23–27).

Good. Everything that proceeds from love is called *good* (n. 31). All *good* things that have existence in act are called uses (n. 336). All *good* is of love (n. 84, 402, 406); of spiritual heat (n. 253); is from the Lord and nothing of *good* is from man (n. 394). The whole power of *good* is by means of truth (n. 406). *Good* acts in truth, thus by means of truth (n. 406).

Grandfathers. Hereditary evils are from the father, thus from *grandfathers* and great-*grandfathers,* successively transmitted to offspring (n. 269).

Greatest. The Divine in things *greatest* and least is the same (n. 77–82). The greatest things in which there are degrees of both kinds (n. 225).

Gyration from right to left tends downward, from left to right, upward. Follows the flow of the interiors (n. 270).

Hands. In the Word, *hands* signify power, and the right *hand* superior power (n. 220). The work of the *hands* of Jehovah means the work of Divine love and Divine wisdom (n. 59). Why inductions into the ministry are performed by the laying on of *hands* (n. 220).

Head. The *head* rules the body under it at will, for the understanding and will have their seat in the *head* (n. 25). Those in hell appear *head* downward and feet upward (n. 275). Several *heads* on one body (n. 24).

Hearing is predicated of attention and giving heed, which pertain to the understanding (n. 363). *Hearing* is effected by means of the lowest atmosphere called air (n. 176). *Hearing* is in the ear, and not in the place where the sound originates, and is an affecting of the substance and form of the ear. Does not go out from the ear to catch the sound, but the sound enters the ear and affects it. It is not something volatile flowing from its organ, but is the organ considered in its substance and form (n. 41). Communicates immediately through fibers with the brains, and derives therefrom its sensitive and active life (n. 365). See Sense.

Heart. The *heart* and the lungs are life's two fountains of motion (n. 291). So long as the *heart* is moved, love with its vital heat remains and preserves life (n. 390). The *heart* is more perfect interiorly according to discrete degrees (n. 201). The will corresponds to the *heart* (n. 378). The heart corresponds to love or good (n. 402). In the Word, *heart* signifies the love of the will (n.

383).

Heat. The *heat* which goes forth from the spiritual sun in its essence is love (n. 5, 32, 363). The first proceeding of love is *heat* (n. 95). In the spiritual world there is continuous *heat* (n. 161). The *heat* of the spiritual world in itself is alive, but the *heat* of the natural world in itself is dead (n. 89). The *heat* of the natural world can be vivified by the influx of heavenly *heat* (n. 88). *Heat* has existence not in love itself, but from love in the will and thence in the body (n. 95). Spiritual *heat* is the good of charity (n. 83, 84). It is obtained by shunning evils as sins (n. 246). Vital *heat*, its origin (n. 379). *Heat* corresponds to love (n. 32). (See also Contents, chapter 2.)

Heaven. The whole *heaven*, and all things therein, look to one God (n. 25, 26). The whole *heaven* in the aggregate resembles a single man (n. 288, 381). *Heaven* is divided into regions and provinces according to the members, viscera, and organs of man (n. 288). There are three *heavens* arranged according to discrete degrees (n. 202, 275). The *heavens* are divided into two kingdoms, the celestial and the spiritual (n. 381).

Heights. In the Word, *height* signifies degrees of good and truth (n. 71). The sun in the spiritual world appears in a middle altitude, why (n. 105).

Hell. There are three *hells*, and they are distinct according to three degrees of height or depth opposite to the three heavens (n. 275). The *hells* are not distant from men, but are about them, yea, within those who are evil (n. 343). (See also n. 339, 341.)

Hemispheres of the brain, why there are two (n. 384, 409). The right is the receptacle of love, the left of wisdom (n. 432).

Herbs. Poisonous *herbs*, etc., their origin (n. 338, 339, 341).

Hereditary evils. *Hereditary evils* are from fathers, thus from grandfathers and great-grandfathers successively transmitted to offspring (n. 269). *Hereditary* corruption is not removed unless the higher degrees are opened, which are the receptacles of love and wisdom from the Lord (n. 432).

Heresy. An abominable *heresy* (n. 130). Every *heresy* is confirmed by its adherents (n. 267).

Higher. In the Word, *higher* signifies inner (n. 206). It is according to order for the *higher* to act upon the lower, and not the reverse (n. 365). "The most *high*" signifies the inmost (n. 103). The *highest* of successive order becomes the innermost of simultaneous order (n. 206).

Hours. In the Word, signify states (n. 73).

House. By the *house* of the will is

meant the whole man (n. 408).

Human Divine. (See n. 11, 12, 233.) In the trinity is called "the Son" (n. 146). The *Human Divine* is the inmost in every created thing (n. 285). The two *humans* of the Lord (n. 221).

Humiliation. Adoration and worship flow forth from *humiliation* (n. 335).

Ideas. Spiritual and natural *ideas* (n. 7, 294, 306). Spiritual *idea* derives nothing from space, but it derives its all from state. In natural *idea* there is space, for it is formed out of such things as are in the world (n. 7). Natural and spiritual *ideas* differ according to degrees of height (n. 294). In all the heavens there is no other *idea* of God than that He is a Man, which is the same as the *idea* of a Human Divine (n. 11). Every nation in the spiritual world has its place allotted in accordance with its *idea* of God as a Man (n. 13). *Ideas* of thought (n. 1, 69, 71, 223, 224). In the natural world man forms the *ideas* of his thought, and thereby his understanding from space and time (n. 69).

Ignorance. *Ignorance* of the man of the church of what love and wisdom are (n. 188).

Image. The created universe, viewed as to uses, is the *image* of God (n. 64, 298). Things created repeat in an *image* things that are in the Lord (n. 223). In all forms of uses there is a kind of image of creation (n. 313); and an *image* of man (n. 317); and of the Infinite and the Eternal (n. 318). All things of the created universe, viewed in reference to uses, represent man in an *image* (n. 319). The natural mind that is in evils and in falsities therefrom is a form and *image* of hell (n. 273). Countless things in the spiritual sun come into existence, as in an *image* in the created universe (n. 155). In Genesis, by the *"image* of God" is meant the Divine wisdom (n. 358).

Impure. *Impure* things of the will in the understanding (n. 421).

Infinite. God is *infinite*, not only because He is very *Esse* and *Existere* in itself, but because in Him there are infinite things (n. 17). An *infinite* without *infinite* things in it is *infinite* in name only (ibid.). The *infinite* things in God-man appear in heaven, in angel, and in man as in a mirror (n. 19, 21). In God-man *infinite* things are one distinguishably (n. 17–22).

Influx. *Influx* is effected by correspondences, and it cannot be effected by continuity (n. 88). There is an unceasing *influx* out of the spiritual world into the natural (n. 340). No physical *influx* into the spiritual operations of the soul is possible

163). There is no word of spiritual *language* the same as any word of natural *language* (n. 295). Natural and spiritual *speech* communicate only by correspondence (n. 306). Angelic *speech* (n. 26, 295).

Last Judgment. Errors concerning it (n. 386). See Judgment.

Left. In the angel and in the man all the *left* parts correspond to wisdom from love, or to truth from good (n. 127, 384, 409).

Length, in the Word, signifies the good of a thing (n. 71).

Lice. Their origin (n. 338, 339, 342, 345).

Life. *Esse* itself is called "Jehovah," and *life* itself, or *life* in itself (n. 4, 76). *life* is the Divine essence (n. 36). God alone is *life,* and His *life* is Divine love and Divine wisdom (n. 363, 400). Man's very *life* is love or will (n. 1, 2, 3, 399). Love and wisdom and will and understanding therefrom, make the very *life* of man (n. 363). The *life* of man in its first principles is in the brains, and in its derivatives in the body (n. 365). Such as *life* is in its first principles such it is in the whole and in every part (n. 366). By means of first principles *life* is in the whole from every part, and in every part from the whole (n. 367). *Life* acts into the natural according to any induced change of form (n. 166). Man is not *life,* but a recipient of *life* (n. 4).

Spiritual *life* is a *life* conformed to the Divine precepts (n. 248). In the Word, by *life* is meant Divine love (n. 38).

Ligaments (n. 403, 408).

Light. The *light* that proceeds from the spiritual sun in its essence is wisdom (n. 5, 32, 363). The first proceeding of wisdom is *light* (n. 95). There is continuous *light* in the spiritual world (n. 161). The *light* of the spiritual world in itself is alive, but the *light* of the natural world in itself is dead (n. 89). The *light* of the world can be illumined by the influx of heavenly *light* (n. 88). *Light* has existence not in wisdom, but in the thought of the understanding, and thence in the speech (n. 95). The *light* of men is Divine truth (n. 383). Spiritual *light* flows in with man through three degrees (n. 242–247). *Light* corresponds to wisdom (n. 32). Spiritual *light* is the truth of faith (n. 83, 84). In the Word, by *light* is meant the Lord's Divine wisdom (n. 38, 98). (See also Contents, chapter 2.)

Likeness. In Genesis the Divine love is meant by the "likeness of God" (n. 358).

Live. Why all men, the good as well as the evil, live forever (n. 240). To *live,* move, and be in God (n. 301).

Liver. From sensation man knows nothing of his *liver* (n. 22). Is more perfect interiorly according to discrete degrees (n. 201).

270, 273). It envelops and encloses the spiritual *mind* and the celestial *mind* (n. 260). It has its seat in the brains in its first principles (n. 273). The *mind* impels the body and all its belongings at will (n. 387). The natural *mind* in form or in image is a world, while the spiritual *mind* in its form or image is a heaven (n. 270). The spiritual *mind* derives its form from the substances of the spiritual world only (n. 270). The natural *mind* is coiled into gyres from right to left, but the spiritual *mind* into gyres from left to right (n. 270). The higher region of the natural *mind* is called the rational, and the lowest region is called the sensual (n. 254). (See Contents, chapters 3 and 5.)

Mineral Kingdom. The forms of the uses of this *kingdom* (n. 313). The relation to man in respect to each and all things of the *mineral kingdom* (n. 61).

Minerals are interiorly more perfect according to discrete degrees (n. 201).

Minute. There can be nothing so *minute* as not to have in it degrees of both kinds (n. 223).

Misuse. *Misuse* of the capacity to raise the understanding above the love (n. 395). *Misuse* of uses does not do away with use (n. 331).

Mites. Their origin (338, 339).

Moon. What is meant by "the light of the *moon* being as the light of the sun" (n. 233).

Moral. Things moral are not abstract but are substances; they are not possible outside of subjects which are substances, but are states of subjects, that is, of substances (n. 209).

Morning. In the Word, *morning* signifies the first state of the church (n. 73).

Moths. Their origin (n. 338, 339).

Motion is produced by forces, and is the outmost degree of conatus; through *motion*, conatus exerts its power (n. 218). In *motion* there is nothing essential except active force (n. 197). Living *motion* in man is action which is produced through living forces by the will united to the understanding (n. 219). Conatus, force, and *motion* are no otherwise conjoined than according to discrete degrees, conjunction of which is not by continuity, but by correspondences (n. 218). Cardiac and pulmonic *motion* (n. 381). See Effort and Force.

Muscle. Its composition (n. 190, 192, 197). Is more perfect interiorly according to discrete degrees (n. 201).

Nation. Every *nation* in the spiritual world has its place allotted in accordance with its idea of God as a Man (n. 13).

Natural. All that springs forth and continues to exist from the sun of the *natural* world is called *natural* (n. 159). There does not exist a natural which does not derive its cause from the spiritual (n. 134). The natural man (n. 251). The spiritual-natural man (n. 429). The sensual-natural man (n. 144, 162, 254). How the *natural* man becomes spiritual (n. 248).

Natural Mind. See Mind.

Naturalism [materialism]. Its origin (n. 69).

Nature in itself is wholly inert (n. 166). In itself it is dead (n. 159, 340). In man and in animals it appears as if alive, because of the life which accompanies and actuates it (n. 159). All things of *nature* are from love and wisdom (n. 46). *Nature* contributes nothing whatever to the production of plants and animals (n. 344). *Nature* has produced and does produce nothing, but the Divine out of itself and through the spiritual world has produced all things (n. 349, 356). To *nature* can be ascribed no more than this, that it serves the spiritual in fixing those things which flow in unceasingly into *nature* (n. 344). The folly of those who ascribe all things to *nature* (n. 162, 166); their state in the spiritual world (n. 357); some are excusable (n. 350).

Neck. All fibers descend from the brains through the *neck* into the body, and none ascend from the body through the *neck* to the brain (n. 365).

Negation. The *negation* of God constitutes hell, and in the Christian world the *negation* of the Divinity of the Lord (n. 13).

Nerves. Their composition (n. 190, 192, 366). (See n. 197, 388.)

Newton. His abhorrence of the idea of nothing applied to vacuum (n. 82).

Night. In the Word, *night* signifies the end of the church (n. 73).

Noon. In the Word, *noon* signifies the fullness of the church (n. 73).

North. In the Word, *north* signifies wisdom in shade (n. 121). In the spiritual world, those who are in a lower degree of wisdom dwell in the north (n. 121).

Nose. The nose corresponds to the perception of truth (n. 254). The appearance is that the *nose* smells, but the understanding smells by virtue of its perception (n. 363). Nostrils in the Word signify perception (n. 383).

Nothing. To make anything out of *nothing* is a contradiction (n. 55, 283). The universe was not created out of *nothing* (n. 283). In *nothing* no real activity of mind is possible (n. 82).

Nuptials. What is understood by the *nuptials* of love and wisdom, or of the will and understanding (n. 404).

Object. The *object* of this work is to uncover causes, that effects may be seen from them (n. 188).

Objects. In spiritual light *objects* of thought are truths, and *objects* of sight are like those in the natural world, but correspondent to their thoughts (n. 70).

Odors. Effect which *odors* have on the blood (n. 420). Foul smells in the hells (n. 339, 341, 420). *Odors* in the heavens (n. 420).

Omnipotence. The *omnipotence* of God (n. 9, 72, 221).

Omnipresence. The *omnipresence* of God (n. 7, 9, 21, 69, 71, 72). God is *omnipresent,* because He is not in space (n. 147).

Omniprovident. It may be seen in a measure how God is able to be *omniprovident* (n. 21).

Omniscience. *Omniscience* of God (n. 9, 21, 72).

One. Love and wisdom proceed from the Lord as *one,* but are not received as *one* by the angels (n. 125). The heat and light in proceeding from the Lord are *one* (n. 99). See Distinguishably one.

Only. That is called the *only* from which everything else proceeds (n. 45). In all things the first is singly supreme in the subsequent things, yea, it is the sole thing in them (n. 197).

Operation. *Operation* by influx into vegetable and animal forms (n. 346).

Order. Successive and simultaneous order of discrete degrees (n. 205–208).

Organic. *Organic* substance (n. 191, 192, 197, 200). *Organic* forms (n. 208).

Organization. *Organization* of the will and understanding (n. 373).

Organs. Their composition (n. 190). *Organs* of sense (n. 366, 407). *Organs* of motion (n. 366). (See n. 207, 370, 376, 377, 384, 385, 400, 401, 408, 410.)

Origin of man (n. 346), of the affections and thoughts (n. 33), of evil (n. 264–270), of vital heat (n. 379), of animals and vegetables (n. 339, 340, 346); of animalcules and noxious insects (n. 342); of substance and matter (n. 302); of earths (n. 302–306).

Outermost. The *outermost* of simultaneous order is the lowest of successive order (n. 206).

Outmost. The *outmost* of each series, that is to say, use, action, and doing, is the complex and container of all things prior (n. 215). Every *outmost* consists of things prior, and these of their firsts (n. 208). Every *outmost* is sheathed about and thereby rendered distinct from its things prior (n. 278). In every *outmost* there are discrete degrees in simultaneous order (n. 207, 208). The degrees of height are in fullness and in power in their *outmost* degree (n. 217–221). The lowest spiritual separated from what is above it produces evil uses (n. 345). All things of the mineral kingdom are last things (n. 65).

form has no *quality,* and what has no *quality* is not anything (n. 15, 223).

Quarters in the spiritual world (n. 119–128). The *quarters* in that world are not determined from the south, as in the natural world, but from the east (n. 120, 132); they are not determined by the sun of the spiritual world, but by the inhabitants there (n. 120); according to their reception of love and wisdom (n. 124–128, 132). The variety of reception of love and wisdom gives rise to the *quarters* in the spiritual world (n. 126). Man as to his spirit is in some *quarter* of the spiritual world, whatever *quarter* of the natural world he may be in (n. 126).

Ramifications of the bronchial tubes of the lungs (n. 405, 412). They correspond to the perceptions and thoughts from the affections for truth (n. 405).

Rational. The *rational* of man is the highest point of the understanding (n. 237, 254). Man's *rational* is in appearance as if it were of three degrees (n. 258). The *rational* man is he who is in natural and in spiritual love both at once (n. 416). Man can become *rational,* by elevation, even to the third degree (n. 258). How the *rational* is perfected (n. 332). The *rational* is the higher region of the natural degree (n.

254).

Rationality. *Rationality* is the capacity by which man is able to understand what is true and what is good; it is a capacity of the understanding (n. 240, 264, 413, 425); it is with every man by creation, consequently by birth, and united with freedom distinguishes him from the beasts (n. 264, 413). A bad man enjoys this capacity equally with a good man (n. 266). It is never taken away from man (n. 247, 258, 264). It does not exist with a man until his natural mind reaches maturity (n. 266). It may be absent when the externals have been injured by accident (n. 259). The *rational* power to think what is false is irrational (n. 425).

Rats. Their origin (n. 339, 341).

Reaction. In everything created by God there is *reaction* (n. 68, 260). *Reaction* is caused by the action of life (n. 68). See Action.

Reason. All things of human reason join and as it were center in this, that there is one God (n. 23). Human *reason,* on what it depends (n. 23). Human *reason* is such as to be unwilling to yield assent unless it sees a thing from its cause (n. 291). How reason becomes unsound (n. 23).

Receive. To *receive* more of heat than of light, and conversely (n. 101). Man is able to *receive* wisdom even to the third degree,

flows into the *respiration* of the body, and produces it (n. 390, 391). There is a correspondence between them (n. 390). These two *respirations* may be separated, and may be conjoined (n. 415, 417). Thought produces *respiration* (n. 412). Angels and spirits breathe just as men do (n. 176, 391). The *respirations* of the lungs correspond to the perceptions and the thoughts of the understanding (n. 420).

Resurrection. The Lord rose again with the whole body, differently from man (n. 221).

Return. *Return* of all things to the Creator (n. 167–172).

Revelation. Every man is taught respecting the Divine precepts, not by immediate *revelation*, but by others who know them from religion (n. 249).

Ribs. Their relation to the lungs (n. 403, 408).

Right. The *right* hand, in the Word, signifies superior power (n. 220). "Sitting at the *right* hand of the power and might of God" signifies to have all power (n. 221). In angel and man the *right* parts correspond to love from which is wisdom or to good from which is truth (n. 127, 384, 409).

Satan. The love of possessing the goods of others by every evil device is called *satan* (n. 273).

Cunning villainies and subtleties are the *satanic* crew (n. 273). See Devil.

Scorpions. Their origin (n. 339, 341).

Seasons. The four *seasons* of the year, in the Word, signify states of the church (n. 73).

See. An angel can See God both within himself and also without himself (n. 130). No one while he is in evil can *see* good, but he who is in good can *see* evil (n. 271). When man thinks from wisdom he *sees* things as it were in light (n. 95). Why those who are in the one world cannot *see* those who are in the other world (n. 91). To *see* from effects only is to *see* from fallacies (n. 187). *Seeing* is predicated of the understanding (n. 363).

Seed. The *seed* which is from the father is the first receptacle of life, but such a receptacle as it was with the father (n. 269). The production of *seeds* was the first production from the earths while they were still new (n. 312). In *seeds* there is an endeavor to multiply and to fructify themselves infinitely and eternally (n. 60). Interiorly they are more perfect according to discrete degrees (n. 201).

Selfhood. The angel's *selfhood,* like man's, is evil (n. 114).

Sensations. *Sensations* are not things abstract from the organs of *sensation* (n. 210). *Sensations* are ultimately derived from love and wisdom (n. 363).

Sense. *Sense* is an affecting of the substance and form of the organ (n. 41). The affecting of the substance and form which causes *sense* is not a something separate from the subject, but only causes a change in it, the subject remaining the subject then as before and afterwards (n. 41). The external *senses* of the body communicate immediately through fibers with the brains, and derive therefrom their sensitive and active life (n. 365). All the bodily *senses* derive their perception from their mind's perception (n. 406).

Sensual. *Sensual* men are the lowest natural men, who are incapable of thinking above the appearances and fallacies of the bodily senses (n. 249). The *sensual* is the lowest region of the natural degree (n. 254).

Series. One thing is from another in a threefold *series* (n. 212). The outmost of each *series* is the complex and container of all things prior (n. 215).

Serpents. Their origin (n. 339, 341).

Sight is possible only by means of an atmosphere purer than air (n. 176). *Sight* is not a something volatile flowing from its organ, but is the organ considered in its substance and form; when this is affected sensation is produced (n. 41). *Sight* is in the eye which is

the subject, and is an affecting of the subject (n. 41). *Sight* does not go out from the eye to the object, but the image of the object enters the eye, and affects its substance and form (n. 41). The sense of *sight* communicates immediately through fibers with the brain, and derives therefrom its sensitive and active life (n. 365). The grossness of bodily *sight* (n. 352). See Sense.

Similitude. Likeness between generals and particulars, or between greatest and least (n. 227).

Simple. The *simple* see more clearly what is good and true than those who think themselves their superiors in wisdom (n. 361).

Simples. *Simples* are more perfect than composites, because they are more naked and less covered over with substances and matters devoid of life (n. 204). The more *simple* anything *simple* is the more exempt from injury it is, because it is more perfect (n. 204). Without such preeminent perfection in things *simple,* neither man nor any kind of animal could have come into existence from seed and could afterwards continue to exist; nor could the seeds of trees and shrubs vegetate and bear fruit (n. 204).

Sirens. Their fantastic beauty (n. 424).

Skin. The *skin* by which man is

enveloped is the subject of touch (n. 41). The substance and form of the *skin* cause it to feel whatever is applied to it (n. 41).

Sleep. In *sleep* the lapse of time is not noticed (n. 74). What becomes of conatus and forces in man during *sleep* (n. 219).

Sloane, Sir Hans (n. 344).

Small. There is nothing so *small* that has not in it degrees of both kinds (n. 223).

Smell. The sense of *smell* is in the nostrils and is an affecting of the nostrils by odoriferous particles touching them (n. 41). The *smell* is not a something volatile flowing from its organ, but is the organ considered in its substance and form; and when the organ is affected sensation is produced (n. 41). The sense of *smell* communicates immediately through fibers with the brains, and derives therefrom its sensitive and active life (n. 365). To *smell* is predicated of perception (n. 363). See Sense.

Societies. In heaven, *societies* are divided according to all the differences of heavenly love (n. 141). Angelic *societies* are countless and in like order as the glands of the brain (n. 366).

Soul. The *soul* in its very *esse* is love and wisdom in man from the Lord (n. 395, 398). There can be no *soul* apart from its body, nor body apart from its *soul* (n. 14). Every man's *soul* is in a

spiritual body after it has cast off the material coverings which it carried about in the world (n. 14). Fruitless researches of the learned into the operations of the *soul* in the body (n. 394). How the *soul* acts upon the body and effects all its operations (n. 398–431). *Soul* of beasts (n. 346). *Soul,* in the Word, signifies the understanding, also the wisdom of the understanding (n. 383).

Sound. *Sound* which is articulated into words all comes forth from the lungs through the trachea and epiglottis (n. 382). The angels recognize a man's love from his tone in speaking, his wisdom from articulation, and his knowledge from the meaning of the words (n. 280). Beasts utter *sounds* in accordance with the knowledge pertaining to their love (n. 255).

South. In the Word, *south* signifies wisdom in light (n. 121). In the spiritual world those in a higher degree of wisdom dwell in the *south* (n. 121).

Space. *Space* is a property of nature (n. 69, 70). *Space* is in each and all things in the world as seen by the eye (n. 7). In the spiritual world there appear to be *spaces,* yet they are only appearances (n. 7). *Spaces* there are not fixed as in the natural world, but are changeable according to states of life (n. 70). States of love correspond to *space* (n. 70). *Space* is in natural, but not in spiritual ideas (n. 7, 111). To think according to *space* concerning God is to think concerning the expanse of nature (n. 9). The Lord cannot advance through *spaces,* but is present with each one according to reception (n. 111). See Time.

Speaking. *Speaking* by degrees is abstract (n. 196).

Speech. See Language.

Sphere. Encompassing *sphere* (n. 291). Everyone in the spiritual world is encompassed by a *sphere* consisting of substances set free and separated from his body (n. 292). A *sphere* flows forth from all things that appear in that world (n. 293). The *sphere* of affections and of thoughts therefrom, which encompasses each angel, manifests his presence to others far and near (n. 291).

Spiders. Their origin (n. 339).

Spiral. The contraction of the spiritual degree is like the twisting back of a *spiral* in the opposite direction (n. 254, 263).

Spirit. Man in the world of spirits is called an angelic *spirit* if he is preparing for heaven, an infernal *spirit* if he is preparing for hell (n. 140). In the Word, *spirit* signifies the understanding and the wisdom of the understanding (n. 383). Corporeal *spirits* (n. 424). Animal *spirit,* what it is (n. 423). The Holy Spirit is the Truth itself which proceeds from the Lord (n. 149). The Holy *Spirit* is the Lord, and not a God who is a person by Himself (n. 359). In the Word, the Holy *Spirit* and *Spirit* of God signify Divine wisdom, and therefore Divine truth, which is the light of men (n. 149, 383).

Spiritual. The heat and light that proceed from the Lord as a sun are what in an eminent sense are called the *spiritual* (n. 100). The *spiritual* flows down from its sun, even to the outmosts of nature, through three degrees (n. 345). The lowest *spiritual* or *spiritual*-natural can be separated from its higher parts (n. 345). Evil uses are effected on the earth by the lowest *spiritual* separated from what is above it (n. 345). The *spiritual* impels nature to act, as what is living impels what is dead (n. 340). It produces the forms of plants and animals, filling them with matters from the earth, that they may become fixed and enduring (n. 340). The *spiritual* furnishes the soul, and the material the body (n. 343). What the *spiritual* and what the natural man is (n. 251). Things *spiritual* are substances, and not abstract; they are not possible outside of subjects which are substances, but are states of subjects, that is, substances (n. 209).

Spiritual Fire. That *fiery spiritual* [substance] which appears before the angels as a sun, is the first proceeding from the Lord's Love and Wisdom (n. 97).

Spleen. From sensation alone man knows nothing of the *spleen* (n. 22).

Spring. In the Word, *spring* signifies the first state of the church (n. 73). There is a perpetual *spring* in all the angelic heavens (n. 105). Springtime corresponds to a state of peace (n. 105).

State is predicated of love, of life, of wisdom, of affections, of joys therefrom and in general, of good and truth (n. 7). In angelic ideas of thought, instead of space and time there are *states* of life; instead of spaces, such things as have reference to *states* of love, and instead of times, such things as have reference to *states* of wisdom (n. 70). Living and dead *states* (n. 161).

Stalks in the forms of the vegetable kingdom are their outmosts. Clothed with layers of bark, they represent the globe clothed with earths (n. 314).

Sternum. Its relation to the lungs (n. 408).

Stomach. From sensation alone man knows nothing of the innumerable things which compose his *stomach* (n. 22). In what way the *stomach* is connected with the lungs (n. 408).

Stones. Their composition (n. 190, 192, 207). There are in them degrees of both kinds (n. 225). They are interiorly more perfect according to discrete degrees (n. 201). A wave of effluvia is constantly flowing forth from *stones* (n. 293).

Striata corpora. (See n. 366).

Structure. *Structure* of the lungs (n. 405, 412, 417).

Subject. A *subject* has substantial existence (n. 373). Men are *subjects* which can be recipients of the Divine love and Wisdom as of themselves (n. 170). That which men think of outside of a *subject* as something hovering or floating is only an appearance of the state of the *subject* in itself (n. 40–42).

Subsistence. The *subsistence* of the universe and of all things belonging to it is from the spiritual sun. *Subsistence* is perpetual existence (n. 152, 153).

Substance. The *substance* that is *substance* in itself is the sole *substance* (n. 197, 300). *Substance* in itself is the Divine love (n. 44–46). All things have been created out of a *substance* which is *substance* in itself (n. 283). Spiritual *substances* become *substances* at rest, and in the natural world fixed *substances* called matters (n. 302). *Substances* of which the earths consist (n. 305, 306, 310). Spiritual and natural *substances* of which the natural mind consists (n. 257,

388). Organic *substances* which are the receptacles and abodes of the thoughts and affections in the brains (n. 191, 192, 197). *Substance* is not possible apart from form (n. 209, 229). *Substance* and form (n. 41).

Substantiated, *Substantiated* in composite things do not arise out of a substance so simple that it is not a form from lesser forms (n. 229).

Suffocation, Swooning. State of the heart and lungs during *suffocation* and in *swoons* (n. 407).

Summer. In the Word, *summer* signifies a state of fullness of the church (n. 73).

Sun. There are two *suns* through which all things were created by the Lord, the *sun* of the spiritual world and the *sun* of the natural world (n. 153). The spiritual *sun* is not the Lord Himself, but is the Divine love and Wisdom proceeding from Him (n. 86, 93, 97, 151– 156, 290, 291). The *sun* of the natural world is pure fire from which everything of life has been withdrawn; but the *sun* of the spiritual world is fire in which there is Divine life (n. 89, 157). The spiritual *sun* is the one only substance from which all things are (n. 300). It appears in heaven at a middle altitude (n. 103–107). In the Word, the *sun* signifies the Lord as to Divine love and Divine wisdom together (n. 98). (See Contents, chapter 2.)

Swammerdam. (See n. 351.)

Swedenborg. The sight of his spirit was opened that he might see the things which are in the spiritual world, and afterwards describe that world (n. 85, 355). He saw the Lord as a sun (n. 131). An entire society of heaven appeared to him as one angel-man (n. 79). He was raised up into heaven to the angels, and was then in the spirit outside the body (n. 391, 394).

Swine. Their origin (n. 339).

Systole. The motions of the heart, *systolic* and diastolic, change and vary according to the affections of each one's love (n. 378).

Taste. *Taste* is an affecting of the substance and form of the tongue; the tongue is the subject (n. 41). *Taste* is not a something volatile flowing from its organ, but is the organ itself considered in its substance and form, and when the organ is affected sensation is produced (n. 41). The sense of *taste* communicates immediately by fibers with the brains, and derives therefrom its sensitive and active life (n. 365). *Tasting* is predicated of perception (n. 363). See Sense.

Tendons. Their origin (n. 304).

Think. To *think* from causes and ends is a mark of higher wisdom, but to *think* of these is a mark of lower wisdom. To *think* from ends is of wisdom; to *think* from causes is of intelligence; and to *think* from effects is of knowledge (n. 202). *Thinking* sensually and materially is *thinking* in nature from nature, and not above nature (n. 351).

Thorax. (See n. 403.)

Thought. *Thought* is not possible except by means of an atmosphere purer than air (n. 176). *Thought* is nothing but internal sight (n. 404). It pertains to wisdom and the understanding (n. 363). Inmost *thought,* which is the perception of ends, is the first effect of life (n. 2). All *thoughts* with man arise from Divine wisdom (n. 33). Affections and *thoughts* are sub-stances and forms, and not entities abstracted from a real and actual substance and form (n. 42, 316). Spiritual *thought* has nothing in common with natural *thought* (n. 163). *Thought* from the eye closes the understanding, but *thought* from the understanding opens the eye (n. 46). The affection which is of love produces thought, and thought produces respiration (n. 412). *Thought* flows into the lungs, and through the lungs into speech (n. 391). *Thought* corresponds to the respiration of the lungs (n. 383). See Affection.

Tigers. Their origin (n. 339).

Time. Time is proper to nature (n. 69, 73, 161). Measures of time (n. 73). In the spiritual world the progressions of life appear to be in time; but since state there determines time, time is only an appearance (n. 73). Time there is nothing but quality of state. Times in the spiritual world are not fixed as in the natural world, but are changeable according to the states of life (n. 70). Times there have relation to states of wisdom (n. 70). It makes one with thought from affection (n. 74). See Space.

Tongue. The appearance is that the *tongue* tastes, but the understanding tastes by virtue of its perception (n. 363). From sensation alone man knows nothing of the innumerable things in his *tongue* (n. 22). It is interiorly more perfect according to discrete degrees (n. 201).

Touch. The sense of *touch* is not in the things which are applied, but in the substance and form of the skin which are the subject; the sense itself is nothing but an affecting of the subject by the things applied (n. 41). The sense of *touch* communicates immediately through fibers with the brains, and derives therefrom its sensitive and active life (n. 365). *Touching* with the hand signifies communicating (n. 220). See Sense.

Trachea. (See n. 382, 408.)

Transmission. Transmission of the love of evil from parents to their offspring (n. 269).

Transparent. The forms receptive of heat and light in man are *transparent* from birth, like crystal glass (n. 245, 255); they transmit spiritual light as crystal glass transmits natural light (n. 245).

Trees and Shrubs. How they are produced (n. 346). There are in them degrees of both kinds (n. 225). A wave of effluvia is constantly flowing forth out of them (n. 293).

Trine. In everything of which anything can be predicated there is the *trine* which is called end, cause, and effect (n. 154, 167–172, 209, 296–301).

Trinity. The *trinity* in the Lord is called Father, Son, and Holy Spirit; the Divine from which [Creative Divine] is called the Father; the Human Divine the Son; and the proceeding Divine, the Holy Spirit (n. 146).

Truth. Everything that proceeds from wisdom is called truth (n. 31). *Truth* is nothing else than a form of affection, that is, of love (n. 411). *Truth* is of the understanding (n. 406, 410). All *truths* are of spiritual light (n. 253).

Truths. Apparent *truths* are appearances according to which everyone may think and speak; but when they are accepted as real *truths*, then apparent *truths* become falsities and fallacies (n. 108).

Turn. Angels *turn* their faces constantly to the Lord (n. 129–134); all their interiors both of mind and body are *turned* to the Lord as a sun (n. 135–139). Every spirit, whatever his quality, *turns* to his ruling love (n. 140–145).

Tyre, in the Word, signifies the church as to knowledges of good and truth (n. 325).

Understanding. The *understanding* is the receptacle of wisdom (n. 360); of intelligence (n. 430). It has an organic form, or a form organized out of the purest substances (n. 373). It is the light by which the love sees (n. 96, 406). It can be in spiritual light even where the will is not in spiritual heat. It does not lead the will, but only teaches and shows the way (n. 244). It does not conjoin itself to the will, but the will conjoins itself to the understanding (n. 410). It corresponds to the lungs (n. 382–384). See Will and Thought.

Union. Union of love with wisdom, and of wisdom with love (n. 35– 37). Of spiritual heat with spiritual light, and conversely (n. 99). Reciprocal *union* causes oneness (n. 35).

Uniting. *Uniting* of two into one, whence it is (n. 15).

Universal. The universal of all things is Love and Wisdom (n. 28).

Universe. The *universe* in general is divided into two worlds, the spiritual and the natural (n. 163). The *universe* regarded as to uses is an image of God (n. 64, 169), All things in the *universe* are recipients of the Divine love and the Divine wisdom of God-man (n. 55). There is a correspondence of each and every thing which takes form in the *universe* with each and every thing of man (n. 52) (See Contents, chapter 4.)

Ureters. Why they are in pairs (n. 384).

Uses. Those things are called *uses* which from the Lord are by creation in order (n. 298, 307, 316, 335, 336). All *uses*, as ends of creation, are in forms (n. 307). *Use* is like a soul, and its form is like a body (n. 310). *Use* has relation to good, and its form to truth (n. 409). All *uses* are brought forth by the Lord out of outmosts (n. 310). All the *uses* in the created universe correspond to *uses* in man (n. 298). Evil *uses* were not created by the Lord, but originated together with hell (n. 336–348). All things that are evil *uses* are in hell, and all things that are good *uses* are in heaven (n. 339). All good things that have existence in act are called good *uses,* and all evil things that have existence in act are called evil *uses* (n. 336). How man may know whether the *uses* he does

are spiritual or merely natural (n. 426). Performing *uses* is acting sincerely, uprightly, justly, and faithfully in the work proper to one's calling (n. 431). (See n. 65–68; and Contents, chapter 4.)

Vacuum is nothing (n. 373, 299). Conversation of angels with Newton on the subject of *vacuum* (n. 82).

Variety. Whence are the *varieties* of all things in the created universe (n. 155, 300). *Variety* of generals, and *variety* of particulars (n. 155). The *varieties* of love are limitless (n. 368). In the *varieties* of things there is an image of the Infinite and Eternal (n. 318). *Variety* obscures (n. 228).

Vegetable kingdom. The forms of uses in that kingdom (n. 314). A relation to man arising out of each and all things of the *vegetable kingdom* (n. 61).

Vegetables. The forms of *vegetables,* whence they are, and how produced (n. 314, 340, 346, 351). Degrees of both kinds are in them (n. 225). Marvels presented in their production (n. 60, 61, 340). A wave of effluvia is constantly flowing forth from *vegetables* (n. 293).

Veins. (See n. 399, 400, 408, 420). Vena Cava (n. 405, 412, 413, 415); bronchial *veins* (n. 405, 407, 413); pulmonary *veins* (n. 405, 407, 412, 413, 420). *Veins* correspond to the affections, and

(n. 14, 358, 368). It is nothing
but an image of love, for in
wisdom love presents itself to be
seen and recognized (n. 358). It is
from love, and is its form (n.
368). It is the cause of which love
is the end, and use the effect (n.
241). It does not beget love, but
only teaches how man ought to
live, and it shows the way in
which he ought to go (n. 244).
Wisdom without love is like an
existere without its *esse;* it is like
the light of winter (n. 139). It is
of *wisdom* to do good from
affection for good (n. 428). See
Contents, chapter 5. See also
Love.

Wise. He that doeth works is called
a *wise* man in the Word (n. 220).
Man is not to be judged of by
wise speaking, but by his life (n.
418).

Wolves. Their origin (n. 339).

Womb. Formation of man in the
womb (n. 6, 356, 400). State of
the infant in the *womb* (n. 407,
410). In the animal kingdom the
body is formed by a seed
deposited in a *womb* or ovum; in
the vegetable kingdom seeds are
the beginnings, the *womb* or
ovum is like the ground (n. 316).

Wonderful things. By the *wonderful
things* which everyone sees in
nature he may confirm himself in
favor of the Divine, if he will (n.
351–356). *Wonderful things* which
the instincts of animals present
(n. 60).

Word. Why the Lord is called the
Word (n. 221). There are three
senses in the *Word,* according to
the three degrees, the celestial
sense, the spiritual sense, and the
natural sense (n. 221). A *word* is
a kind of resultant, involving
tone, articulation, and meaning
(n. 280). In each single *word* of
the *Word* there is something
spiritual from Divine wisdom
and something celestial from
Divine love (n. 280).

Work. In every Divine *work* there
is a union of love and wisdom
(n. 36).

Works, deeds. All things which are
of the three degrees of the
natural mind are included in
deeds (n. 277–281). From the
deeds of a man we judge of the
thought of his will (n. 215). All
things of charity and faith are
present in good *works* (n.
214–220). On this account *works*
are so often mentioned in the
Word (n. 215, 220).

World. There are two *worlds,* the
spiritual and the natural (n. 83,
163). In external appearance they
are entirely alike, but as to
internal appearance they are
entirely unlike (n. 163, 173, 321).
They are totally distinct, and
communicate only by
correspondences (n. 83). In the
spiritual *world* there are all
things that take form in the
natural *world* in its three
kingdoms (n. 52, 321). All these

things are correspondences, and take form according to the affections and consequent thoughts of the angels (n. 322). The spiritual *world* is wherever man is, and in nowise away from him. Every man as regards the interiors of his mind is in the spiritual *world* in the midst of spirits and angels there (n. 92). The spiritual *world* includes heaven, and hell, and the *world* of spirits (n. 140, 339).

World of Spirits. Every man after death comes first into the *world of spirits,* which is midway between heaven and hell (n. 140).

Worms. Noxious *worms,* their origin (n. 339, 341, 342). Metamorphosis of worms (n. 354). *Silkworms* (n. 61, 356).

Write. Why some can think and speak well, but cannot *write* well (n. 361).

Writing. There is nothing of spiritual *writing* like natural *writing* except the letters, each of which contains an entire meaning (n. 295). These two *writings* have communication only by correspondences (n. 306).

Zenith. Why in the spiritual world the sun never appears in the *zenith* (n. 105).